Barray
minor

Barray maior.

DVCALIDO

Leuis

Vnsalcage loc

Radamah

Patri
rius.
st.

S Clemens

Durna

Noys

Tlen le
bet

SStoj
castel

Fladdan

Waternesse

Trantneß

Cnoknorveyn

ohan

Skye

Freford

Tranta

Dunwegen

S.Nicolas

mort
c.

Altmeke

Rona

Fladda

Ronavza

Grunzo

Brent

Ilertons

Stone

Keser
lac

Feuris

Dureneße

naheru

Wrayght
Faro head

Straits

Foullis

Laxford

NIVS

Ardur
neße

TI
A.

Beane
Roffen.

Dridon

Hen Conne

Ardwiton

Howyp
Tunge

Hen.Marten
Ship iland

Sudert

# Mapping
# Shakespeare

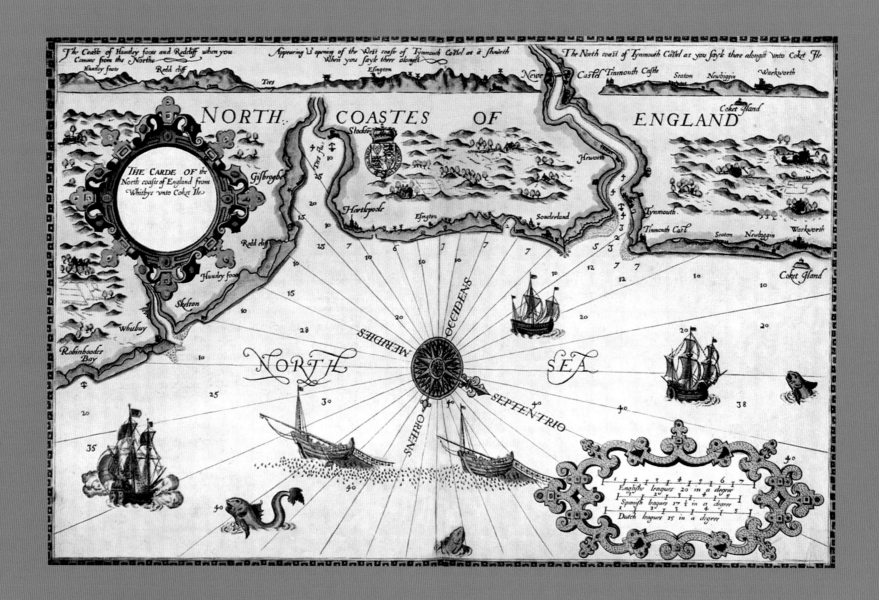

# Mapping
# Shakespeare

An exploration of
Shakespeare's world
through maps

Jeremy Black

C❖NWAY
LONDON · OXFORD · NEW YORK · NEW DELHI · SYDNEY

FOR EILEEN COX

CONWAY
Bloomsbury Publishing Plc
50 Bedford Square, London, WC1B 3DP, UK

BLOOMSBURY, CONWAY and the Conway logo are trademarks of Bloomsbury Publishing Plc

First published in Great Britain in 2018

A catalogue record for this book is available from the British Library

Library of Congress Cataloguing-in-Publication data has been applied for.

ISBN:   HB:      978-1-8448-6517-8
        eBook:   978-1-8448-6516-1
        ePDF:    978-1-8448-6515-4

2 4 6 8 10 9 7 5 3 1

Design by Nimbus Design
Printed and bound in India by Replika Press Pvt. Ltd.

To find out more about our authors and books visit
www.bloomsbury.com
and sign up for our newsletters

Map of the north coast of England from *The Mariner's Mirrour*, 1588, a ground-breaking publication designed for sailors. As well as navigational information, the book contained 45 large-scale coastal views of European harbours and ports. The maps were engraved by three Flemish map-makers – De Bry, Hondius and Rutsinger – and one Englishman, Augustine Ryther. **PAGE 2**

The Chandos portrait of William Shakespeare (c.1600–10) has never been fully confirmed to be a likeness of the playwright. It has often been ascribed to his friend and fellow playwright, Richard Burbage who was also a talented painter. **RIGHT**

# Contents

PREFACE . 6

MEDIEVAL BACKGROUND . 8

THE RENAISSANCE LEGACY . 16

PROJECTIONS, ACCURACY AND PRINTING . 30

ASTROLOGY AND ASTRONOMY . 38

MAPPING ENGLAND . 58

MAPPING LONDON . 98

MAPPING HISTORY . 108

SHAKESPEARE'S EUROPE . 120

'AN ETHIOP'S EAR': BEYOND EUROPE
IN THE AGE OF SHAKESPEARE . 158

IDEAS OF SPACE . 178

INDEX . 188

PICTURE CREDITS . 192

# Preface

Shakespeare's world was that of space and time, the experiences and understandings he had, and those of the spectators and readers. These, in turn, were dynamic in nature due to the amazing explorations of the age and the descriptions of them that were published, as well as the appearance of historical works that threw light on the past. For the first, Shakespeare lived in the age of voyagers into the unknown – such as Francis Drake, the first Englishman to sail round the world, Martin Frobisher and Henry Hudson – and in the shadow of those of an even bolder set of trailblazers, notably Christopher Columbus, Vasco da Gama, and Ferdinand Magellan. Exploration by these men, 'discoveries' to Europeans (but not to those who were already aware that they existed), affected not just the knowledge of places and peoples that was available, but also the very way of seeing and explaining the world. This was the case from the existence, number and shape of its continents, particularly the understanding of the existence and scale of the Americas, to the extent of the world's circumference; and from the projections employed by map-makers to the perspectives deployed. Maps and globes literally changed, and these changes, and the very nature of change itself, encouraged an awareness of a world that was at once known and knowable and yet also in the process of discovery and thus uncertain.

Shakespeare's choice of setting for his works reflected this changing geography. In his plays, there were places that were very familiar and/or well understood by his audiences – notably the street life and social geography of London. However, there was also an understanding of the geography of England, such that the places where Shakespeare set action, for example Dover, Bristol, London, Southampton and York, were understood, even though a smaller percentage of the population would have travelled widely in England than is the case today. Moreover, some places abroad were close enough to be presented as similar, notably in order to make archetypal points, such as the Vienna of *Measure for Measure* and the Venice of *The Merchant of Venice*.

Yet Shakespeare also moves further afield: Europe's peripheries and neighbours come into view in the shape of characters from them, such as the Prince of Morocco who was an unsuccessful suitor of Portia in *The Merchant of Venice*, or a unit of Muscovite troops in Italy in *All's Well That Ends Well*. Such individuals resonated with the news of Shakespeare's lifetime. For instance, the Moroccans had routed a Portuguese invasion in 1578, and Elizabeth I of England had subsequently sought an alignment with Morocco against Spain. Under Ivan IV, 'the Terrible' (r.1533–1584), Russia had become a major and expansionist power, and England had sought good relations with that country, too.

Turning to potent non-Western powers, there is mention of the threat from the expansionist Turkish Empire; it is this that leads Othello, a Venetian general, to the Venetian colony of Cyprus – although by the time Shakespeare wrote the play it had actually already fallen to the forces of the Turkish Sultan, Selim II. In addition, in *All's Well That Ends Well* there is mention of the Turks fighting the Safavids of Persia, which they did for much of the period from the 1500s to the 1630s. Shakespeare does not engage in a comparable fashion with China, India and Japan, but the sense of new lands is represented by the voyages taken by characters, and their shipwrecks on strange shores. Distance alone should place Prospero's Island in *The Tempest*, its travellers shipwrecked on a voyage from Tunis to Italy, somewhere in the Mediterranean. However, the imaginative world had been expanded by recent English voyages, notably to Bermuda and Virginia, and they therefore became the point of reference for the audience – as, indeed, they remain.

The situation was less transformative as far as history was concerned. Nevertheless, Renaissance Humanism had affected people's engagement with the past, notably in encouraging a broader-based understanding of the Classical world – the ancient world of Greece and Rome – and this was an important aspect of Shakespeare's plot-setting as well as of his imagery and language. Authors such as Plutarch, whom Shakespeare knew through the 1579 English edition, provided guidance. Thus it was an ancient world, although not that of the Middle East, that was readily available, and led to figures such as Julius Caesar, whose character Shakespeare based closely on accounts by Plutarch, striding the boards.

Moreover, this was not the only source of new information. The system of chronicles that had been so important for the national history of England had been upgraded, and especially so in the cases of the works of historians Edward Hall and Raphael Holinshed, who was responsible for the *Chronicles of England, Scotland, and Ireland* (1577), which was expanded in a second edition in 1587. In particular, the coverage of the fifteenth century was fleshed out, notably in Hall's *The Union of the Two Noble and Illustrious Families of Lancaster and York* (1548), and the early sixteenth century, too, was brought within the historical span. Shakespeare's works reflected all this.

In this atlas, I engage with this changing awareness, by discussing developments in cartography and by publishing maps that throw light on contemporary understandings. The mental maps of the audiences are far harder to recreate and assess, but the settings conjured up in the plays are a key guide to them.

I am most grateful to my editor, Lisa Thomas, who is as effective and efficient as she is calming and helpful. It is a great pleasure to dedicate this book to Eileen Cox, a good friend who is a superb guide to London's history.

A **16th century map** of Lombardy by Giacomo Gastaldi. Engraved on a copper plate and printed on parchment, the map includes the cities of Milan, Verona, Padua, Mantua, Parmaå, Modena, Bologna and Venice, many of which featured in the plays of William Shakespeare.

# Medieval Background

Shakespeare's world is known to us through the plays he wrote. Visually and in terms of perception, this includes not only productions on the stage, but also in film and on television. For contemporaries, however, this world was represented in and by maps – of the physical and mental kind. Maps reflected both knowledge about the wider world and the way in which this information was understood, capturing cultural assumptions about territory and identity. In Shakespeare's lifetime, this world was changing greatly as a result of Western exploration and also religious division within Christendom. The former contributed greatly to an awareness of change through time as a transformative rather than cyclical process, as had been previously generally believed and as was conveyed in some Shakespearean imagery and speeches. Because of this emphasis on transformation, there was, at least for some, a sense of modernisation and modernity, and the sense of a coming to the present offered an account of time, and therefore of space as well, that was markedly different to that of earlier centuries.

First, however, we should examine the medieval background because this provides the context for inherited values in Tudor England and also created a legacy of beliefs, ideas and collective experiences that can be seen in Shakespeare's plays. In Christendom, these values were initially represented by *mappae mundi* (world maps), and the world view they communicated. These charts conveyed geographical knowledge in a Christian format, offering a combination of belief and first-hand observation, and employed a tripartite internal division, depicting three regions: namely, the regions of the world divided between Noah's sons – Asia, Europe and Africa. All of these were contained within a circle, the O, with the horizontal bar of the T within it separating the regions representing the waterways differentiating Asia from the other two.

This was not a case of separate continents – all three were regions of one world to medieval Western thinkers. There were no Americas and no Australia.

These maps were full of religious symbolism. The T was a symbol of the Christian cross and, most powerfully, Jerusalem was placed at the centre of the world, reflecting the fact that as a destination it was the inspiration for and major goal of Christian pilgrimage. Jerusalem represented the key moment in history, that of Christ's redemptive mission, and was also central to human space. As the symbol of Creation, a pre-Christian idea, the circle acted to contain the ephemeral nature of human activity. The use of a circle also suggested the Wheel of Life and Fortune, and, separately, but linked through the influence of the zodiac, the movement of the heavenly spheres. *King Lear* offers the most striking instance of Shakespeare's use of the idea of a wheel, with the king 'bound Upon a wheel of fire' (4.7), although no action in any of the plays is set in Jerusalem.

Alongside the religious symbolism, wondrous creatures were depicted in *mappae mundi*, as well as in other accounts of lands outside Europe, and notably in sub-Saharan Africa. These creatures echo in *Othello* when the protagonist describes his earlier travels, including details of:

> 'being taken by the insolent foe
> And sold to slavery'. (1.3)

Moreover, he had seen:

> '... hills whose heads touch heaven
> ... the Cannibals that each other eat,
> The Anthropophagi, and men whose heads
> Do grow beneath their shoulders.'
> (1.3)

The *Hereford Mappa Mundi* (*World Map*) was made in c.1300 and bears the name 'Richard of Haldingham or Lafford'. It conveyed geographical knowledge in a Christian format, offering a combination of belief and first-hand observation. Such maps employed a tripartite internal division, depicting three regions, namely, the regions of the world divided between Noah's sons – Asia, Europe and Africa – all contained within a circle, the O. The use of a circle also suggested the Wheel of Life and Fortune, a theme captured in King Lear's 'I am bound Upon a wheel of fire' (4.7). Christ in Majesty presides over the world in this map, which was probably placed between pictures, or reliefs, of Heaven and Hell. The British Isles are on the lower left.

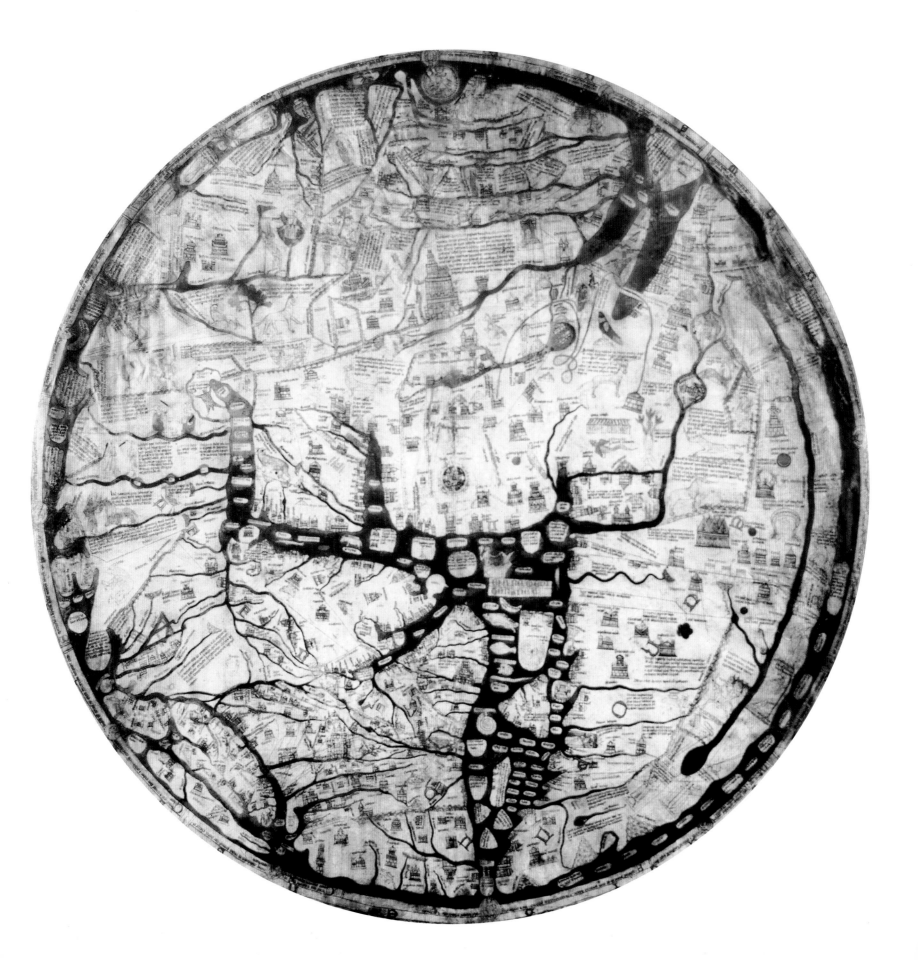

Such accounts went back to the Classics and suggested a known world shadowed by a mysterious present.

By the late sixteenth century, the *mappae mundi* might appear to depict a redundant mental world, one that had been overthrown by a secularising transformation in the shape of the Renaissance, the Age of Discovery, the Reformation and the Scientific Revolution, with printing and the rise of the middle class acting as assistants. That is certainly one way to present Shakespeare's age, yet it suffers from the tendency to downplay the dynamism of the earlier medieval society, and to define the two periods as being more different than they actually were. In the case of medieval map-making, for instance, contemporaries had available to them more than just the *mappae mundi*. One alternative was the *Gough Map*, a practical map of Britain of about 1375 that was possibly produced for administrative use. This provided an effective route map and showed nearly 3,000 miles of roads, which transmitted goods, demands, information and innovations in an increasingly market-driven and economically sophisticated society.

Up until the mid-fourteenth century, the overwhelming use of Western maps appears to have been in scholarship and display – with the *mappae mundi* clearly featuring in the latter category – but from that period onwards there was an increase in the number made for practical purposes or, looked at differently, *other* practical purposes. Local maps covering towns and some estates appeared, especially in England, France, Germany and, most prominently, Italy. These maps included drawings – for example, of buildings and bridges – indicating the extent to which elements of pictograms were featured. The visual was an important means and product of information, although written surveys remained common. Most local maps date from after

Matthew Paris' map of Great Britain, 1250, is the most comprehensive and artistically successful of four maps of the nation drawn by the thirteenth-century historian Matthew Paris, who was a monk at St Albans' Abbey. These can be considered as base maps for how medieval England viewed itself and are the earliest surviving maps of Britain with such a high level of detail; many geographical features are recognisable. They stand out in the history of medieval map-making as the first attempts to portray the actual physical appearance of the country rather than to represent the relationship between places in simple schematic diagrams. The map is mainly delineated by its rivers and coastlines on either side of a north–south axis.

It is particularly rich in the number of named cities, towns, hills and rivers – more than 250 of them. Panels around the margins of the map identify the nearest land in each direction.

The boundary between England and Scotland is clearly marked by Hadrian's Wall – 73 miles long and built between 122 and 130 by the Roman Emperor Hadrian to protect the Empire's most northerly border. Further north is the Antonine Wall, which was constructed by Hadrian's successor, Antonius Pius. Both are shown schematically as battlemented features, although the Antonine Wall was, in fact, a ditch and turf-wall structure.

London is acknowledged on the map as the country's largest city by having the most elaborate towered and battlemented frame surrounding its name. Windsor Castle is shown upstream on the banks of the river Thames. The Isle of Thanet appears (wrongly) off the south coast, not yet joined to the mainland by silting and land reclamation. In north-west Wales, the peaks of Mount Snowdon are roughly indicated and labelled 'Snaudun'.

1400, suggesting that it was at this point that mapping began to play a role in local disputes as maps ceased to be novelties and as people sought to demonstrate the boundaries of landholdings.

Maps were also slowly adopted to delineate some Western frontiers from the fifteenth century onwards. They helped to make the understanding of frontiers in linear terms, rather than zones, easier: an important distinction, and an understanding that came to play a role in frontier negotiations. There were, however, major conceptual and methodological problems in comprehending frontiers and in assessing and presenting them in these terms. As a result, a case law and literature developed. For example, in his treatise *De Fluminibus seu Tiberiadis* (1355), Bartolo de Sassoferrata considered the difficulties of mapping meanders, changes of river courses and new islands in rivers.

A different form of information for mapping was provided by portolan charts – navigational maps based on compass points that supplemented spoken or written sailing instructions by offering coastal outlines that helped pilots plot courses from one harbour to another. This form of navigation was the basis of most of the voyages Shakespeare describes in the Mediterranean, the majority of which sought to be within sight of the coast. In *Pericles*, for example, the storm-tossed protagonist asks a sailor 'what coast is this' and is told 'We are near Tarsus.' (3.1)

The charts were covered in rhumb lines: radiating lines resembling compass bearings. The use of the compass for navigation by Westerners had begun in the twelfth century and, as with other innovations – for example astrolabes, which also became a navigational tool – the compass was not a one-stop change. Initially a needle floating in water, it went on to become a pivoted indicator and, by the fifteenth century, compensation had

been made for the significant gap between true and magnetic north – a major improvement. Moreover, portolan charts became more accurate in terms of time, and new discoveries could be incorporated into this format – a key element in any information system.

At first, new geographical information in the three centuries before Shakespeare largely arose from journeys across Asia, such as the one undertaken by William of Rubruck in 1253–1255 on behalf of Louis IX of France, 'St Louis', to the Court of the Mongol khan, Möngke, at his newly constructed capital, Karakorum. The Crusades greatly encouraged the acquisition of information, partly because so many travelled from Western Europe to the Near East and North Africa but also due to strong support for the idea of finding allies from beyond the world of Islam. This led, in particular, to interest in the Mongols – who, in the thirteenth century, were a scourge of the Muslim world – and also in Prester John, the mythical head of what was in fact the Christian kingdom of Abyssinia (Ethiopia), a place that echoes in Shakespeare's references to the country. Louis IX, who led crusades to Egypt and Tunis before dying of disease on the latter in 1270, was interested in Mongol support against the Mamluks of Egypt – a people who in the thirteenth century, having defeated the Mongols and the Crusaders, came to dominate the Holy Land and Syria.

In the case of William of Rubruck, as in so many other travellers' experiences both before and during Shakespeare's lifetime, the information presented was a mixture of accurate reporting and assumptions based on the Bible and on apocalyptic prophecies about non-Christian peoples – assumptions that affected the reports made by travelling friars – with scant guidance to help readers determine the differences.

More famously, benefiting from the trans-Asian trading routes that were made more accessible by the order enforced by the Mongols, Marco Polo claimed to have left Venice in 1271 and to have reached the summer palace of Kublai – the ruler of China and grandson of Chinggis (Ghengis) Khan – at Shangdu four years later. Then, in 1292, Polo was given, he claimed, the task of escorting a Mongol princess from China to Hormuz on the Persian Gulf, and from there he returned home in 1295.

The accuracy of Polo's account was challenged by some contemporaries and has been questioned since by some scholars, but despite its dubious veracity it nevertheless had a major impact on Western knowledge about the Orient: by inaccurately assuming that he had travelled 16,000 miles from Venice to Beijing, instead of, in fact, 7,000, and thus locating China further from Europe than it is, Polo helped to create a misunderstanding about the distance from Europe to China across the Atlantic. This encouraged the idea that by sailing west it would be relatively easy to reach an Asia that, allegedly, was further east than is really the case. Indeed, Polo's account was to be one of the sources used for the 1492 globe by the Nuremberg geographer Martin Behaim that depicted only islands between Europe and China, and not a landmass, and which underestimated the distance. Behaim also showed a large island called Antilla between Africa and China, an island that, since 1424, had been linked with the long-held and inaccurate notion that seven bishops and their flocks, fleeing the Islamic invasion of Portugal in the eighth century, had established seven islands, or cities, beyond the Atlantic horizon. Such fictions were, however, to be relocated as European transoceanic exploration developed in the fifteenth century, with the Atlantic becoming in large part known by Shakespeare's lifetime.

Towns are depicted on *Itinerary from London to Dover* from Matthew Paris' *The Itinerary from London to Jerusalem* by means of pictograms. The linear nature of the route was not too inappropriate for an age in which there was much use of Roman roads, and it also captured the role of the journey as a spiritual task. Dover and its environs were important in *King Lear* and *King John*. In the former, the blind Gloucester tries to leap off the cliffs, but is tricked into falling over safely onto dry land by his son Edgar.

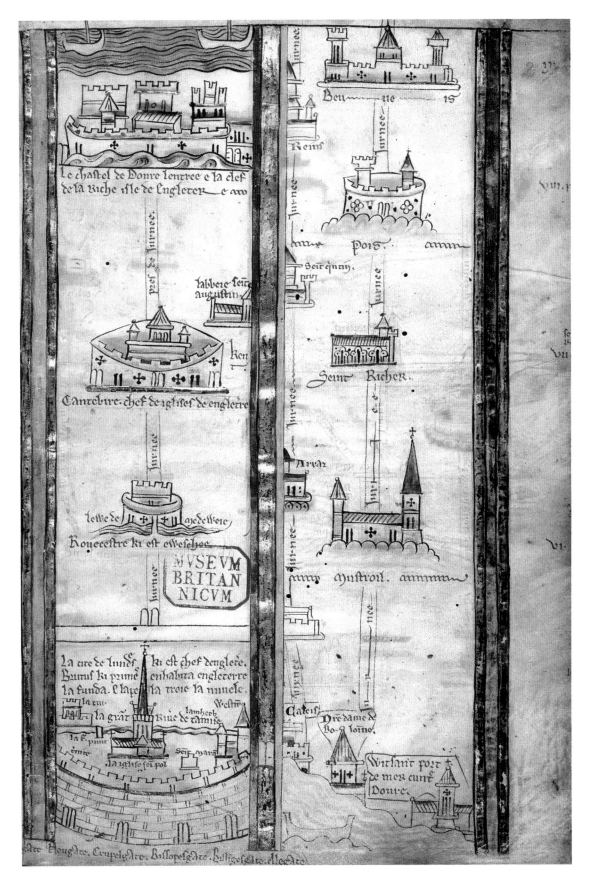

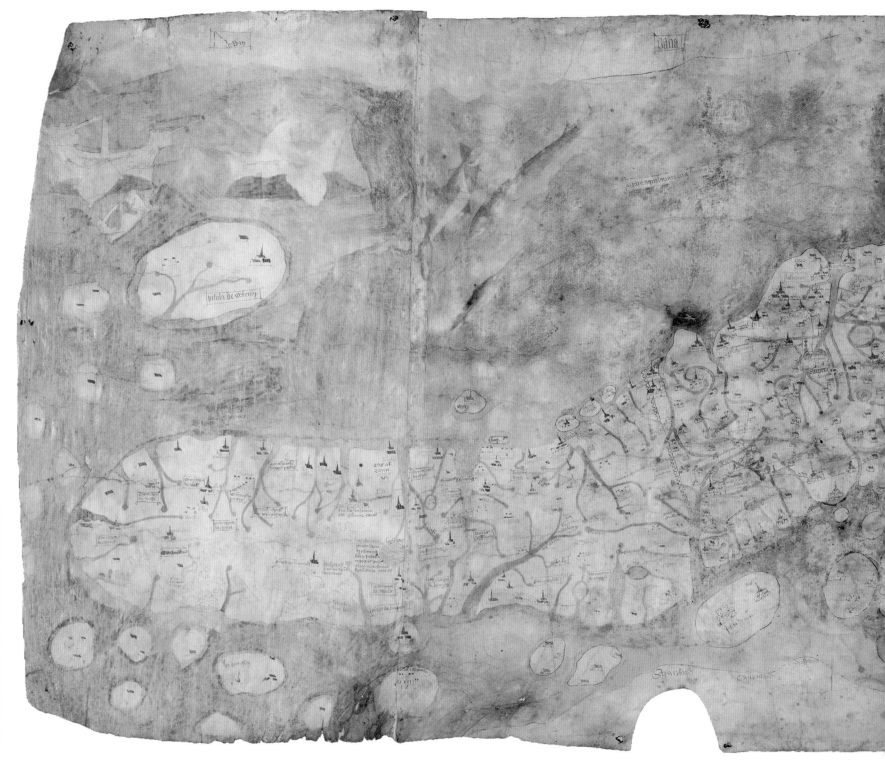

The precise date and the identity of the mapmaker of the Gough Map are unknown, although it is thought to date from about 1375. It was named after Richard Gough, who bequeathed the map to the Bodleian Library in Oxford in 1809. A practical map possibly produced for administrative use, it provided an effective guide to routes, and showed nearly 3,000 miles of roads – many of which followed Roman routes – that transmitted goods, demands, information and innovations in an increasingly economically sophisticated society. Eastern England is presented with more accuracy than western. Journeys were a frequent plot device and theme in Shakespeare's plays, as in *Two Gentlemen of Verona*.

# The Renaissance Legacy

While the mental world of many in Shakespeare's time was still strongly affected by the medieval understanding of space and time, the Renaissance legacy was particularly significant for map-makers. In part, this legacy was a result of the recovery of aspects of Classical knowledge. In particular, Ptolemy's *Geographia*, a second-century CE gazetteer, was translated from Greek into Latin in 1406. This work included material about three projections (representations on a plane surface of the curved, three-dimensional surface of the Earth), and thus encouraged the idea that the world could be presented through different projections – an important source of relativism. Moreover, Ptolemy's use of latitude and longitude in his gazetteer encouraged an emphasis on the mathematisation of location, and, thus, on accurately measured data that was recorded with reference to a graticule. This grid was to become a central feature of Western mapping and made it relatively easy to treat knowledge in a cumulative fashion by locating and adding new pieces of information.

Maps that drew on the coordinates from Ptolemy's translation appeared in the fifteenth century, with printed versions being produced after 1475. There were major errors – notably the Indian Ocean being shown as enclosed by land east from southern Africa – but nevertheless the consequences of the emphasis on geometry meant that mathematical proportionality was applied to the known world and to what was discovered. Moreover, the imposition of mathematical rules on representation lessened the sense of a spiritual connection with the Earth that had been seen in the T–O maps centred on Jerusalem.

Similarly in the arts, firm mathematical rules were being used in order to produce a sense of accurate perspective. This was a goal encouraged by the artist and mathematician Piero della Francesca (c.1415–1492) in his *De Prospectiva Pingendi* (*On Painting Perspective*). Infinity thus became a readily depicted mathematical proposition while perspective, in providing a method for organising spatial reality, offered a theory – at once visual, intellectual and spiritual – that engaged with the need to stabilise and reify perception. Perspective geometry was to be combined with a grid of latitude and longitude in map-making. Meanwhile, astronomical navigation developed, notably in Iberia (Spain and Portugal), where it benefited from Arab and Jewish influences. There was an important development of astronomy in Salamanca in Spain after 1460.

Science combined with a need to improve the information available to mariners. The use of the compass encouraged the recording, systematisation and use of navigational information. Dead reckoning was no longer an adequate method. The printing of sailing directions became more frequent in England in the sixteenth century.

The Renaissance also fostered and focused interest in the Classical world, which ensured a greater degree of knowledge of its geography. In *Antony and Cleopatra*, Augustus is shown in Rome telling his principal advisors that Mark Antony in Alexandria, the capital of Cleopatra's kingdom, had divided up the Middle East:

> 'Unto her [Cleopatra]
> he gave the 'stablishment of Egypt; made her
> Of Lower Syria, Cyprus, Lydia,
> Absolute queen...
> His sons he there proclaim'd the kings of kings;
> Great Media, Parthia, and Armenia
> He gave to Alexander; to Ptolemy he assign'd
> Syria, Cilicia, and Phoenicia.
> .... who now are levying
> The kings o'the earth for war.

A key Ottoman figure was Piri Reis (Captain Piri), who was born Ahmed Muhiddin Piri in about 1465 in Gelibolu (Gallipoli). Having followed his uncle into the Ottoman fleet, Piri prepared both a world map of 1513 that incorporated information from Portugal and Spain and the Kitab i-Bahriye [Book of the Sea], a manual for sailors that provided information on routes, distances, watering locations and safe harbours around the Mediterranean. It contained more than 200 maps, including nautical charts, coastal plans and city maps, but the number varies as there were different editions, in 1521 and 1526, and numerous copies thereafter. More than 30 original manuscript copies survive. In 1552, Piri Reis with 30 warships and 850 soldiers, sailed from the naval base at Suez, sacking the Portuguese base at Muscat and then besieging that at Hormuz. Its successful resistance led him instead to plunder the island of Qeshm. He was executed for his failure.

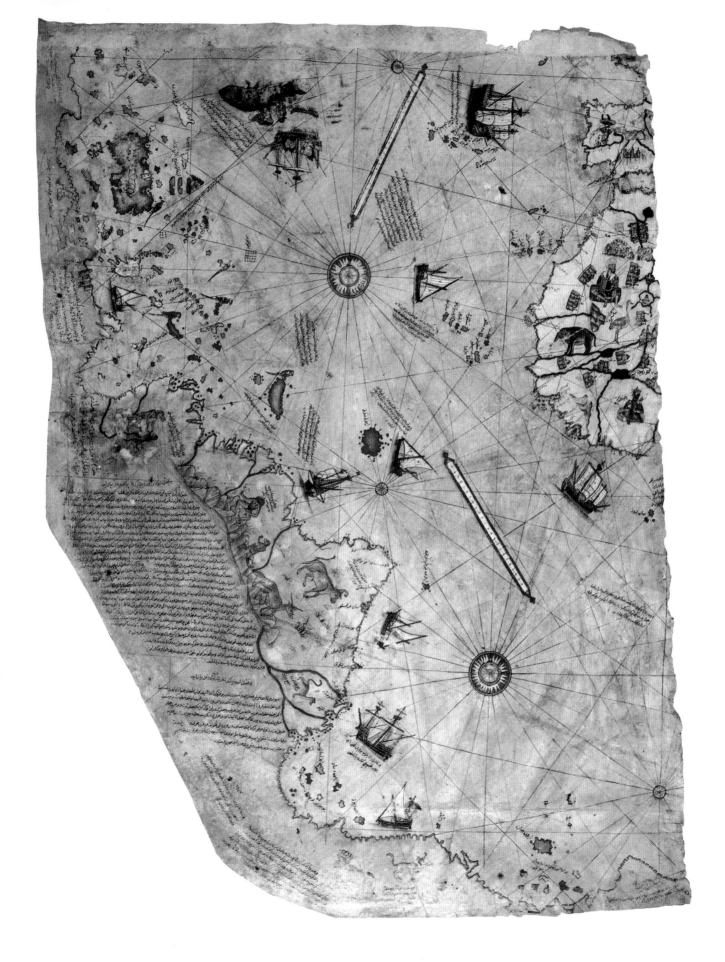

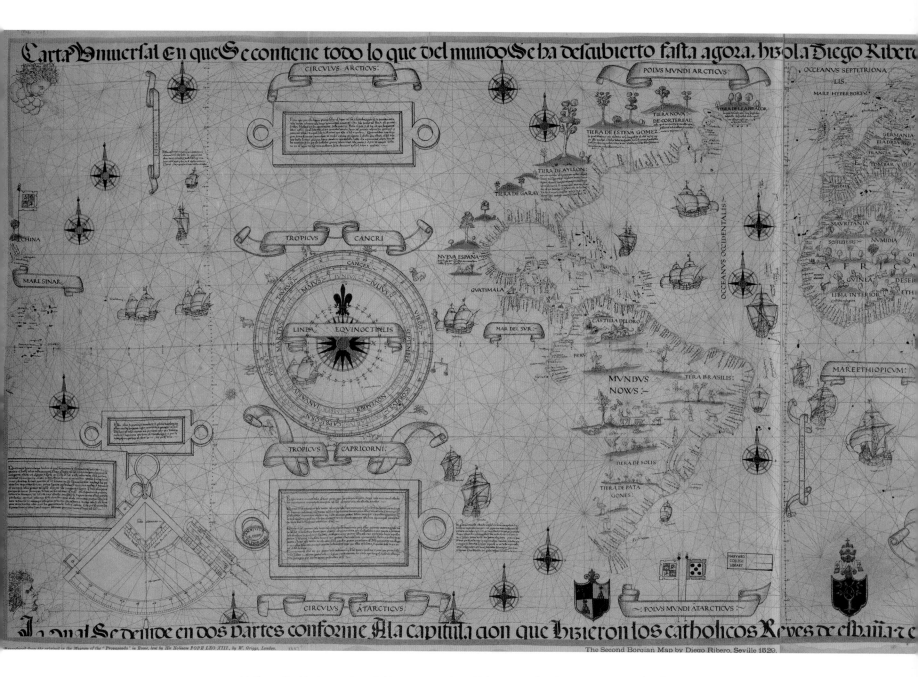

**Mathematical instruments** and ships are both depicted in this *World Map* by Diego Ribero, Seville, 1529. Seville, a centre of Spanish exploration and of Spain's trade with the New World, was in 1545 the place of publication of Pedro Medina's navigational treatise, which was translated into English, French, German and Italian. Medina also made astrolabes and other navigational tools. 'I'll put a girdle round about the earth in forty minutes', boasts Puck to Oberon in *A Midsummer Night's Dream* (2.1) in response to the instruction to get hold of a flower, and he duly returns in only a few minutes of the play's time. A contemporary awareness of maps and the span of the Earth would have made apparent the magical nature of Puck's achievement.

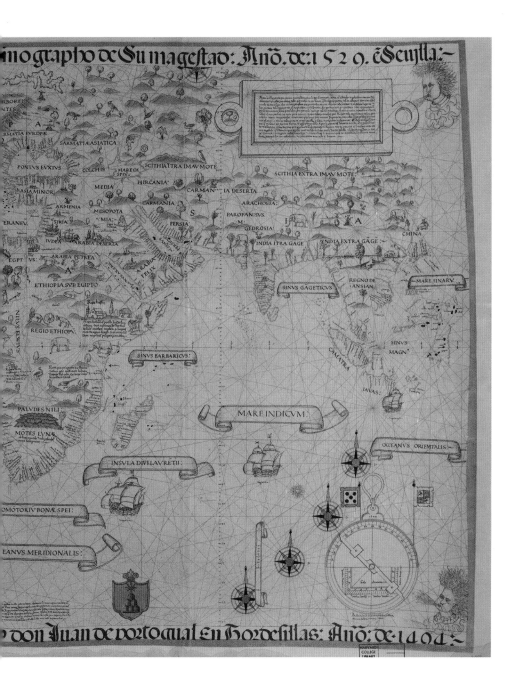

*He hath assembled*
*Bocchus, the King of Libya; Archelaus,*
*Of Cappadocia; Philadelphos, King*
*of Paphlagonia; the Thracian king, Adallas;*
*King Malchus of Arabia; King of Pont;*
*Herod of Jewry; Mithridates, King*
*of Comagene; Polemon and Amintas,*
*The Kings of Mede and Lycaonia,*
*With a more larger list of sceptres.'*
(3.6)

This is a version of Oriental power that linked Renaissance interest in the Ancient world to the Oriental-style drama conjured up by Christopher Marlowe in his play *Tamburlaine the Great*, which was performed to great success in London in about 1587.

Meanwhile, exploration and travel provided and confirmed new geographical information, such as that offered, supposedly in Messina in Sicily, by Benedick, in *Much Ado About Nothing*, when affirming his wish to travel far rather than to talk with Beatrice:

> 'I will go on the slightest errand now to the Antipodes that you can devise to send me on. I will fetch you a tooth-picker [toothpicks were made of precious materials] now from the furthest inch of Asia; bring you a length of Prester John's foot; fetch you a hair off the great Cham's [Emperor of China] beard; do you any embassage to the Pigmies.' (2.1)

The last was a reference to sub-Saharan Africa, while Prester John referred to Ethiopia, and to the Antipodes, which were known as the mysterious Southern Continent. Knowledge of the Arctic waters is seen in *Twelfth Night* when Fabian says: 'you are now sailed into the north of my lady's opinion, where you will hang like an icicle on a Dutchman's beard' (3.2) – a reference to the voyage of William

Barentz around the north of Novaya Zembla in 1596–1597.

Interest in gold had encouraged Portuguese explorers to sail south along the coast of West Africa in the fifteenth century. Religion was also a dynamic, with the Portuguese, notably under Prince Henry the Navigator, seeking allies against Islam in the drive to reconquer Jerusalem, which was seen as a crucial preliminary to the Second Coming of Christ. Similarly, Christopher Columbus – in his *Book of Prophecies*, compiled before his fourth voyage to the Caribbean in 1502 – argued that the end of the world would occur in 155 years, and that his own discoveries had been foretold in the Bible. By sailing west to discover a route to Asia, Columbus hoped to raise money to retake the Holy Land and, thus, redeem the Christian world. More generally, the recovery of Jerusalem was a key theme, one that indicated the continuing significance of Crusading ideology.

Columbus had set sail westwards in 1492, bound, he thought, for Japan but, instead, had reached the West Indies. Information about his achievement was rapidly disseminated, with the second voyage of 1493 being significant as it helped establish a viable and repeatable route. In 1500, Pedro Álvares Cabral, the commander of the second Portuguese fleet to India, discovered Brazil as far as Europeans were concerned.

The first circumnavigation of the world in 1519–1522, begun by Ferdinand Magellan – although he was killed in 1521 on the island of Cebu in the Philippines en route – greatly affected an understanding of its shape. This was the first expedition (in late 1520) to round the southern point of South America, and subsequently achieved the first recorded crossing of the Pacific, although Polynesian travellers had already made long voyages across that ocean.

The circumnavigation also exemplified how new information required new ways to display and consider it. It made the globe a more obvious tool, indeed the basic map, for understanding the world, and thus emphasised the need to give greater attention to the projections used in depicting that world. Perhaps it is little wonder, then, that the idea of a globe was repeatedly used in Shakespeare's plays. For example, appearing at the start of *Henry IV, Part Two*, before the castle of Henry, 1st Earl of Northumberland of the Percy family, at Warkworth, Rumour announces:

*'I, from the orient to the drooping west,*
*Making the wind my post-horse, still unfold*
*The acts commenced on this ball of earth.'*
*(Prologue)*

This is not the sole reference, either: Oberon remarked in *A Midsummer Night's Dream*:

*'We the globe can compass soon,*
*Swifter than the wandering moon.'*
*(4.1)*

In *Troilus and Cressida*, Ulysses refers to the danger that disorder will 'make a sop of all this solid globe' (1.3), and in *The Comedy of Errors*, at a more popular level, Dromio of Syracuse describes Nell the 'kitchen-wench' as being 'No longer from head to foot than from hip to hip: she is spherical, like a globe' (3.2).

Furthermore, new information clarified the amount of additional information that had to be acquired, for the map of the globe had to be filled. More particularly, by drawing attention to the size of the Pacific, the circumnavigation made more clear not only the size of the Earth but also how much remained to be mapped. The possibilities that

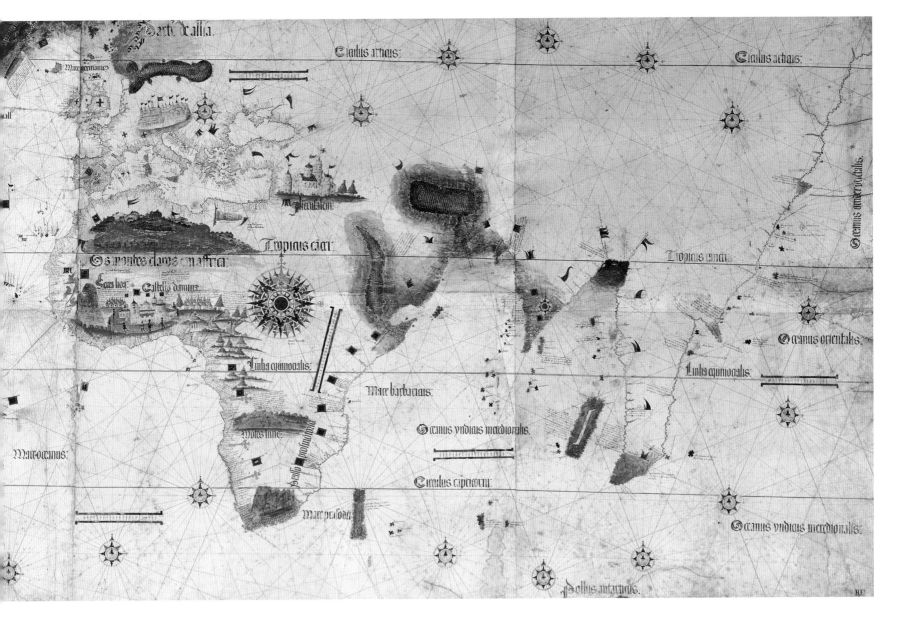

Commissioned by Alberto Cantino, the envoy at Lisbon of Ercole d'Este, Duke of Ferrara, for the Duke, *The Cantino Planisphere* (1502) includes details of Portuguese discoveries, and accompanied an account of the second voyage of Gaspar Corte-Real to American waters in 1501, a voyage on which he and his ship disappeared. The coast of Brazil is depicted rather vaguely, complete with trees and parrots, while that of West Africa, where the Portuguese had been sailing for longer, is revealed in greater detail. As yet the Portuguese were far more knowledgeable about India than about coasts further east, notably South-East Asia and China. Shakespeare's plays were first produced in Brazil in the early nineteenth century. Jerusalem is clearly shown as is the division of the, to Europeans, expanding world in 1494 by Pope Alexander VI.

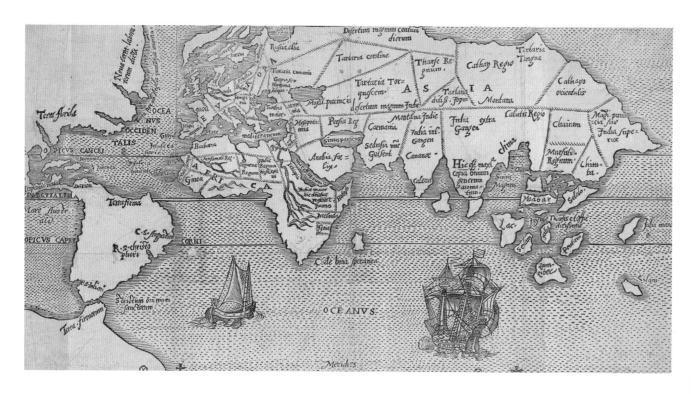

**Robert Thorne's world map, 1527**. An English merchant resident in Seville and Bristol, Richard Thorne the Younger (1492–1532) urged Henry VIII to try to gain for England the benefits of trade with the newly explored Indies of East and West. In particular, he advocated use of a North–East passage to Cathay (China). This world map was published in 1576 for the Muscovy Company, who wanted to show North America as an impenetrable bulk, such that there could not be a North–West passage above it from the Atlantic to the Pacific. Instead, the emphasis is on trade via Asia and via the Indian Ocean. An engraved version of the map was incorporated in Richard Hakluyt's *Divers Voyages* (1582). Willem Barentsz (c.1550–1597), a Dutch explorer who sailed to the Arctic seeking a North-East Passage, is referred to by Shakespeare. In *Twelfth Night*, Fabian says: 'You are now sailed into the north of my lady's opinion, where you will hang like an icicle on a Dutchman's beard' (3.2). **ABOVE**

22

This immensely detailed map from 1500 – *Venice* by Jacopo de' Barbari (*c.*1440–1515) – shows us the position of canals that no longer exist. In addition, de' Barbari used the views from three bell towers to develop his map of Venice, which means that it effectively has three different perspectives. Both of these factors make it difficult to correlate the map with modern street information, although the Rialto Bridge (near the Rialto Market) and the Arsenal are clearly visible. The former gets a mention in *The Merchant of Venice*, for it is 'upon the Rialto' (3.1.1.) that Shylock hears of Antonio's trading voyages, and he later refers to Antonio 'who dare scarce show his head on the Rialto' (3.1.41). The presence of Neptune and Mercury suggests that the city has been divinely blessed with control of the seas and maritime wealth, and gives a nod to Classical mythology. **BELOW**

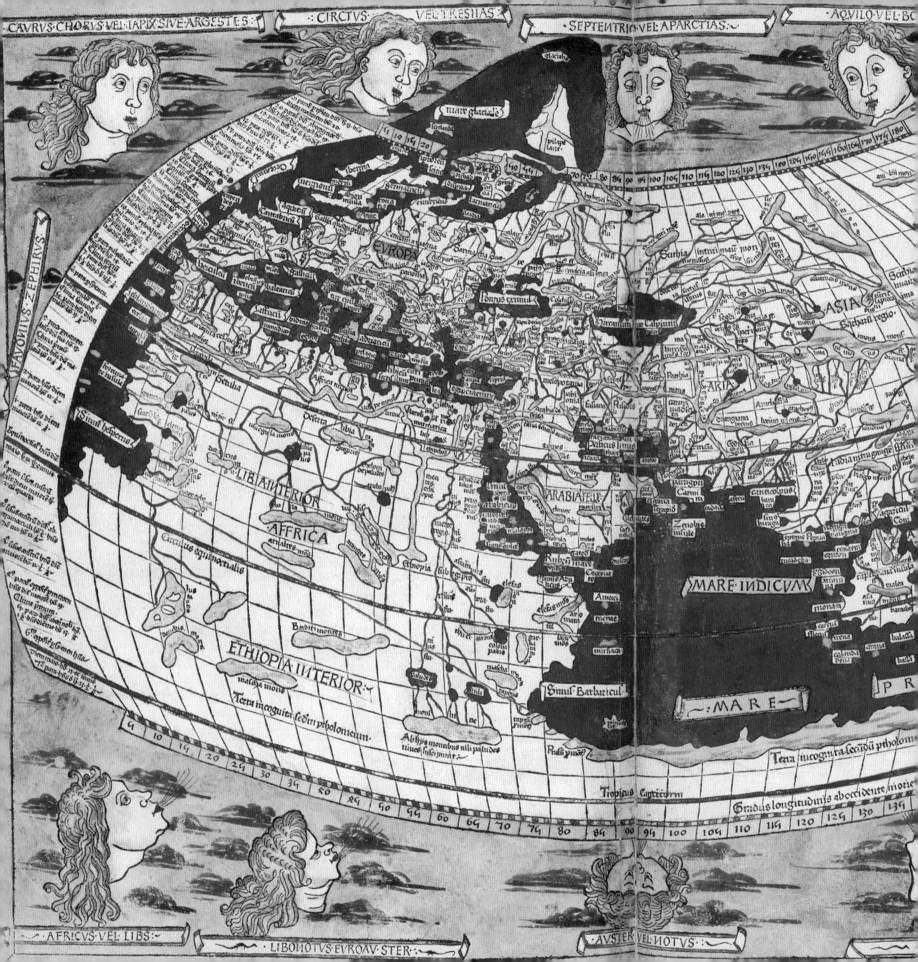

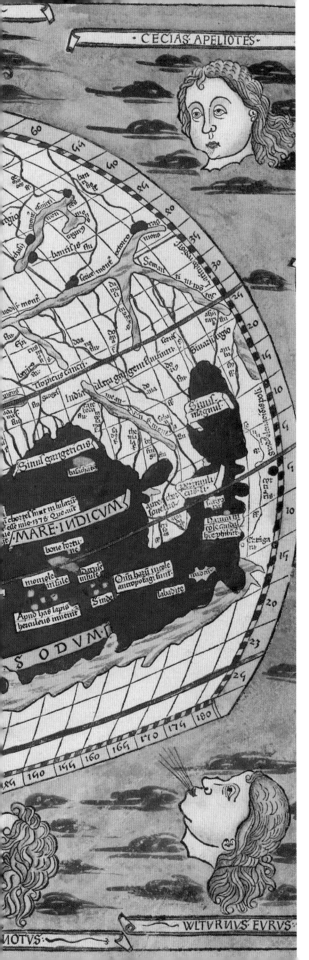

Ptolemy (*c.*100–178), a Greek geographer who worked in Alexandria, produced in his *Geographia* a gazetteer of the ancient world providing latitude and longitude based on astronomical data. His *Geographia* was translated from Greek into Latin in 1406, and maps drawing on the coordinates from this translation appeared over the following decades, with printed versions being produced after 1475. This copy was produced in 1482. There were major errors, notably with the Indian Ocean shown as being enclosed, but Ptolemy's use of latitude and longitude furthered an emphasis on the mathematisation of location and, thus, on accurately measured data, recorded with reference to a graticule. Ptolemy's *Geographia*, which made no concessions to religious geography, served as the basis for the knowledge of the geography of the ancient world drawn upon by Shakespeare's contemporaries.

landmasses existed to the north or south of Magellan's route across the Pacific encouraged attention, the latter landmass being seen as necessary in order to balance the greater known landmass in the northern hemisphere. Despite not having actually been found, a southern continent was depicted on maps, for example by Ortelius, and was even shown with a full set of place names. As observers on ships could only see the distance allowed by the human eye (a distance expanded by sending someone to the top of the mast and benefiting from the curvature of the Earth's surface) and, subsequently, by the supplement of the telescope, most of the Pacific remained a matter of speculation.

The sixteenth century did not produce the dramatic news of the late fifteenth, but there was still an increase in geographical information and its dissemination, both in books and in map form. The sources were varied. For example, the capture of individuals helped the transmission of information, notably between Islam and Christendom. Print spread the resulting information, as with Leo Africanus' *La Descrittione dell'Africa* (1550).

Maps provided increased detail of coastlines, but far less so of hinterlands. For example, Diego Gutiérrez's 1562 map of South and Central America offered a complete account of the coastline that captured the general configuration, but the interior was only poorly covered. The charts of the Indian Ocean produced by Sebastião Lopes in his portolan atlas published in Lisbon in about 1565 reflected a growing awareness of the coastline, for example of the island of Sumatra in the East Indies, with which the Portuguese traded, notably for spices.

Much of the greater knowledge stemmed from non-English explorers, especially the Portuguese and Spaniards, and their insights were often not readily available in England. In part, this was due to a determination to control information, and this was certainly the case with Portugal and Spain, which from 1580 to 1640 were under the same ruler, the King of Spain. There were also delays in publication and translation. Thus, in 1625, Samuel Purchas published in England the rutter (advice for pilots) of João de Castro, describing the routes this Portuguese traveller took in the Red Sea in 1541. By 1625, though Samuel Purchas, a London cleric, had already published *Purchas his Pilgrimage, or Relations of the World and the Religions observed in all Ages and Places discovered from the Creation unto this present* (1614).

Moreover, there could be a reluctance to take on new ideas. In 1622, the publication of the history of Ethiopia by the Spanish Jesuit missionary priest Pedro Páez (1564–1622) provided up-to-date information that helped resolve disputes about the size of Ethiopia and the source and course of the Nile. Whereas earlier ideas about Ethiopia were derived from the Classical and medieval world, notably with regard to Prester John, Páez's information provided the foundation for more realistic mapping, not least in refuting earlier views about the great size of Ethiopia. Nevertheless, older ideas about Ethiopia and Africa persisted, especially concerning the Mountains of the Moon and King Solomon's Mines. A different form of the persistence of old ideas, notably their application to the present, was seen with the response to the gold and silver of the Americas, which led to the claim that the New World was the Ophir and Tarsis from where King Solomon had supposedly obtained bullion and ivory.

What's more, in further contradiction of the notion that knowledge is always incremental and mapping therefore a matter of progress, some erroneous ideas, for example about the interior of Africa, were fostered by information obtained, assembled and distributed during sixteenth-century exploration. Some of this was accurate, notably

about coastlines, including river mouths, but there were also many rumours as well as mistaken speculations based on it, for example the idea that California was an island.

Páez's work reflected the extent to which exploration and information had ideological dimensions. It was an aspect of a Jesuit body of knowledge intended to further understanding of the world, an understanding that would contribute to missionary activity, and thus to the glory of God, as well as to the reputation of the new and ambitious Jesuit Order. Founded in 1534, the Jesuits were a Catholic missionary order that expanded greatly in Shakespeare's lifetime, exciting fear in Protestant England. The Order was particularly important for the exploration of South America. More generally, Christian purpose overlapped with cartography, for, aside from concern with the geography of the Holy Land – the key element of *Geographia Sacra*, which was an important aspect of Western geography – maps in part were designed to encourage consideration of God's work.

For Shakespeare's audiences, it was English exploration that was more to the point. Aside from news of exploration by others, a great extension of direct English interaction with the world occurred during Shakespeare's lifetime, one in which the key, but not the only, names were Drake, Cavendish, Frobisher, Davis, Hudson and Raleigh. This exploration left echoes in the plays, as when Sir John Falstaff in *The Merry Wives of Windsor* contemplates the appeal and wealth of the two women he mistakenly thinks desire him: 'she is a region in Guiana, all gold and bounty. I will be 'cheator to them both, and they shall be exchequers to me: they shall be my East and West Indies, and I will trade to them both' (1.3). In this, Shakespeare draws on Sir Walter Raleigh's exploration of modern Venezuela in 1595, exploration that had led to his *The Discovery of the Large, Rich and*

**This world map** is by Antonio Milo, a captain and cartographer who was active from 1557 to 1590, and whose map-making included the production of portolan charts. He lived part of his life in Venice, as shown from the records of the Greek community there. The contrast between, on the one hand, knowledge of the Mediterranean and Black Seas and the shape of Africa, and, on the other, knowledge of much of the rest of the world is readily apparent.

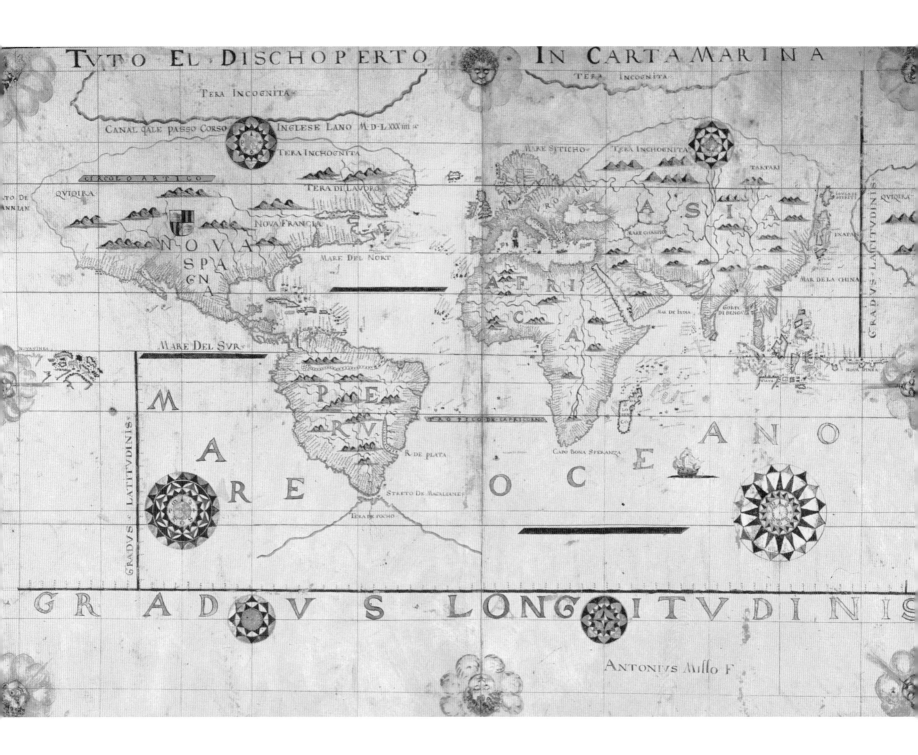

*Beautiful Empire of Guiana* (1596). Alongside other accounts of the Americas, this book influenced the background to Shakespeare's *The Tempest*.

Raleigh knew the playwright Christopher Marlowe and the mathematician Thomas Harriot, and advised Richard Hakluyt, who compiled information on overseas travel. Searching for El Dorado, Raleigh claimed to have found gold in the Orinoco Valley. He continued to be committed to his quest – for example sending out ships in 1596 and 1597 – a quest that helped maintain interest in the region. In the 1610s, Raleigh focused on the issue even though in 1604 peace had been negotiated with Spain, which claimed the area. Against Raleigh's orders, a detachment of the expedition he organised in 1617 attacked the Spaniards, ignoring James I's insistence that he was not to do so, and it did not find any gold mines. As a result, because of Spanish demands for his punishment, Raleigh was beheaded in the Old Palace Yard at the Palace of Westminster in 1618, allegedly saying of the axe: 'This is a sharp medicine, but it is a physician for all diseases and miseries.'

These maps were originally created in 1540 in the *Sala dello Scudo* – a reception room in the Doge's Palace, Venice, which was restored after fire gutted the palace in 1577. The maps were repainted in the eighteenth century. The 'Scudo' Room takes its name from the coat of arms of the reigning Doge, which was exhibited here while he granted audiences and received guests. The largest in the Doge's apartments, the room runs the entire width of this wing of the palace and was used as a reception chamber. Its decoration with large maps was designed to underline the prestige and significance of geographical knowledge. The two globes in the centre of the hall date from the same period. One shows the Earth, the other the Stars, a division also seen in Philip II of Spain's library in his palace at the Escorial. **ABOVE**

This section of the *Sala dello Scudo* covers Greece and the Aegean, which were areas of traditional Venetian interest. Venice retained Crete until lost to the Ottomans in a long war in 1645–69. The Ionian Islands were retained but, other possessions, including Euboea, Coron and Modon, had been lost earlier. Ephesus, the setting of *The Comedy of Errors*, is shown, as is Mitylene, a key site in *The Winter's Tale*, where Helena is sold to work in a brothel, only to thwart the bawd. **RIGHT**

# Projections, Accuracy and Printing

As more maps were produced, different projections were devised in response to the extension of Western knowledge about the physical shape of the world. They did not all have a long-term impact. For example, Petrus Apianus (1495–1552), a German Humanist who became the official cosmographer to the Emperor, Charles V, devised in 1530 the first cordiform (heart-shaped) map to be printed. This had far less impact than the work of the mathematician and map-maker Gerard De Kremer (1512–1594), whose name was Latinised as Mercator. A Fleming, he worked for the Emperor Charles V, the nephew of Henry VIII's first wife, Katherine of Aragon, before in 1552 moving to Duisburg to work for the more pacific Duke of Cleves. In 1569, Mercator produced a nautical chart with a projection that treated the world as a cylinder, so that the meridians were parallel, rather that converging on the North and South, Poles. In this projection, the poles were expanded to the same circumference as the Equator, although in 1569 Mercator produced a separate, fanciful map of the Arctic, presenting it as a rock surrounded by a large body of water from which four channels crossed a continent, dividing it into four islands. Beyond that, there was a continuous ocean to the north of the various continents.

The maps that utilised Mercator's projection greatly magnified the temperate landmasses to the north and south of the Equator at the expense of tropical ones. Taking into account the curvature of the Earth's surface, Mercator's projection kept angles, and thus bearings, accurate in every part of the map. A course of constant bearing (a loxodrome), such as Mercator put on globes, could therefore be readily charted as a straight line across the plane surface of the map. A crucial tool for navigation, this was a huge achievement. It was one unmatched, for example, by the non-Western traders of the Indian Ocean, who were unable to use a grid of latitude and longitude in order to create practical navigation charts. Mercator was also the influential progenitor of putting italic lettering on maps.

To achieve his navigational goal, the scale was varied in the Mercator projection, and thus size was distorted. Mercator's projection affords negligible distortion on large-scale detailed maps of small areas, but relative size is markedly misrepresented on Mercator charts because of the increased poleward separation of parallels required to straighten out loxodromes, the name given to arcs crossing all meridians of longitude at the same angle – in other words, paths with constant bearing as measured relative to true or magnetic north. This, however, was not a problem for Western rulers and merchants keen to explore the possibilities provided by exploration and conquest in the middle latitudes to the west (America) and east (South Asia). Indeed, by providing a way to understand distance, and thus to overcome it, conceptually and practically, the projection highlighted Western transoceanic activity, such as circumnavigations of the world and colonialisation.

It was, therefore, an appropriate accompaniment to the circumnavigations of Francis Drake and Henry Cavendish (the second and the third circumnavigations of the world after the first, the Magellan mission), both by English navigators, as well as to the success of Philip II of Spain (only son of Charles V), in creating, in the 1560s, the first global empire – the first on which the Sun literally never set. The Philippines, named by the Spaniards after Philip, demonstrated another characteristic of imperial power: appropriation through naming, as with Hudson Bay. The name has survived to the present.

The Mercator projection also underlay the idea of the Earth as habitable and open to communication, as opposed to the Classical Greek concept of

**By the mid sixteenth century** it was clear that there was a need for a flat map that allowed seaborne navigators to plot long distances using a straight line that took into account the curvature of the Earth's surface. The result was Gerard Mercator's enormous 1569 world map, called a *Description of the Earth for Use in Navigation*. It employed a projection that lengthened the parallels north and south of the Equator. As can be seen on this map, such a method created maximum distortion at the polar regions, but was remarkably accurate either side of the equatorial regions, particularly when sailing east or west (as shown by the tiny ships in the Indian and Pacific oceans). By the eighteenth century, the projection had been adopted almost universally by European navigators, and was adapted by nineteenth-century atlases extolling the virtues of the British Empire. This led to Mercator (1512–1594) being criticised for 'Eurocentrism', an unreasonable criticism of the map and the man. Mercator, meanwhile, had his own problems with authority, standing accused of heresy by the Catholic authorities in 1544.

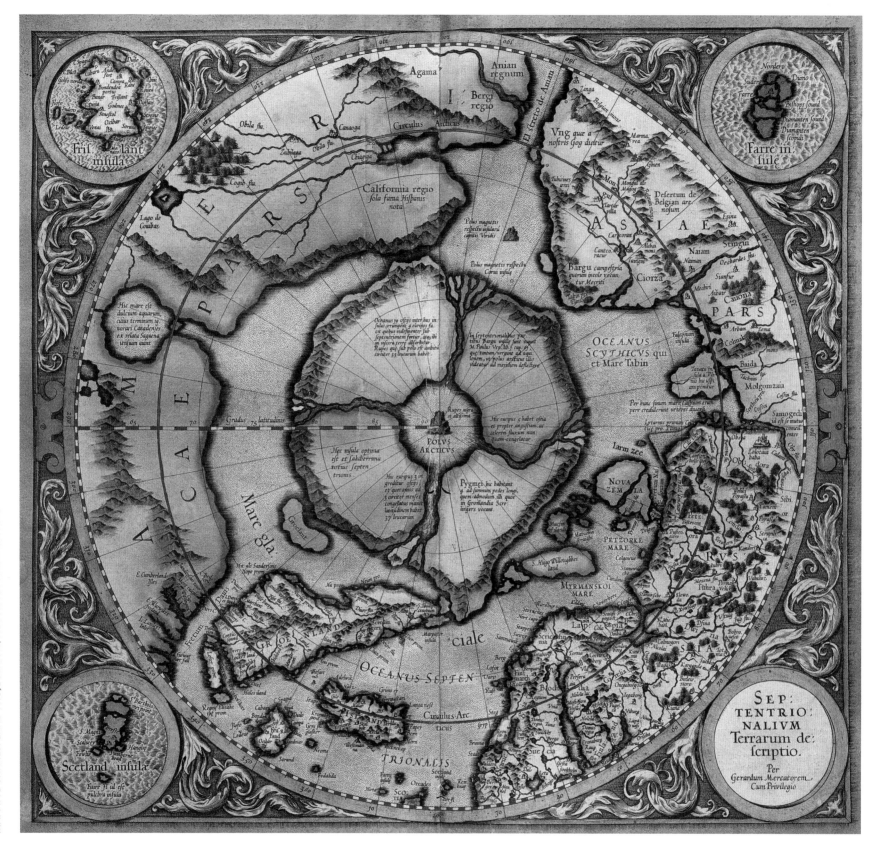

four continents, the inhabitants of which could not communicate with each other. A Mercator projection need not necessarily include more of the northern hemisphere than the southern, nor position Europe at the top centre. However, Mercator placed Europe at the top centre, while also giving the southern hemisphere less than half the map. This reflected both a sense of relative importance and what was easiest to map. However, these practices created misleading assumptions.

More generally, there were (and are) practical problems in providing a two-dimensional representation of the three-dimensional curved globe. The problem that a straight line on a plane chart was not a straight course because of the curvature of the Earth had been highlighted by Pedro Nunes in his 1537 *Tratado da Sphera* (*Treatise of Spheres*), a work that introduced new methods and instruments in navigation. It is not possible to provide both accurate bearing and equal-area mapping.

Mercator looked back to Ptolemy in employing coordinate geometry as both a guarantee of and a means of producing and applying a mathematically consistent plan and a logically uniform set of rules. The combination of the grid of latitude and longitude with perspective geometry proved a more effective way to locate places, and thus to adapt to the range of new information. In contrast, the earlier portolan charts had a variety of scales and units of measure, and the rhumb lines on different charts did not coincide. As a result, these charts were more personalised than the consistency offered by a mathematical formulation of a projection.

Separately to the issue of projection, exploration posed problems over how best to integrate new information with existing material. Additions could be inaccurate because they included material from explorers who, generally understandably, had not comprehended what they saw. In 1522, for example,

Following Gerard Mercator's death in 1594, his son Rumold (1545–1599) published the last of the three parts of his famous atlas, which contains this map. It is the first full map of the Arctic, an expansion of Gerard Mercator's inset of the area in his world map of 1569, here showing recent Northwest and Northeast Passage discoveries. In the east, 'S. Hugo Willoughbes land' is named for Sir Hugh Willoughby (*d*.1554), who, leading the English Company of Merchant Adventurers' three-ship expedition in 1553, became locked in the ice off the coast near Murmansk in Russia with two of his ships.

Willem Barentsz (*c*.1550–1597), the Dutch navigator, while commanding three expeditions in search of a navigable passage to eastern Asia across the top of Europe and Russia, reached Novaya Zemlya and discovered Spitsbergen (1596). 'Fretum Forbosshers' and 'Fretum Dauis,' in the west, refer to discoveries by the Englishmen Martin Frobisher and John Davis in the 1570s and 1580s. The roundels in the corners contain the title and maps of the Shetland Islands, the mythical island of Frisland, and the Faroe Islands.

Mercator depicts the North Pole as a large magnetic rock, surrounded by four mountainous islands that are separated by four major rivers converging upon it. Mercator explained the source for his cartography in a 1577 letter to John Dee, an English mathematician and astrologer:

*'In the midst of the four countries is a Whirl-pool … into which there empty these four indrawing Seas which divide the North. And the water rushes round and descends into the earth just as if one were pouring it through a filter funnel. It is four degrees wide on every side of the Pole, that is to say eight degrees altogether. Except that right under the Pole there lies a bare rock in the midst of the Sea. Its circumference is almost 33 French miles, and it is all of magnetic stone.'*

Giovanni de Verrazano, a Florentine explorer in the service of Francis I of France, followed the coast of North America from Georgia to Nova Scotia. He thought, when sailing off the Outer Banks of North Carolina, that he was seeing a long isthmus between the Atlantic and the Pacific, and this was shown in the world map of 1529 by his brother, Gerolamo de Verrazano. The erroneous idea was later adopted by other map-makers, too.

The New World was the cause of much error. In his *Universale*, or world map, of 1546, Giacomo Gastaldi, who in 1548 became the official cartographer of Venice, captured the eastern seaboard of the Americas and the western seaboard of South America with some accuracy, but he had Asia and North America as a continuous landmass, with the join between the main sections no mere land bridge but as wide as Europe. This was an influential model for other maps of the period. Nevertheless, growing knowledge of North Pacific waters, in particular as a result of voyages from the Indian Ocean to Japan (where the Portuguese and Dutch established trading outposts), led to an abandonment of the land link in many Western maps by the late sixteenth century.

As an admission of a lack of information, and therefore of the expectation that more would be obtained, it was possible to leave the coastlines of the North Pacific blank, as with Edward Wright's map of the world published in the second edition of Richard Hakluyt's *Principal Navigations* (1599) – the map referred to in Maria's description of Malvolio smiling in *Twelfth Night*: 'he does smile his face into more lines than are in the new map with the augmentation of the Indies' (3.2). Despite this, it was not until Vitus Bering's voyages in the early eighteenth century that the idea of a land link between Asia and North America would be conclusively rejected. There was also an erroneous idea of a large north-west passage between Canada and an Arctic landmass to the north, and the belief that California was an island – both assumptions that remained significant into the eighteenth century.

Nevertheless, the accumulative nature of cartographic information was readily apparent. Abraham Ortelius' atlas, the *Theatrum Orbis Terrarum* (*Theatre of the World*), published in Antwerp in 1570, contained 53 maps, and was expanded in the 1584 edition to include a map of the Azores by the Portuguese map-maker Luis Teixeira; interest in the Azores had risen in the early 1580s as Spain conquered them in 1582–1583, beating a Portuguese claimant and his French supporters. In 1582, in the battle of Punta Delgada – one of the major sea battles of the century, which involved 90 sailing ships – the Spaniards intercepted and defeated a larger French fleet. The 1595 edition also contained a map of Japan based on Teixeira's work. Editions appeared in a number of languages, including Dutch, French, German and Spanish.

John Norton (*c.*1556–1612), Printer to James I, Master of the Stationers' Company and Alderman of London, published a handsome English edition of Ortelius in 1606, the first in English. The largest book ever published in England up to that date, this was based on the Latin edition of 1603. The maps were printed in Antwerp and then shipped to London, where the text was added, probably having been translated by William Bedwell (1561–1632), a cleric who is regarded as the father of Arabic studies in England, and who was also a keen mathematician and astronomer. The edition carried the arms of James I.

Like Mercator, Ortelius (1527–1598) captured the idea of mapping as a continuous process, rather than representing the proclamation of a supposedly complete body of knowledge. Thus, his *Theatrum* made reference to the sources used for its maps, a practice that carried with it the implication that new

This 1554 *Map of Europe* by Mercator, a printed work, correctly shows Bohemia far from the coast, unlike Shakespeare in *The Winter's Tale*, who draws on his literary source, Robert Greene's prose romance *Pandosto: The Triumph of Time* (1588). Mercator also depicts political boundaries, many of which are linked to mountain ranges. Cyprus, still then a Venetian possession, is shown, as is Tarso (Tarsus), which is mentioned in *The Winter's Tale*, and Ephesus, the setting of *The Comedy of Errors*. The handling of the Arctic is wrong, but most of the Mediterranean is covered reasonably well, although there are errors in depiction and alignment.

EVROPA,
ad magnæ Europæ Ge:
rardi Mercatoris P. imitati:
onem, Rumoldi Mercatoris F.
cura edita, seruato tamen
initio longitudinis ex ratio:
ne magnetis, quod Pater
in magna sua vniuer:
sali posuit.

Medius Meridianus eo reliqui ad hunc
inclinantur pro ratione 60. & 40.
parallelorum.

information would lead to new maps. Mercator, who was committed to the search for new sources, had correspondents as far away as Goa in India, the major Portuguese base in the Indian Ocean.

Ortelius' work was extensively drawn on by the playwright Christopher Marlowe, who took many place names and geographic features from the *Theatrum*, as well as from illustrations in the atlas. It is apparent that Marlowe had the atlas open when he wrote. Shakespeare, by contrast, certainly did not, given the description of Bohemia in *The Winter's Tale* as 'A desert Country near the Sea' (3.3) to which a ship could sail. Shakespeare took this information from Robert Greene's *Pandosto: The Triumph of Time* (1588), but the description has been seen by some as part of the play's function as a moral fable. From Ben Jonson onwards, there have been complaints about the description, although Bohemia also had a positive reputation as a land of Protestantism.

For the Americas, the accumulation of cartographic information was easier when it came to their coastlines than it was for their interiors. Nevertheless, progress was made with the latter. Thus, in the 1570s, Philip II of Spain commissioned an extensive survey of his territory, the *Relaciones Geográficas*, partly with the aim of elucidating the political boundaries or tribute-reach of pre-Conquest states. Indigenous artists were, in the main, responsible for the maps that emanated from New Spain in response to Philip's commission. This mixture of native and European mapping conventions and symbols marked a transition stage that reflected the syncretic character of Spanish imperialism: its ability to adopt and adapt as part of its rule, seen, for example, in the way in which native religious cults were given a place within Christianity. The Spaniards, however, became increasingly concerned with having standard European-style documentation to support titles to land and other claims, and

this contributed to the decline of native mapping.

More generally, the organisation of information about the outside world was a matter in part of a systematic response to accumulation, as with the Dutch East and West India Companies, whose ship pilots began to produce charts employing sheets of paper with pre-drawn compass lines. This also applied to the concept of a map-book or atlas. The idea of maps systematically produced to a common purpose fused utility and the consequences of the technology of printing, including predictability and quantity.

Printing was a key element. Manuscript maps continued to be produced, for example from 1536 to 1564 by Battista Agnese, who worked in Venice – a major centre of cartography as well as an important subject of maps. However, the printing of maps began in Europe in the 1470s and became central to most map production in the sixteenth century. Thanks to the use of woodblocks, maps could be more speedily produced and more widely distributed, and could therefore be profitable as a format designed for a non-personalised market.

From the mid-sixteenth century, woodblocks gave way to engraved copper plates as the latter were easier to correct and revise – both important factors in a map-making world that emphasised novelty and precision. At the same time, copper lacked durability and had to be re-engraved, which, again, encouraged the incorporation of new material through revision. New machinery, too, played a part in changes in the production process. In place of the screw press came the rolling press, which was used for printing from copper plates, and which offered speedier output and greater uniformity. Faster output was important to the entrepreneurial character of map publishing, since it made it easier to test demand and to switch to new editions.

Information was cumulative and, as a result of printing, most map-makers had more and more recent maps to which they could refer. Printing therefore facilitated the exchange of information and the processes of copying and revision that were so important for map-making. By contrast, hand copies were prone to variations, and thus to corruption. However, this contrast was far less the case for an atlas because the latter was a compilation of maps, each of which could have a separate publication history, not least with the use of old sheets after newer versions were printed. The compilation could thus vary greatly.

The Mariner's Mirrour, a book of sailing directions and printed charts, with an opening section on the art of navigation, was published in 1588. It was called a *waggoner* because of the author of the Dutch original, *Spieghel der Zeevaerdt* (1583–1584), Lucas Janszoon Waghenaer. The frontispiece of the book depicts public interest, with a crowd waiting for a blank globe to be completed. A French pilot book covering more limited waters had been translated into English earlier in the century.

Printing also led to an emphasis on the commercial aspects of map-making, and encouraged a wider public interest in maps, and thus created a new dynamic for their production – one that copperplate engraving was well placed to satisfy. In addition, map-making was linked to new techniques for acquiring information – notably triangulation, the way to measure a straight line over the Earth's curved surface – and this was explained in works such as *The Cosmographical Glasse* (1559) by William Cuningham, while John Davis's *The Seaman's Secrets* (1595) provided advice on how to read charts and use instruments.

Maps thus became a more important form of applied knowledge, one in which, as with geography books, knowledge could be accumulated, organised and deployed for reasons of pleasure and profit. However, as Shakespeare shows, this issue could become contentious. In *Troilus and Cressida,* for instance, Ulysses has to respond to the criticisms of Greek war-making made by Achilles and Patroclus, criticisms that extend to 'mappers':

> 'They tax our policy, and call it cowardice;
> Count wisdom as no member of the war;
> Forestall prescience, and esteem no act
> But that of hand; the still and mental parts,
> That do contrive how many hands shall strike,
> When fitness calls them on, and know by measure
> Of their observant toil the enemies' weight, –
> Why, this hath not a finger's dignity:
> They call this bed-work, mappery, closet-war;
> So that the ram that batters down the wall,
> For the great swing and rudeness of his poise,
> They place before his hand that made the engine
> Or those that with the fineness of their souls
> By reason guide his execution.'
> (1.3)

Title page from *The Mariner's Mirrour*, 1588. The book is an English version of the world's first sea-atlas, containing a ground-breaking collection of charts, coastal views and directions intended to help sailors navigate the coastlines of Western Europe, from southern Spain to northern Norway. **ABOVE**

# Astrology and Astronomy

The measurement, presentation and understanding of physical space on the Earth's surface scarcely exhausted the geographies of Shakespeare's world: an important geography was presented by the stars. This indeed was a geography that appeared far more present than that of distant continents, in part due to the influence, if not control, that the zodiac was believed to wield over people's lives. The zodiac was part of an ordered world, and this can be seen repeatedly in Shakespeare. In *Troilus and Cressida*, for example, Ulysses declares:

'Degree being vizarded,
The unworthiest shows as fairly in the mask.
The heavens themselves, the planets and this centre
Observe degree, priority and place,
Insisture, course, proportion, season, form,
Office and custom, in all line of order;
And therefore is the glorious planet Sol
In noble eminence enthroned and sphered
Amidst the other; whose medicinable eye
Corrects the ill aspects of planets evil,
And posts, like the commandment of a king,
Sans cheque to good and bad: but when the planets
In evil mixture to disorder wander,
What plagues and what portents! what mutiny!
What raging of the sea! shaking of earth!
Commotion in the winds! frights, changes, horrors,
Divert and crack, rend and deracinate
The unity and married calm of states
Quite from their fixure! O, when degree is shaked,
Which is the ladder to all high designs,
Then enterprise is sick! How could communities,
Degrees in schools and brotherhoods in cities,
Peaceful commerce from dividable shores,
The primogenitive and due of birth,
Prerogative of age, crowns, sceptres, laurels,
But by degree, stand in authentic place?*

*Take but degree away, untune that string,*
*And, hark, what discord follows!' (1.3)*

Ulysses is presented as a skilled speaker, indeed manipulator, and what he says may be comprehended in this context. Moreover, it is not necessary to understand speeches as necessarily reflecting Shakespeare's views. Nevertheless, Ulysses' remarks reflected a widespread opinion: the world – not just the Earth, but the wider world within which the Earth was located – had order, and therefore purpose. Humans needed maps to understand this order and its underlying structure, and these maps were both mental and physical. The zodiac was a key form and process of this structure.

Astrology, almanacs and witchcraft were thus all part of the process, one that could variously be benign or malign, or both. Life, fertility, health, livelihood, fortune in war or love – all were at stake in a form of, at once, control and pursuit of knowledge that replicated that of the oracles of Antiquity. Justice, free will and determinism all played a role. The tales of Antiquity, notably Ovid's *Metamorphoses*, which was extensively used by Shakespeare, described unpredictable change, but also change that reflected the transformative ability of phenomena, including change of shape and the coming loss and recovery of life, and, with it, of identity and love. These were stories about becoming. Ovid was Shakespeare's favourite Classical writer, and most of his references to Classical mythology relate to stories in that work, which Shakespeare knew in both Latin and in the 1567 English translation. The influence of the *Metamorphoses* is especially strong in *A Midsummer Night's Dream*, *Titus Andronicus* and *The Winter's Tale*, but it can also be seen elsewhere, for example in *The Tempest*; Shakespeare's Classical education at Stratford left an important legacy in his writings.

Globes showing the signs of the zodiac, 1511. Astrology was heavily dependent on information that was depicted in a variety of forms, including globes. Shakespeare's characters regularly make astrological references. In *Much Ado About Nothing*, for instance, Don John says to Conrade, a fellow villain: 'I wonder that thou – being, as thou sayest thou art, born under Saturn – goest about to apply a moral medicine to a mortifying mischief' (1.3). This is a reference to the gloomy and 'saturnine' character of those born under this sign. Astrology represented a powerful continuation from medieval thought, one made stronger and more dynamic in Shakespeare's lifetime by the attempt to revive the supposed purity of its ancient roots and by the incorporation of new astronomical and mathematical knowledge.

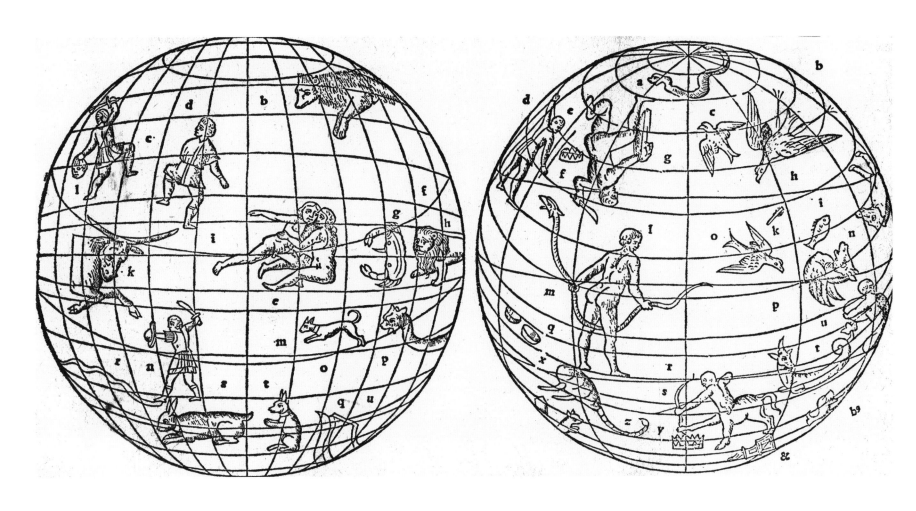

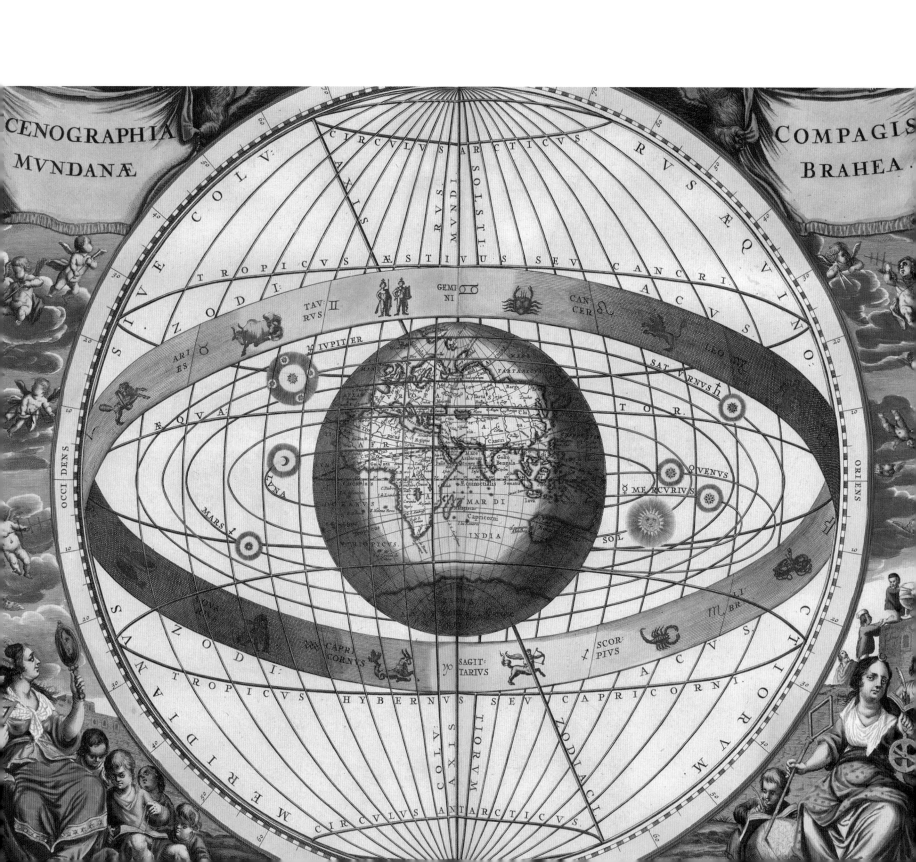

The impact of the zodiac was also seen in both character and change. This crucial issue fired up the debate between determinism and free will – a debate found throughout Shakespeare and in works by other playwrights of the period. This could be horrific, as the spell-casting witches lure Macbeth to regicide, or comic, as lovers seek to influence their intended. Other issues, too, could be involved.

There was also neglect or criticism of the influence of astrology. At the start of *Cymbeline*, for example, the First Gentleman observes that:

*'our bloods*
*No more obey the heavens.' (1.1)*

In *King Lear*, there is a bitter attack on astrology and the zodiac, though it is given to the morally bankrupt villain Edmund, which compromises the attack.

The common characteristic for those who believed in, or at least were aware of, the zodiac, was of a geography as well as a moral sphere that needed to be navigated. This was a geography of the factors that affected fate, one that, in practice, brought the occult into people's lives and enabled its possibilities to be understood. The magician was therefore the great geographer, for the magician could range beyond Christian magic to conjure up evil or seek to lessen it, although, again – not least for dramatic effect and to avoid Calvinistic predestination – space had to be left for individual will. Prospero was the most impressive instance of Shakespeare's magicians, but he was scarcely alone. The magicians could scan the skies, indeed generally did so, but they also looked at a full range of means to gauge the future, many of which were reading natural runes on Earth, from human health to the behaviour of animals or other equivalents. Casca tells Cassius in *Julius Caesar* that:

*'It is the part of men to fear and tremble*
*When the most mighty gods by tokens send*
*Such dreadful heralds to astonish us.' (1.3.54–56)*

This was a geography that was respectable in Shakespeare's London, notably with the reputation of John Dee (1517–1608), a leading mathematician and cartographer. Indeed, the date of Elizabeth's coronation was fixed only after consultation with Dee and, in 1575, Elizabeth and the Privy Council came to visit his large library. As a reminder of the overlaps of careers and interests, Dee, author of *General and Rare Memorials Pertaining to the Perfect Art of Navigation* (1577), gave advice on navigation to explorers and coined the term the 'British Empire'. On the Continent, meanwhile, the court of the Emperor Rudolf II (r. 1576–1612), located in Prague, was a major centre of astrology. Those involved sought to be at the cutting edge of advances in astronomy, mathematics and other subjects; they were not 'reactionary' figures. More humble astrologers lacked such patronage, facilities and education, but benefited from the knowledge and information provided by publications.

Again, this was a world comprehended and presented by Shakespeare. Fortune telling was a matter of the small talk of young men discussing marital prospects, as much as a risk to souls, as in *Macbeth*, or an engagement with affairs of state. In *Henry IV, Part One*, Owen Glendower and Hotspur row about the astral signs, which were frequently cited as highly significant, that allegedly accompanied the birth of the former. In *King John*, the villainous king is told:

*'... they say five moons were seen tonight:*
*Four-fixed, and the fifth did whirl about*
*the other four in wondrous motion...*
*Old men and bedlams [the insane] in the streets*
*Do prophesy upon it dangerously.'*
*(4.2)*

**The world's location** according to Danish astronomer Tycho Brahe (1546–1601). Financed from 1576 to 1597 by the Danish Crown, Brahe built a large observatory. He also built on the Ptolemaic Earth-centred view of the universe, and provided many observations and, in 1600, went on to Prague to work as Court Astronomer to the Emperor Rudolf II, a position later filled by Kepler. Famously, he devised a geo-heliocentric system in which the five then known planets orbit the Sun, while the Sun and the Moon orbit the Earth. In *Antony and Cleopatra*, Octavius, Julius Caesar's great nephew and adopted son, better known as Augustus, responds to Antony's suicide, regretting:

*'... that our stars,*
*Unreconcilable, should divide*
*Our equalness to this.'*
*(5.1)*

Astronomy was, then, a key element in the understanding of the world, and one that was developing rapidly. Thomas Addison's *Arithmetical Navigation* (1625) provided detailed knowledge about the effective use of maritime charts and about the celestial bodies. The heliocentric system of Nicolaus Copernicus (1473–1543), namely, that the Earth moved about the Sun, was rapidly disseminated by print, while the *Rudolphine Tables* (1627) of Johannes Kepler (1571–1630) provided tables of planetary positions based on his discovery that the orbits of planets were elliptic and on his ability to ascertain their speeds. Kepler, the author of *Astronomia Nova* (1609), succeeded Tycho Brahe (1546–1601) as court astronomer to Rudolf II. Copenhagen, from where James I's wife, Anne, came, was also an important centre of astronomy, with King Christian IV a major supporter. Kepler's *Harmonice Mundi* (*Harmonies of the World*, 1619), reflected both his continuing research in planetary motion and the belief that astronomy was necessary to understand the inherent design and order of the universe, and therefore its capacity for good. Jeremiah Horrocks (1618–1641), an English astronomer, made use of the *Rudolphine Tables* to predict, and observe, the transit of Venus across the Sun in 1639 – the first such prediction.

There was also an interest in the idea of other inhabitants of the cosmos, which helped to explain concern with the Moon, where such inhabitants were believed to exist. The predictive power of the imagination was seen in written accounts of fictional lunar voyages, such as Kepler's *Somnium* (*Dream*) of about 1609 and Francis Godwin's *The Man in the Moone: or A Discourse of a Voyage Thither* (1638).

Astronomical research encouraged an interest in mathematical understandings of the cosmos and its workings. This was particularly seen with the work of Shakespeare's contemporary Galileo Galilei (1564–1642), Professor of Mathematics at the University of Pauda, and then Mathematician to Grand Duke Cosimo of Tuscany. His first publication, *Le Operazioni del compasso geometrico e militare* (1606), focused on military engineering, not navigation, but there was an emphasis on using an instrument (a compass) and on the importance of applying mathematical rules. Subsequently, Galileo's empirical research centred on the newly invented telescope. First appearing at The Hague in 1608, this was an instrument greatly improved by Galileo. His research helped make Copernicus' ideas relevant and convincing. Moreover, in revealing what he had discovered with his telescope which, by the close of 1609, magnified 20 times, Galileo's *Sidereus Nuncius* (*The Sidereal Messenger*, 1610) transformed the understanding of the Moon by showing it to be like the Earth: uneven and with mountains and valleys.

Such a similarity challenged the view of an essential contrast between the nature and substance of the Earth and the Heavens, an argument made by Aristotle. Drawing on his authority, the thinkers of medieval Christendom saw the Moon as being like the planets – perfect in shape and orbit, and unchanging – whereas the Earth was prone to change and decay. As a result, the Earth was the appropriate setting for redemption. By revealing that Jupiter had four satellites, Galileo also showed that the Earth's moon was not unique.

In 1613, Galileo's astronomical ideas were attacked on scriptural grounds. A self-conscious rationalist as well as an empiricist, he subsequently fell foul of Church authority, in part because of his *Dialogo sopra i due massimi sistemi del mondo* (*Dialogue on the Two Principal World Systems*, 1632), which compared the Copernican and Ptolemaic systems, and supported the former. In 1633, the Inquisition condemned Galileo for holding that the Earth moves

**The Sun at the Centre** is the heliocentric model of the Solar System that placed the Sun, not the Earth, at the centre of the system, the latter being the view of the Bible and Ptolemy. Drawing on Classical ideas, the heliocentric model was advanced by Nicolaus Copernicus (1473–1543) in his *De Revolutionibus Orbium Coelestium* (*On the Revolution of Heavenly Spheres*, 1543). At the start of *Cymbeline*, the First Gentleman observes that: 'our bloods/No more obey the heavens' (1.1).

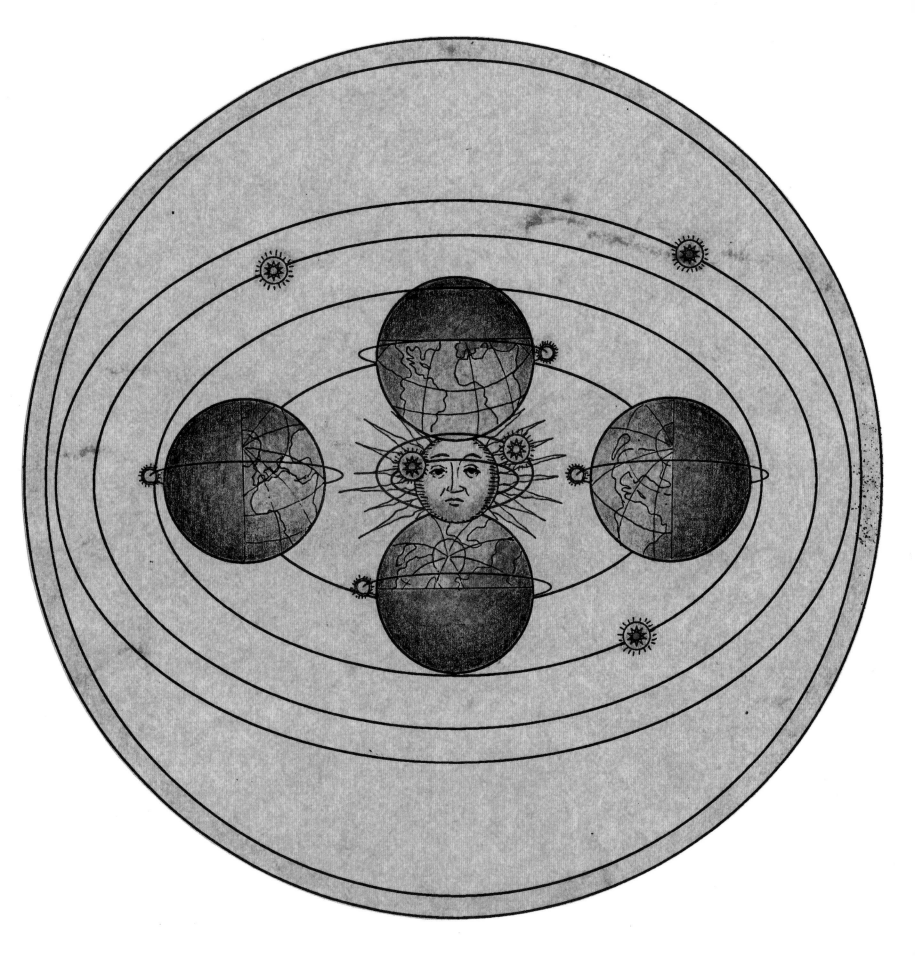

and that the Bible is not a scientific authority. In addition, his views on atomism were a challenge to the Catholic doctrine of transubstantiation, and thus to its practice of the Mass, the nature of matter being significant in both cases.

Galileo was duly confined to house imprisonment. The Inquisition had been introduced into Tuscany as part of the process in which the Medici became Grand Dukes, identifying himself with the authority of the Church. Condemnation by the Inquisition, a Papal institution, saved Galileo from being tried by the Tuscan government on issues related also to religion, a trial that might have led to a death sentence. Thus, rival jurisdictions played a major role in the crisis of Galileo's life. Astronomy continued to offer new perspectives, and these were recorded and rapidly disseminated. Since measurement was crucial, improvements in telescopes played a role. As with advances in knowledge through voyages of exploration, astronomy led to mapping, naming and systematisation. Lunar map-making was taken forwards, and for long fixed, with Johannes Hevelius' *Selenographia* (1647), while Giovanni Riccioli's *Almagestum Novum* (1651) established the system for naming lunar features. Advances in astronomy also helped resolve major issues in geography and navigation on Earth, for example determining longitude on land.

The impact of the telescope was matched (less dramatically) by that of the microscope, which was also used from the early seventeenth century onwards. Like the telescope, the microscope unlocked another world, and again served to suggest linkages, with Robert Hooke, in his *Micrographia* (1655), arguing that the micro-world helped explain how that at the human scale worked.

Map of the constellations in the Northern Hemisphere. The geography of the stars appeared far more present than that of distant continents in part due to the influence, if not control, the zodiac was believed to wield. There was considerable debate about the legitimacy and accuracy of astrology, including criticism from Christian commentators. In 1601, John Chamber (1546–1604), an Oxford academic who lectured and wrote on astronomy, published his *Treatise against Judicial Astrology*. In reply, Sir Christopher Heydon (1561–1623) published *A Defence of Judiciall Astrologie* (1603), which in turn led George Carleton, Bishop of Chichester, to publish *The Madnesse of Astrologers* (1624). 'Rapt in secret studies' (1.2), Prospero is a potent instance of a holder and user of the secret knowledge offered by the zodiac. **OPPOSITE**

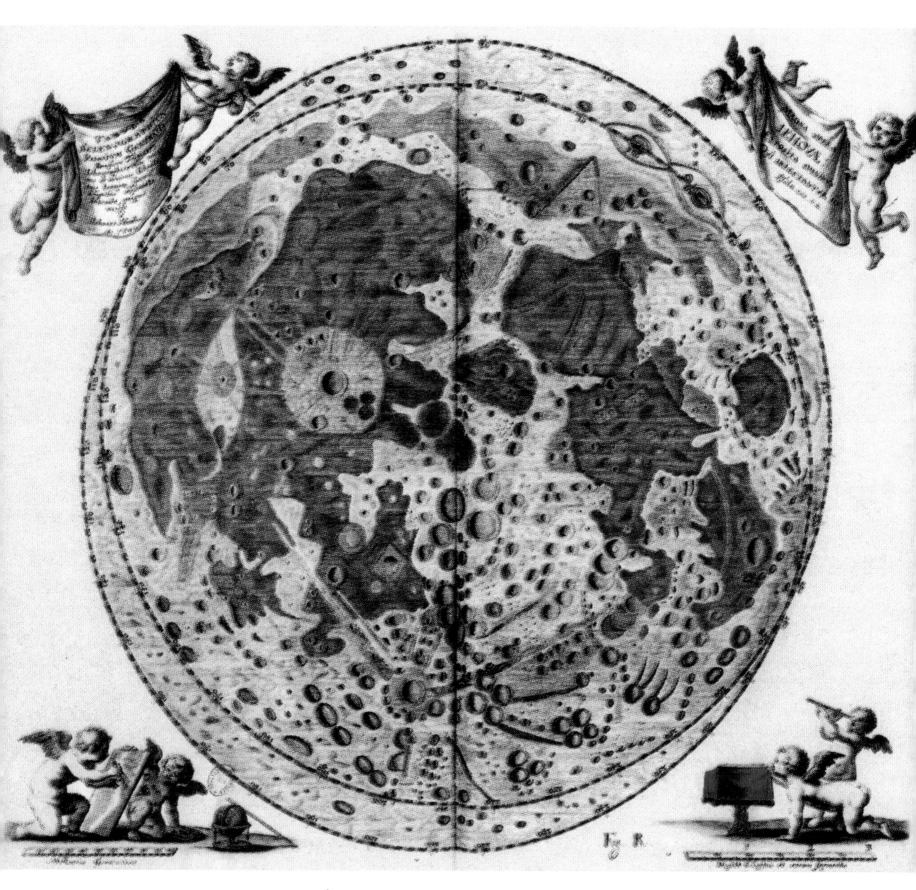

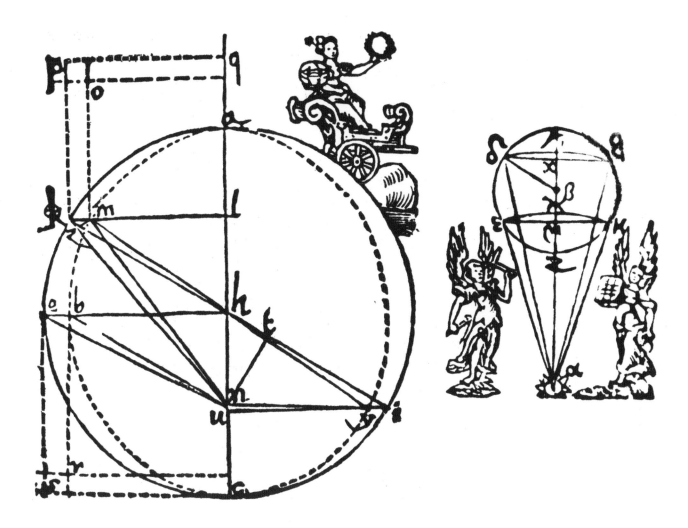

Map of the Moon, 1654, by Johannes Hevelius. In *The Tempest*, Stephano tells Caliban that he had been 'the man i th'moon' (2.2) and had come from the Moon to the island, while Prospero describes Caliban's mother, the witch Sycorax, as:

> '... one so strong/That could control the moon'. (5.1)

Elsewhere, the predictive power of the imagination was seen in written accounts of fictional lunar voyages, such as Kepler 's *Somnium* (*Dream*) of about 1609 and Francis Godwin's *The Man in the Moone: or A Discourse of a Voyage Thither* (1638). Playwrights were less adventurous. **LEFT**

Drawing showing the calculation of the orbits of planets from Johannes Kepler's *Astronomia Nova* (1609). Kepler succeeded Tycho Brahe as Court Astronomer to the Emperor Rudolf II, a major sponsor of astrology. In his *Rudolphine Tables*, Kepler provided tables of planetary positions based on his discovery that the orbits of planets were elliptic and on his ability to ascertain their speeds. In *Titus Andronicus*, Aaron asked 'was't not a happy star led us to Rome' (4.2). **ABOVE**

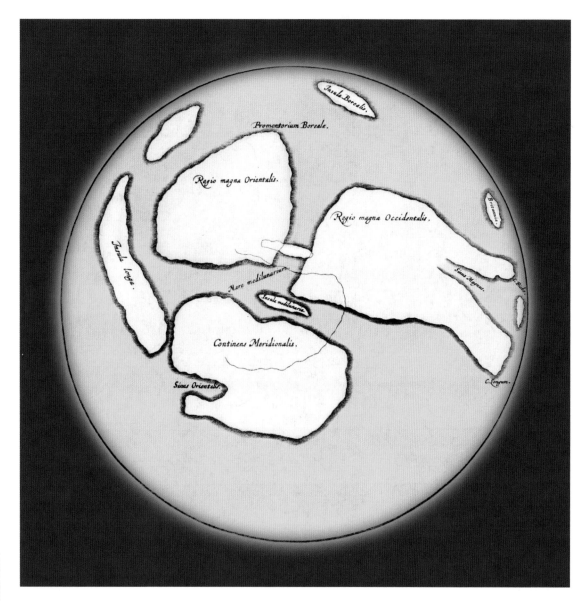

**A map of the Moon**, made before the invention of the telescope, drawn by William Gilbert (1544–1603). Gilbert was a Cambridge academic who became physician to Queen Elizabeth in 1601 and then James I. He wrote several major works on magnetism, publishing in 1600 *De Magnete, Magneticisque Corporibus, et de Magno Magnete Tellure* (*On the Magnet and Magnetic Bodies, and on the Great Magnet the Earth*) – an important study. Gilbert made the first attempt to map the surface markings of the Moon. He argued that the light spots on the Moon were water. **ABOVE**

*Constellations in the Southern Sky,* based on a map by Albrecht Durer (1515) and decorated with the crest of Cardinal Lang von Wellenberg. The Southern sky was opened up to Europeans by voyages of exploration from the late fifteenth century. Astrology resulted in a geography as well as a moral sphere needing to be navigated, a geography of the factors that affected fate. The difficulties in interpreting the stars in relation to fate can be seen in Sonnet 14:

*'Not from the stars do I my judgement pluck;*
*And yet methinks I have astronomy,*
*But not to tell of good or evil luck,*
*Of plagues, of dearths, or seasons' quality;*
*Nor can I fortune to brief minutes tell,*
*Pointing to each his thunder, rain, and wind,*
*Or say with princes if it shall go well,*
*By oft predict that I in heaven find:*
*But from thine eyes my knowledge I derive,*
*And, constant stars, in them I read such art*
*As "Truth and beauty shall together thrive,*
*If from thyself to store thou wouldst convert";*
*Or else of thee this I prognosticate:*
*"Thy end is truth's and beauty's doom*
*and date."'* **RIGHT**

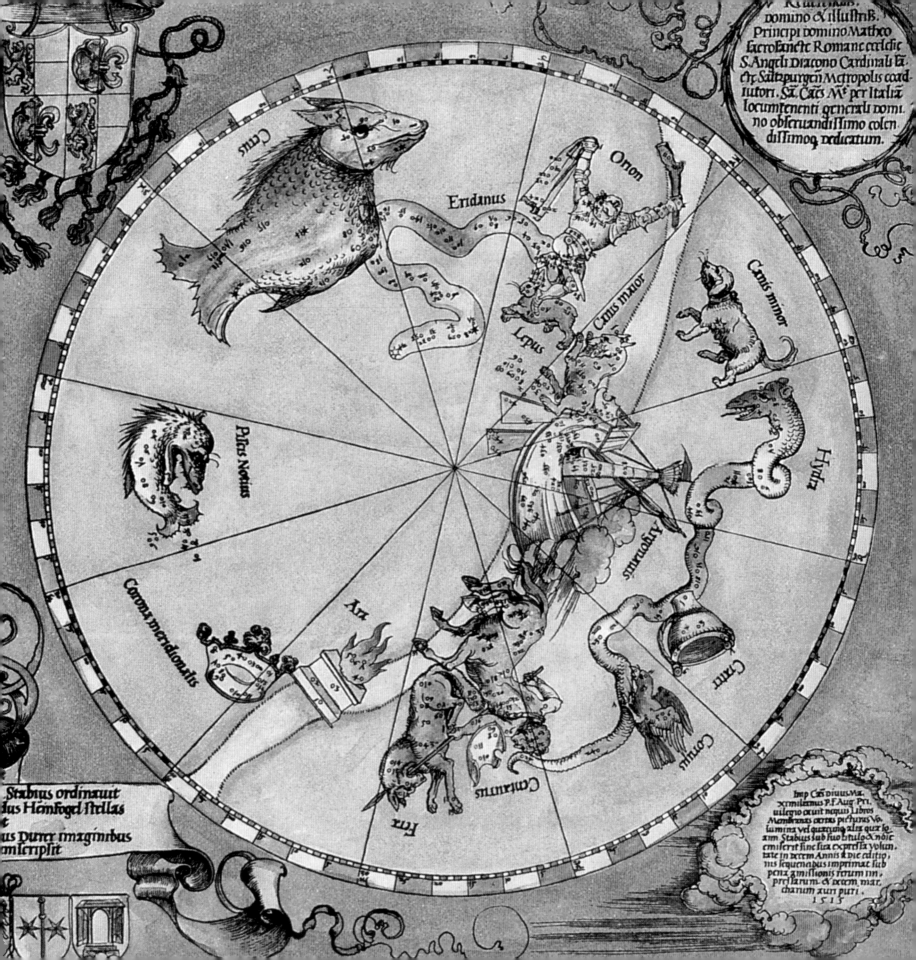

ARCIS VRANIBVRGI, A TYCHONE BRAHE, DÑO DE KNVDSTRVP, IN INSVLA HELLESPONTI DANICI HVENNA CONSTRVCTÆ, QVO AD TOTAM CAPACITATEM, DESIGNATIO.

In *Troilus and Cressida*, Ulysses declares:

> 'Observe degree, priority and place,
> Insisture, course, proportion,
>     season, form,
> Office and custom, in all line of order;
> And therefore is the glorious planet Sol
> In noble eminence enthroned
>     and sphered
> Amidst the other;
>     whose medicinable eye
> Corrects the ill aspects of planets' evil,'
>     (1.3)

**LEFT**

*On the Revolutions of the Celestial Spheres*, 1543, by Nicolaus Copernicus. The astronomical model developed by Copernicus placed the Sun near the centre of the Universe. The Sun is shown as motionless, allowing the Earth and other planets to orbit around around it in circular paths at uniform speeds. It was a significant departure from the Ptolemaic model which placed the Earth at the centre of the universe. **RIGHT**

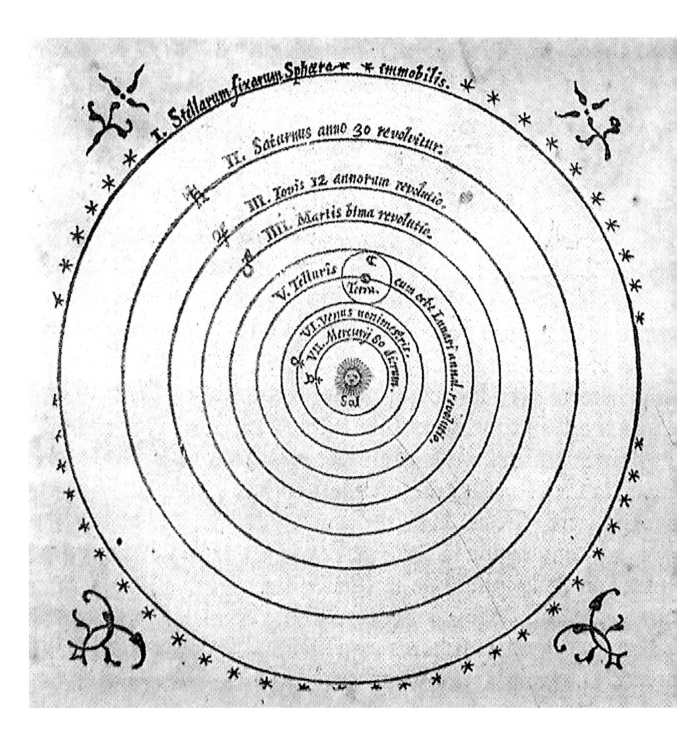

Pages from *Sidereus Nuncius* (*The Sidereal Messenger*, 1610) by Galileo Galilei (1564–1642). In revealing what he had discovered with his telescope – which, by the close of 1609, magnified 20 times – this book transformed the understanding of the Moon by showing it to be like the Earth: uneven and with mountains and valleys. Such a similarity challenged the view of an essential contrast between the nature and substance of Earth and the Heavens, an argument made by Aristotle. Drawing on his authority, the thinkers of medieval Christendom saw the Moon as being like the planets: perfect in shape and orbit and unchanging. Galileo offered a different interpretation.

This fascination with all things lunar can be seen in *A Midsummer Night's Dream*, when Robin Starveling, the tailor, plays the Moon, accompanied by dog, thorn-bush and lanthorn, and Theseus facetiously discusses whether he should 'be put into the lanthorn: how is it else the man i' the moon?' (5.1)

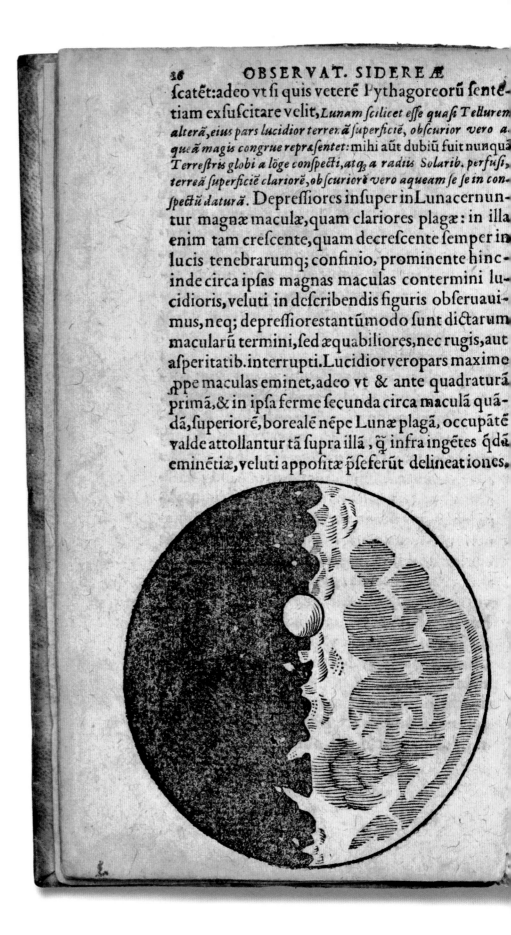

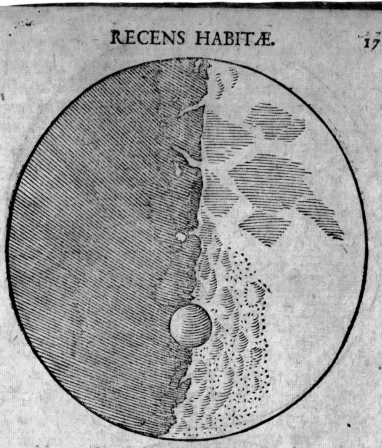

Hæc eadē macula ante secundam quadraturam ni-
grioribus quibusdam terminis circumuallata conspi-
citur, qui tanquam altissima montium iuga ex parte
Soli auersa obscuriores apparent, qua vero Solem re-
spiciunt, lucidiores exstāt, cuius oppositum in cauita-
tibus accidit, quarum pars Soli auersa splendens appa-
ret, obscura vero ac vmbrosa, quæ ex parte Solis sita
est. Imminuta deinde luminosa superficie, cum pri-
mū tota ferme dicta macula tenebris est obducta, cla-
riora montium dorsa eminenter tenebras scandunt.
Hanc duplicem apparentiam sequentes figuræ com-
monstrant.

B

**This 17th century celestial map** by Dutch cartographer Frederik de Wit (1630–1706) shows star groups and astrological and zodiac signs. The importance of the stars is revealed repeatedly in Shakespeare's works, for instance in Sonnet 15, when he writes: '... this huge stage presenteth nought but shows/Whereon the stars in secret influence comment' (3–4); or in *Much Ado About Nothing*, when Beatrice remarks that 'there was a star danced, and under that I was born' (2.1). Other examples occur in *All's Well That Ends Well*, when Parolles is told he must have been born under Mars when it was moving backwards because he is inclined to flee when fighting, and in *Twelfth Night*, when Toby Belch points out to Andrew Aguecheek that they were both 'born under Taurus' (1.3) and should therefore be able to dance.

In *King Lear*, however, Shakespeare provides a bitter attack on astrology and the zodiac, although, since the words are delivered by the morally bankrupt Edmund, it is greatly compromised: 'This is the excellent foppery of the world ... we make guilty of our disasters the sun, the moon, and the stars' (1.2).

<u>Macbeth and the three witches</u> from Raphael Holinshed's *Chronicles of England, Scotland, and Ireland ... from the First Inhabiting unto the Conquest*. The spell-casting witches lure Macbeth to regicide (the murder of Duncan) and the loss of his soul. The witches operate in the dark or in misty vapours, while Macbeth's evil is encapsulated by his willingness to call on the dark to cover the murder of his erstwhile friend, now imagined rival, Banquo. King from 1040 until 1057, Macbeth in fact replaced Duncan I (r. 1034–1040), who had been killed in battle by Macbeth's forces. In turn, Macbeth had to face an English invasion in 1054. He was killed in 1057 at the battle of Lumphanan by forces loyal to Duncan's son Malcolm III (r.1058–93) who gained the throne after assassinating Macbeth's stepson Lulach (r.1057–58). **ABOVE**

<u>Map of the universe</u> from *The Tales of Luqman*, an Arabic manuscript, 1583. It is a miniature showing the Globe, the seven saints of the heavens, the Zodiac and the position of the 28 days of the month. **RIGHT**

# Mapping England

In Tudor England, maps grew in potency, both as a symbol and as reality. Their visual splendour encouraged their display, but maps were also used. Their authority increased when one illustrating the Exodus route of the Bible was printed in 1535, which meant that the Bible story could be fixed. John Dee noted that men began to collect maps:

*'Some to beautify their halls, parlours, chambers, galleries or studies or libraries with ... some other[s] to view the large dominion of the Turk, the wide empire of the Muscovite, and the little morsel of ground where Christendom ... is certainly known ... some other[s] for their own journeys ... into far lands, or to understand other men's travels.'*

In Shakespeare's *King John*, Philip the Bastard, a positive and energetic character, mocks the conversation of polite society:

*'And talking of the Alps and Apennines,*
*the Pyrenean and the river Po,*
*It draws toward supper in conclusion so.*
*But this is worshipful society*
*And fits the mounting spirit like myself.'*
*(1.1)*

The development of map-making in Europe in the period can be seen in the attractive maps produced in England by Christopher Saxton, about whose early life little is known. Born in about 1542–1544 in Yorkshire, Saxton learned surveying and was commissioned by Thomas Seckford, Surveyor of the Court of Wards and Liveries, to produce his county maps. Seckford was close to Elizabeth I's leading minister, William Cecil (1520–1598), Secretary of State from 1550 to 1553 and 1558 to 1572, and Treasurer from 1572 until his death. Cecil, who was made Lord Burghley in 1571, had a substantial collection of maps, some annotated in his own hand, and had been a patron of Laurence Nowell in his interest in mapping and other scholarly work in the 1560s.

Cecil had manuscript maps, including early proof states of Saxton's printed county maps, bound together in a bespoke reference atlas. One included was an unsigned, undated map with the title 'This platte ys made for the description of the river of Humber and of the sea and seacoast from Hull to Skarburgh.' The map includes the coast of East Yorkshire, showing possible landing places, as well as the harbours and warning beacons, and depth soundings in the waters off the coast. The map reveals concern about the prospect of invasion by the French, who raided Tynemouth in the winter of 1559/60. The map indicates that Saxton built on a widespread competence in map-making practice. The primary purpose of this map, however, was unlike that of Saxton's 1577 map of the county, in that it was hydrographic not topographical. Indeed, the map includes directions for entering or leaving port or riding at anchorage in different winds. It also depicts Ravenspur at the mouth of the river Humber, a sand spit where, as Shakespeare recorded, the future Henry IV had landed in 1399 in order to overthrow Richard II.

Military purposes, indeed, were a key element of map-making, although the surveying of land for economic reasons was separately significant. In 1512, a map-maker accompanied the English army sent by Henry VIII to Spain for the invasion of South-West France and drew a map of the latter.

The pressure of defence was more significant, as with the map of the Humber. Thus, the fortifications built from 1538, as fears developed about the prospect of French and/or Spanish invasion, led to concern about the location and strength of fortifications. The focus was on designs for the latter,

*A New Description of Kent* by Philip Symonson (*d.*1598) of Rochester. This map was engraved in London by Charles Whitwell as two sheets to be joined down the middle, and first published in 1596 at around the same time as the second edition of William Lambarde's *A Perambulation of Kent*, in which it was recommended; the first edition was in 1576. Lambarde (1536–1601) and Symonson were both connected with Rochester Bridge: Lambarde had been a member of the governing body since 1585 and Symonson was appointed Paymaster in 1593. Almost all the surviving specimens carry the added imprint of the London print-seller Peter Stent, who embellished the map with inset views of Dover and Rye. Coastal fortifications were an important aspect of Kent's significance, notably with Dover and Deal castles. In *Richard III*, a rising in Kent against the King is reported prior to the battle of Bosworth. In *King Lear*, Edgar describes 'the murmuring surge' (4.6.20) on Dover beach.

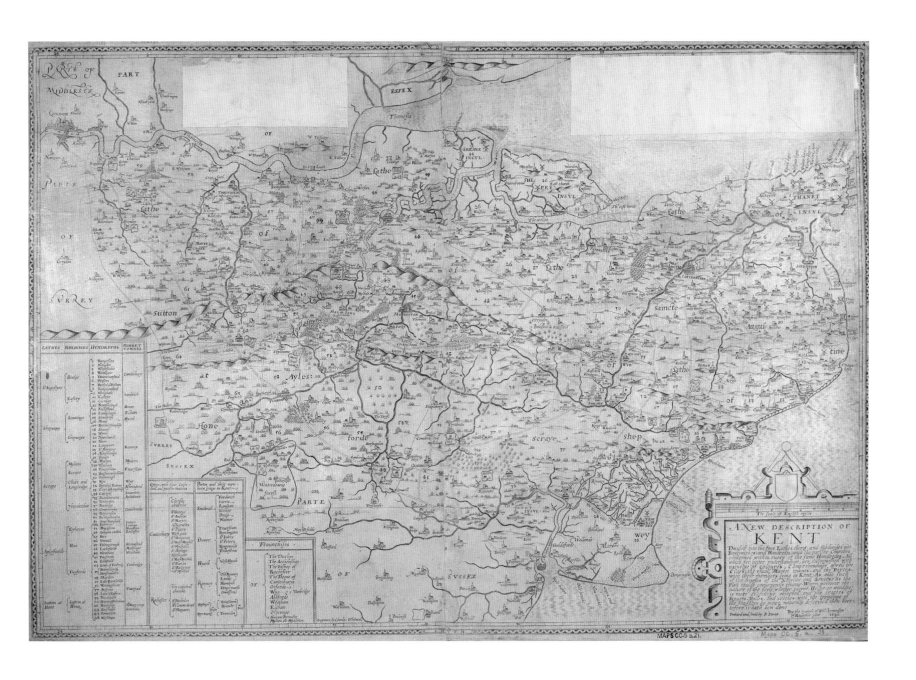

59

which included Deal and Walmer castles, but that concern also entailed an interest in the wider geographical situation.

Cannon had altered the situation even if Shakespeare was being anachronistic in *King John* when Philip the Bastard says of Angers (which fell to King Philip Augustus of France in 1204–05):

'*By east and west let France and England mount*
*Their battering cannon charged to the mouths,*
*Till their south-fearing clamours have brawl'd down*
*the flinty ribs of this contemptuous city.'*
(2.1)

Artillery produced a dynamic element in the location and character of fortifications, not least because of issues of range, bearing, impact and vulnerability. These factors encouraged greater precision in measurement and representation. The need for angular measurement and for the use of a surveying compass with sights was discussed in *Questiti et inventioni* (1546), dedicated to Henry VIII by Niccoló Tartaglia, a pioneer in the mathematical understanding of ballistics, notably with his *Nova Scientia Inventa* (1537). His work influenced Leonard Digges, the author of *Pantometria* (1571), a work finished by his son Thomas, and William Bourne, in his *Arte of Shooting in Great Ordnance* (1587), dedicated to Ambrose, Earl of Warwick, the Lord of the Ordnance and elder brother of Robert, Earl of Leicester, favourite to Queen Elizabeth.

Bourne had presented a version to Burghley in 1572 in a manuscript covering a range of topics, including a call for maps. Bourne's writings indicate the overlap of navigation, mapping and almanacs. He published several of the latter, as well as *A Regiment of the Sea, containing Rules, Mathematical Experiences, and Perfect Knowledge of Navigation for all coasts and countries: most needful and necessary for all seafaring men and travellers,* as *pilots, mariners, merchants, etc* (1573). Maps became more useful in the period of warfare that began in 1585, not only in the defence of England from invasion but also for operations in Ireland, where Richard Bartlett produced valuable campaign maps following on from earlier ones by Robert Lythe and John Browne. This was different to the challenge of the measurement of larger areas, but Saxton's surveys showed how this challenge was met.

Saxton's project was presumably backed by the government: in 1576, the Privy Council instructed the Justices of the Peace and Mayors in Wales to give him all assistance in travelling and viewing the country there. Burghley was sent proof copies of Saxton's county maps, which formed the core of his personal atlas. He added his own notes to the margins, recording, for example, possible enemy invasion sites on the map of Dorset, a county with a long coastline on the English Channel. This was an aspect of the relationship between government and experts, ministers, men of business and scholarship – a relationship that was to be praised by James I's Lord Chancellor as well as noted philosopher, Francis Bacon.

Saxton's sources, including earlier maps, are not known, but he carried out surveys that led to the engraving of 34 county maps. That of Norfolk (1574) may have been the first of the Saxton county maps to be printed. Most of the maps covered a single county, such as Cornwall, Devon and Northumberland, although some covered several: Kent, Surrey, Sussex and Middlesex appeared on one map published in 1575, and Northamptonshire, Bedfordshire, Cambridgeshire, Huntingdonshire and Rutland in another of 1576. The coastlines indicate the extent of subsequent change to the landscape as, on the map for Kent, Sheppey and Thanet appear as islands.

The scale of Saxton's maps varied, as did the degree of pictorial detail. Woods, bridges and hills

**Humphrey Llwyd's introduction** to Ortelius was brought about by his affluent merchant friend Sir Richard Clough, also of Denbigh, who lived for a time in Antwerp. As a result, Llwyd prepared the manuscript for a map of Wales, shown here, and a map of England and Wales – both of which first appeared in 1573, in a supplement to the *Theatrum*. In the letter accompanying the manuscript, Llwyd explained that the map of Wales gave the ancient names of rivers, towns, people and places, as well as the modern English names, and that the map of England and Wales included the ancient names mentioned by Ptolemy and other ancient writers. The map of Wales continued to be reprinted until 1741.

Elizabeth's reign was a period of rising population and expanding agriculture in Wales. The more fertile lands of South Wales ensured that it had the highest population. Welsh sites in Shakespeare's plays include Milford Haven (*Cymbeline*; *Henry IV*; *Richard III*); Haverfordwest (*Richard III*); Brecon (*Richard III*); Monmouth (*Henry V*); Harlech (*Henry V*); and Flint Castle (*Richard II*). Owen Glendower was one of the conspirators in *Henry IV, Part One*.

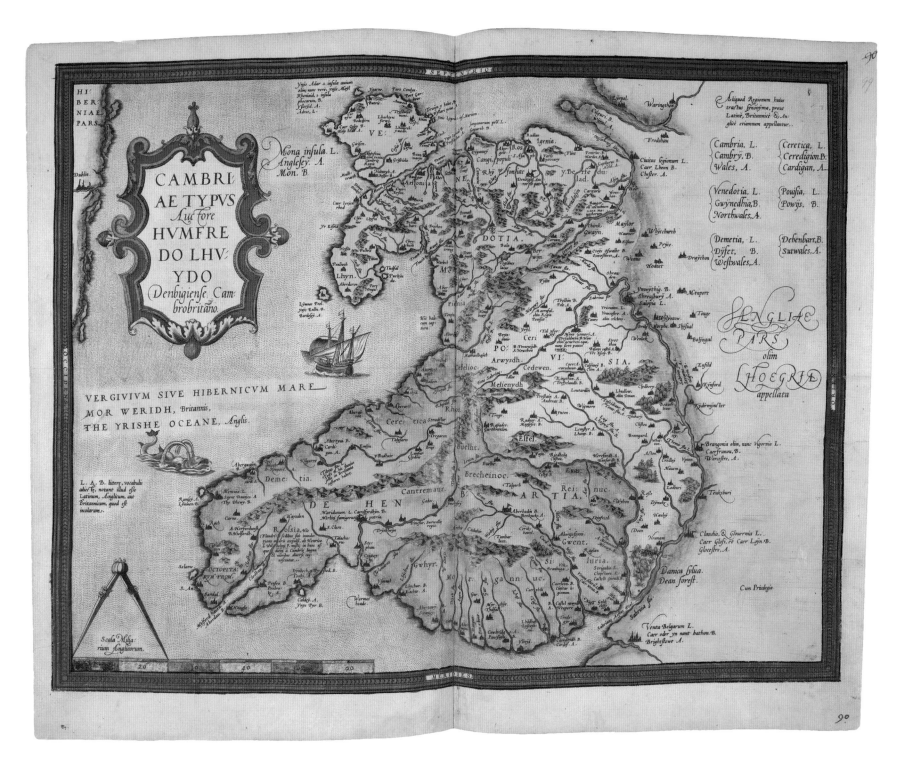

HI-
BER-
NIAE
PARS

Dublin

**CAMBRI-
AE TYPVS**
Auctore
**HVMFRE-
DO LHV-
YDO**
Denbigiense, Cam-
brobritano.

Miona insula. L.
Anglesey. A.
Mon. B.

VE

DOTIA

Aliquod Regionum huius
tractus synonyma, prout
Latinè, Britannicè & An-
glicè etiamnum appellantur.

Cambria. L.  Ceretica. L.
Cambry. B.  Ceredigion. B.
Wales. A.  Cardigan. A.

Venedotia. L.  Pouisia. L.
Gwynedhia, B.  Powijs. B.
Northwales. A.

Demetia. L.  Dehenbart, B.
Dyset. B.  Sutwales. A.
Westwales. A.

ANGLIAE
PARS
olim
LHOEGRIA
appellata

**VERGIVIVM SIVE HIBERNICVM MARE**
**MOR WERIDH,** *Britannis,*
**THE YRISHE OCEANE,** *Anglis.*

L. A. B. litterae, vocabulis
adiectae, notant illud esse
Latinum, Anglicum, aut
Britannicum, quod est
incolarum.

Ceretica

Demetia.

DE HEN

Cantremaur

B ARTIA.

Brecheinoc.

Gwent.

Claudia, & Glouernia L.
Caer Glofs, et Caer Leyn B.
Glocestre. A.

Danica sylua.
Dean forest.

Cum Priuilegio

Morgannuc.

Venta Belgarum L.
Caer oder yn nant bathon B.
Brightstowe A.

Scala Milia-
rium Anglicorum.

10   0   40   60

61

were drawn in, as were the fenced-off parks of major landowners, but not roads, which must have affected the maps' value to travellers. The visual prominence given to the scale affirmed the mathematical surveying values underlying the map. The level of accuracy was high, although there were some significant errors, such as the shape of Cornwall in that the Lizard Peninsula was overly large.

Saxton also produced, in 1579, the first printed atlas of the counties of England and Wales. His large general map of England and Wales was printed in 1583, and like the atlas, bore the royal arms. Such maps were an aspect of majesty, a proclamation of the extent of the state and its unity in and under the Crown. Marcus Gheeraerts the Younger painted Elizabeth standing on a rendering of the 1583 Saxton map, and she was also pictured on the title page of Saxton's atlas.

The popularity of Saxton and Saxton-derived maps reflected the desire for images drawn to scale in which crucial physical outlines – coastlines and rivers – were precisely marked. North was at the top of these maps. Saxton's maps also indicated the increased use of uniform conventional symbols to depict, for example, forests and hills. In 1573, Humphrey Llwyd, an MP and a noted antiquarian, produced the first map of Wales with a considerable degree of accuracy.

Saxton's maps were copied with few, if any, changes for two centuries, largely because the cost and effort of new surveys appeared redundant not only for commercial reasons, but also due to the authority of the Saxton maps. Saxton's copper plates were reused, but with alterations, for example by William Webb in 1645 and Philip Lea in about 1690. Roads were added to Saxton derivatives, notably in Lea's maps, and some included distance tables and a key. As a result, map publishers took over from map-makers. Saxton's surveys were the basis for maps by later cartographers – such as John Norden (1548–1629), a surveyor who was an advocate for enclosure and agricultural improvements – and their maps further helped to establish and consolidate the visual image of counties. This was an important aspect of the extent to which particular images were propagated in introducing maps to a wider public and encouraging map use. There was an equivalent in Shakespeare helping to fix the usage of words and phrases.

Norden planned a series of county maps and descriptions, the *Speculum Britanniae (Mirror of Britain)*. A Privy Council order, dated from the palace of Hampton Court on 27 January 1593, instructed Lord Lieutenants to help Norden, who was 'authorised and appointed by her Majesty to travel through England and Wales to make more perfect descriptions, charts, and maps'. Middlesex was published in 1593, after a draft had been corrected by Burghley, and Hertfordshire five years later. Norden's patron, Burghley, had reiterated his backing in 1594, issuing a recommendation of 'Norden, who has already imprinted certain shires to his great commendation, and who intends to proceed with the rest as true and ability permit'. In 1595, Norden produced a manuscript, 'Chorographical Description of the several Shires and Islands, of Middlesex, Essex, Surrey, Sussex, Hampshire, Wight, Guernsey and Jersey, performed by the travel and view of John Norden, 1595', which was dedicated to the Queen. However, no other maps were published in his lifetime and, beset by financial problems, the project was abandoned, leaving surveys of five other counties in only manuscript form. Norden did, however, produce maps for the 1607 edition of William Camden's *Britannia* (first published in 1586) and for John Speed's *Theatre of the Empire of Great Britain* (1611).

Other county maps included that of Kent in

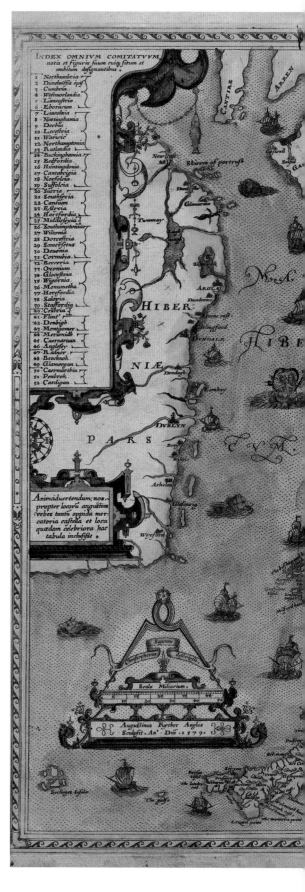

*Map of England and Wales, 1579*, Christopher Saxton. Drawing on his county surveys, this impressive map had flaws, as in the coverage of the neighbouring areas of southern Scotland and the Isle of Man, but showed Wales more accurately than did Humphrey Llwyd's map. The coasts are full of shipping and large fish, providing pictorial detail to complement the land, where counties are differentiated by colour. Differences emerge clearly, as in the scarcity of towns in the Fens and the Breckland.

1596 by Philip Symonson. This took the pictorial image further by depicting churches with spires as opposed to towers.

Speed was quick to see the commercial value of maps, and printed town maps as insets on his county maps. Speed's town maps indicate the importance of local topographical features, as in the 1610 map of Newcastle. His *Theatre of the Empire of Great Britain* appeared in a second edition in 1614 and a third in 1627. This entrepreneurial activity was important because royal and official patronage of cartography declined, especially after 1612. This may have been due to the financial problems of the Crown as well as the lack of a foreign threat.

Mapping of Scotland also improved in the mid-sixteenth century. John Elder and Lawrence Nowell both produced maps, and others followed in the seventeenth century. A more accurate depiction of the Scottish coastline emerged, although the Highlands remained poorly mapped, as can be seen in Speed's map of Scotland. Timothy Pont (c.1565–1614), who sought to emulate Saxton, faced a much tougher task in Scotland, where he travelled widely in the 1580s and 1590s. The pressing commercial imperative that existed in England was missing, as was indicated by the fact that the manuscripts with their 78 identifiable maps were not published in his lifetime. Instead, they proved the basis for the maps of Scotland in a Dutch work, the 1655 extension of Joan Blaeu's *Atlas Novus*, which appeared as the sixth volume of Blaeu's *Atlas Major*. Using the significant image of the hazards of maritime travel, Blaeu presented his role as that of rescuing material that was otherwise at risk of being lost 'like sacred objects from a shipwreck ... deposited ... with us in the safe harbour of Amsterdam, where we engraved them for the use of posterity, to live again (in case they should perish) in copper'. A similar process characterised much map publication, but, in most cases,
information about sources is lacking.

Shakespeare's characters are shown making some use of maps. In the first scene in *King Lear*, for instance, the vain protagonist calls for the map in order to display his division of his kingdom between his daughters, telling one of them, Goneril:

'Of all these bounds, even from this line to this,
With shadowy forests and with champains [open country] riched,
With plenteous rivers and wide-skirted meads,
We make thee lady...' (1.1)

Located in pre-Christian history, this story depicted the use of a map that could not, and would not, have occurred then. However, for Shakespeare's audience, such an action would have appeared possible, not least because maps of England, however imprecise, were adequate for such purposes.

Partition on a map clearly interested Shakespeare. In *Henry IV, Part One*, the conspirators against Henry IV meet in Bangor in North Wales, with 'Hotspur' at first angry that he has 'forgot the map'. Already competing and bitter with each other, Hotspur and the Welsh leader, Owen Glendower, then row over the distribution of their projected gains:

'Glendower: Come, here's the map: shall we divide our right
        According to our threefold order ta'en
Mortimer: The archdeacon hath divided it
        Into three limits very equally.
        England, from Trent and Severn hitherto,
        By south and east, is to my part assign'd:
        And westward, Wales beyond the Severn shore,
        And all the fertile land within that bound,
        To Owen Glendower; and dear coz [Hotspur], to you
        The remnant northward, lying off from Trent'
        (3.1)

**John Speed (c.1551–1629)** conceived the *Theatre of The Empire of Great Britain* as a supplementary volume to his monumental *History of Great Britain* (1611). Finally published as a complete work in 1612, the atlas was the culmination of several years' work during which pre-existing maps by Saxton and Norden were updated, information was gathered and collated, and new surveys were completed before the plates were engraved, mainly by Jodocus Hondius of Amsterdam. Many of the maps bear earlier dates and would have been available for sale as loose sheets prior to the completion of the atlas. This map shows the Anglo-Saxon kingdoms, which were conventionally presented as seven different territories, although the boundaries displayed here would not have coincided chronologically. The term Heptarchy dates to the sixteenth century. The tradition of the seven kingdoms dates to the twelfth century, although the term heptarchy dates to the sixteenth. The Isle of Man was seriously misrepresented on the map. Speed, a Londoner, had published a wall map of Biblical Canaan in 1595 and in 1598 was appointed a Customs Waiter (official) by Elizabeth I, to whom he had presented the map. In 1627, Speed's *Prospect of the Most Famous Parts of the World* was published. **OPPOSITE**

'Hotspur: 'Methinks my moiety, north from Burton here,
    In quantity equals not one of yours:
    See how this river comes me cranking in,
    And cuts me from the best of my land
    A huge half-moon, a monstrous cantle out.
    I'll have the current in this place damm'd up,
    And here the smug and silver Trent shall run
    In a new channel, fair and evenly:
    it shall not wind with such a deep indent,
    To rob me of so rich a bottom here.
Glendower: Not wind! it shall, it must; you see it doth.
Mortimer: Yea, but
    Mark how he bears his course, and runs me up
    With like advantage on the other side;
    Gelding the opposed continent as much,
    As on the other side it takes from you.
Worcester: Yea, but a little charge will trench him here,
    And on this north side win this cape of land;
    And then he runs straight and even.
Hotspur: I'll have it so; a little charge will do it.
Glendower: I will not have it alter'd.' (3.1)

Their quarrel makes the division appear ridiculous, as does the idea of changing the course of the river Trent, one of the major rivers in the country. However, the use of a map is instructive.

More generally, audiences were expected to know, or at least accept, geographical references, for example, in *Cymbeline*, that Milford Haven was in Wales. In *Richard II*, the audience was given an account of the campaign that led to the overthrow of the King, with Bolingbroke, the future Henry IV, landing at 'Ravenspurgh' in Yorkshire. Subsequently, 'in the Gloucestershire Wolds', in other words, the Cotswolds, Bolingbroke asks Henry, 1st Earl of Northumberland of the Percy family: 'How far is it, my lord, to Berkeley now?' (2.3) receiving the reply:

    'Believe me, noble lord,
    I am a stranger here in Gloucestershire:
    These high wild hills and rough uneven ways
    Draw out our miles and make them wearisome.' (2.3)

Outside Berkeley Castle, Bolingbroke resolves to attack Richard's supporters in Bristol Castle. The campaigning then switches to Wales, and, as with Bangor, the audience is assumed to know where Flint Castle is.

In *King John*, the play moves from Angers, with references to parts of France – 'Then do I give Volquessen, Touraine, Maine, Poitiers, and Anjou' (2.1) – and to England, where the French invasion:

    'All Kent hath yielded; nothing there holds out
    But Dover Castle.' (5.1)

The move is both historical – a key aspect of the highly speeded-up narrative offered by the play – and psychological, with pressures building on the evil John.

There was also geography as prospectus. In *King John*, the Duke of Austria, the ally of France, gives John's nephew Arthur an account of England as a maritime realm:

    '... that England, hedg'd in with the main,
    That water-walled bulwark, still secure
    And confident from foreign purposes.' (2.1)

*Elizabeth I*, commonly known as 'The Ditchley portrait', was painted *c*.1592 by Marcus Gheeraerts the Younger (*c*.1561–1636). Produced for Sir Henry Lee (1533–1611), who had served as Elizabeth's Champion from 1559 to 1590, the portrait shows Elizabeth standing on the globe, with her feet on Oxfordshire. The counties of southern England are differentiated by colour. The clouds in the stormy sky are parting to reveal sunshine, which perhaps reflects the fact that by the early 1590s Elizabeth had surmounted the crises posed by Mary, Queen of Scots and the Spanish Armada (1588). However, war with Spain (1585–1604) proved intractable and expensive, and this exacerbated difficulties over the public finances and with Parliament. Elizabeth was also affected by the death of the advisers who had helped her govern for most of her reign, notably Burghley, Leicester and Walsingham. The text on the picture makes mention of divine power. It is likely that the painting commemorates an elaborate and highly symbolic entertainment that Lee organised for Elizabeth in 1592, probably in the grounds of his house at Ditchley or in nearby Woodstock – an entertainment similar to that referred to by Theseus in *A Midsummer Night's Dream* (2.1.). **OPPOSITE**

Such an approach employed the resonances of geography in order to underline views on national identity and destiny, and was seen at greater length with John of Gaunt's speech in *Richard II*:

'*This royal throne of kings, this scepter'd isle,
this earth of majesty, this seat of Mars,
this other Eden, demi-paradise,
This fortress built by Nature for herself
Against infection and the hand of war,
this happy breed of men, this little world,
This precious stone set in the silver sea,
Which serves it in the office of a wall,
Or as a moat defensive to a house,
Against the envy of less happier lands,
This blessed plot, this earth, this realm, this England.'*
(2.1)

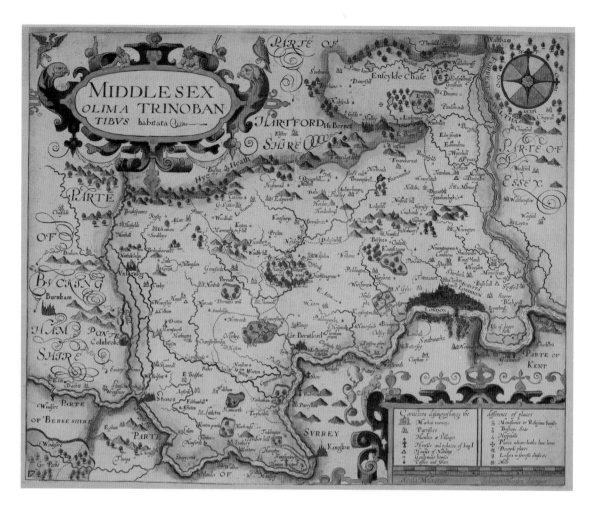

*Middlesex*, 1593, by John Norden, an Oxford graduate who lived most of his time near London. A surveyor who was an advocate for enclosure and agricultural improvements, Norden (*c*.1547–1625) planned a series of county maps and descriptions, the *Speculum Britanniae* (*Mirror of Britain*), but only two were published. Norden's patron, William Cecil, Lord Burghley, was also a supporter of Saxton, and Norden too enjoyed government patronage, being appointed Surveyor of Crown woods and forests in Southern England in 1600, and adding the Surveyorship of the Duchy of Cornwall in 1605.

Norden's work included estate plans in more than 20 counties, for instance a manuscript atlas showing the Suffolk estates of Sir Michael Stanhope.

Middlesex, depicted in this map, benefited greatly from London's growing demand for food as the city expanded; market gardening was particularly important, notably in the area now covered by Heathrow Airport. The map of the county was the first in England to mark roads. In *Henry VI Part Three*, Edward IV has 'the best at Barnet field' (5.3) where Warwick the 'Kingmaker's' defeat and death in 1471 are depicted. **ABOVE**

Norden's map, *Hertfordshire*, made in 1597, was of interest to the Cecils, not least because it depicted their seats of Hatfield and Theobalds. Norden's map was located and enhanced by also showing sections of other counties. The representation of hills as if they were mountains is somewhat ridiculous, but also a consequence of the limited range of symbols that were available. St Albans shows up in Shakespeare's History Plays (*Henry VI, Parts One* to *Three* and *Richard III*) because of the battles fought there in 1455 and 1461, during the Wars of the Roses, though there is no real sense of place in the plays.
**RIGHT**

HERTFORDIÆ
Comitatus A. cat
tifuclanis olim.
Inhabitatus.

The names of the Hundreds of this mappe.
Caiſho Hundred . 5 Odſey Hundred .
Dacorum Hundred . 6 Eduuiſtree Hundred .
Hitch halfe Hudred . 7 Braghinoe Hundred .
Bread water Hundred . 8 Hartforde Hundred .

PARTE OF CAMBRIDGE SHIRE

PARTE OF

BEDFORD SHIRE

PARTE OF BVCKIG HLM. SHIRE

ESSEX

Scala Milliarum

Iohannes Norden perambulauit & deſcripſit
W Haelius kip Sculpſit

16

PARTE OF MIDDLESEX.

69

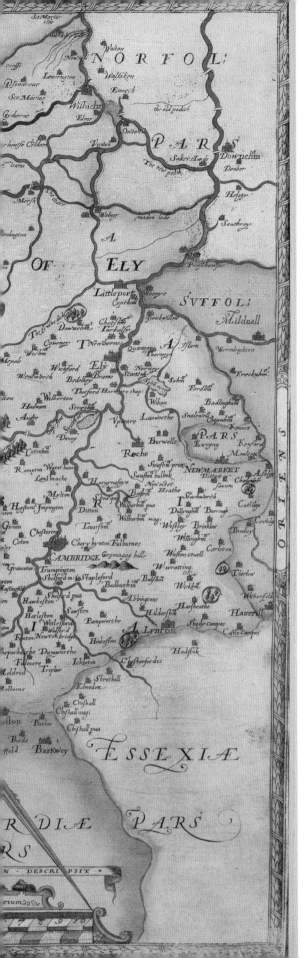

**Map of Northamptonshire** and adjacent counties, 1576, from Christopher Saxton's *Atlas of England and Wales*. Northampton was mentioned in the History Plays, but only in a tangential way; there was even less attention given to Bedfordshire, Cambridgeshire, Huntingdonshire and Rutland.

Although a centre of agriculture, the heavy claylands of the Midlands were difficult to work. Despite this, Northamptonshire was important for grazing, whereas flatter Huntingdonshire and Cambridgeshire were significant for grain. Aside from grazing land, the Jurassic limestone band in Northamptonshire was the site of a number of grand country seats, including that of one of Elizabeth's favourites, Sir Christopher Hatton, a Northamptonshire landowner and MP, who became Lord Chancellor in 1587. Fotheringay Castle, where Mary, Queen of Scots was tried and executed in 1587, was also in Northamptonshire, near Peterborough. In *King John*, Arthur is held in Northampton Castle.

This 1574 *Map of Norfolk* may have been the first of the Saxton county maps to be printed. Norwich, with a population of 15,000, was England's second city in 1550 and a major centre of manufacturing, notably of woollen cloth supplied by the sheep of East Anglia and Lincolnshire. Despite this, the county was not significant in Shakespeare. One of the few references appears in *Henry VI, Part Three*, when Edward IV is released from captivity while hunting in Yorkshire and urged to escape to Flanders by means of boarding a ship at King's Lynn, a major port.

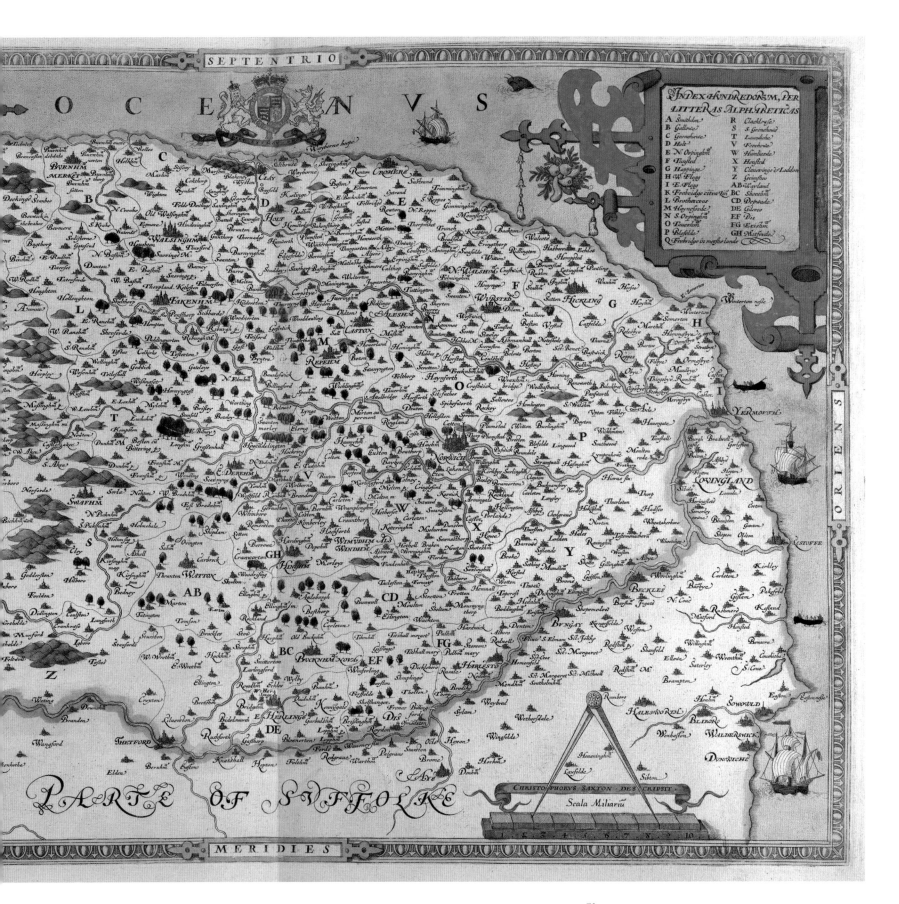

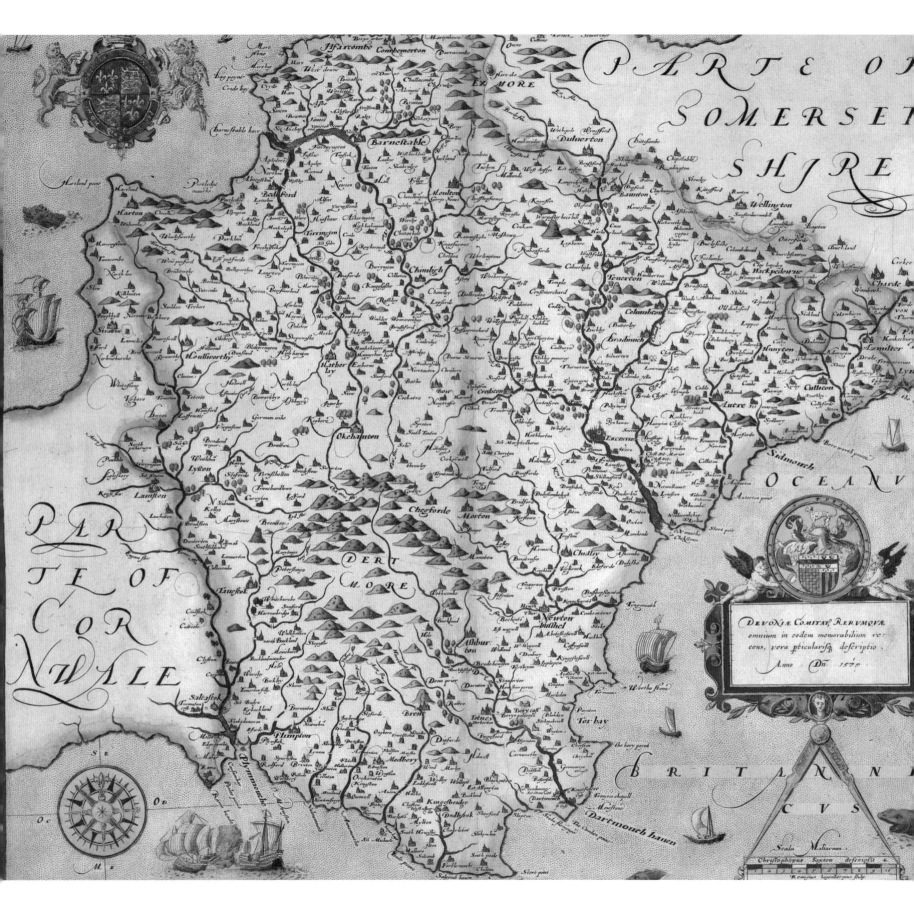

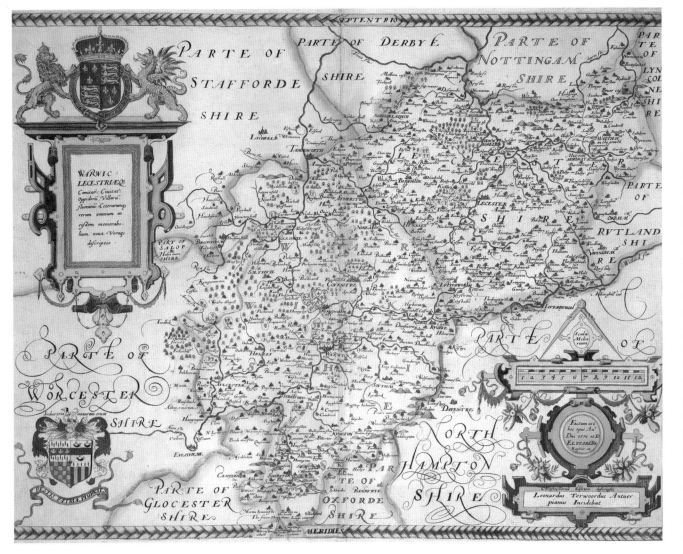

1577, Saxton. Warwickshire was Shakespeare's native county. It was heavily wooded, but the part between the river Avon and Edge Hill was described as the 'very granary' of the whole county, with the Vale of Avon also being noted for its cattle-grazing and the limestone belt for its sheep pastures. The wooded part of the county, on the far side of the river Avon, included Kenilworth, the seat of Robert, Earl of Leicester, the magnificence of which was praised by the traveller William Camden. Elizabeth was entertained at Kenilworth in 1585 and it has been suggested that this was the basis for allusions in *Twelfth Night* and *A Midsummer Night's Dream*. Much of Warwickshire and Leicestershire were affected by rural disturbances in 1607. Most of the Forest of Arden, the setting of *As You Like It*, was in Warwickshire. **LEFT**

*Map of Devon*, 1575, Saxton. This map did not include economic aspects, such as tin and copper workings on Dartmoor, nor important industries – notably the production of cloth, a trade that linked rural spinning and weaving to finishing in urban centres – nor the extent to which grain was grown in the east and south of the country but not further north. Exeter and Dartmouth were at the time major ports yielding good customs revenues, and Devon was important for fishing. Dartmoor emerges clearly on the map, not least as an area with low population density. The map also does not include roads, which were significant in the region, too.

Then Devon appears in Shakespeare in *Richard III* as part of a pun that gives the evil king reason to pause:

Richmond? When last I was at
   Exeter,
The mayor in courtesy show'd me
   the castle,
And call'd it Rougemont: at
   which name I started,
Because a bard of Ireland told me
   once
I should not live long after I saw
   Richmond.' (4.2)

Later, a rising in Devon against Richard is reported to the king before Bosworth. **LEFT**

_Northumberland,_ Saxton, 1576(?). Northumberland, the great border county, encompassed the economic change already present in coal-based industrialisation near Newcastle, for example salt pans and glasshouses, and what William Camden termed 'the wastes' of much of the upland, where 'you would think you see the ancient nomads ... a martial sort of people, that from April to August lie in little huts (which they call sheals and shealings) here and there, among their several flocks'.

The Percy interest of the Earls of Northumberland – the basis of the opposition to Henry IV in the two plays of that name by Shakespeare – was brought under royal control under Elizabeth as a result of the suppression of the Northern Rising of 1569, while the accession of James I in 1603 was followed by a firm campaign of repression against the lawless border reivers (raiders) or moss-troopers who dominated the Anglo-Scottish border lands. Many were killed and one of the most persistently troublesome clans, the Grahams, was forcibly transported to Ireland in 1606. With the Wardenships of the Marches ending, the government of the English frontier regions became more like that of ordinary shires. _Henry IV, Part Two_ begins with Rumour appearing before the Earl of Northumberland's powerful castle at Warkworth, still today a potent ruin, and the first Act is set there, as is a subsequent scene in the second Act.

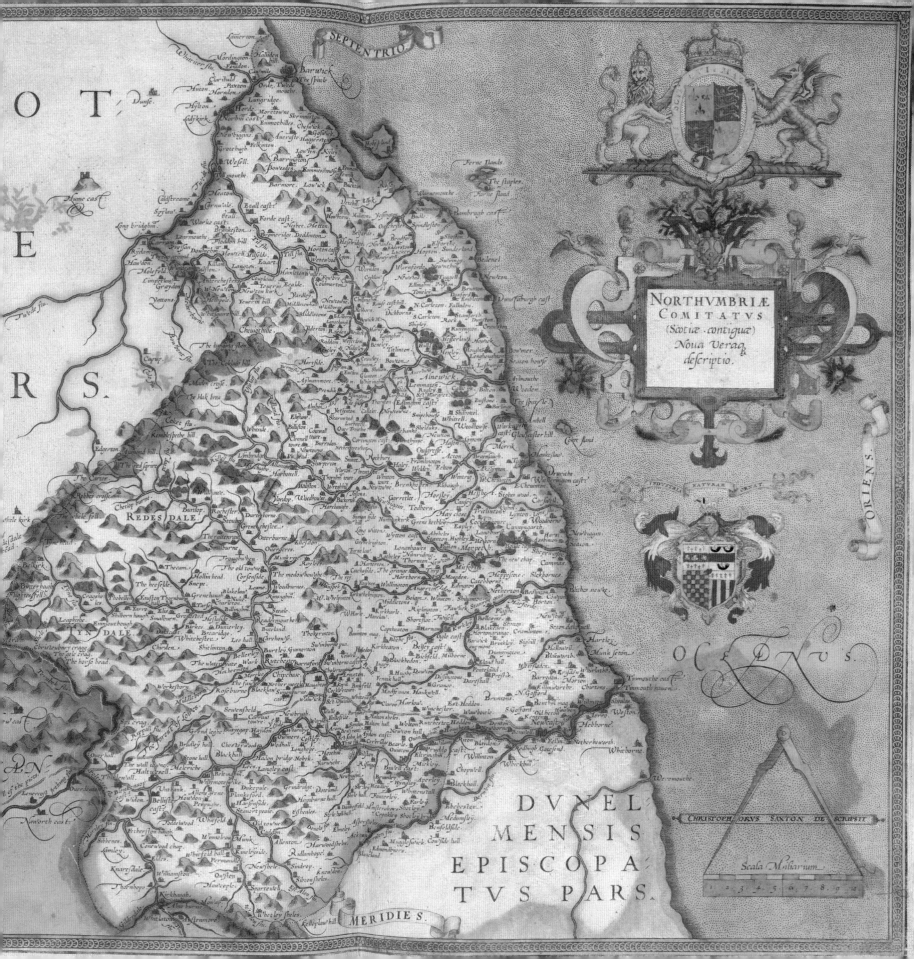

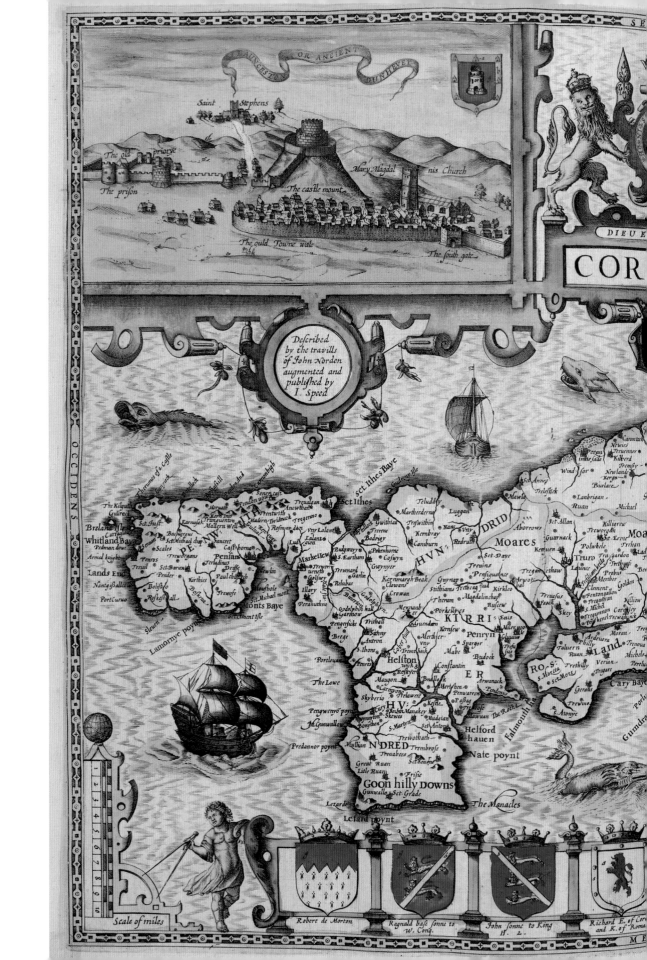

The other halfe stone

ꝺOΠI
ЄꝚV:ꝚO
ꝫϹVIɅ
ꝔMOꝚꝚ
IIIꝭ

THE HURLERS

THE CHESEWRING

*Iodocus Hondius Celavit Anno Domini 1610*

BRITISH SEE

Theise Mappes are to be solde in Popes-heade alley against ÿ Exchange by John Sudbury and G. Humble. Cum Privilegio.

Edward sonne to K.E.I.    Piers Gaveston, Erle of Cornwall    John of Eltham, Erle of Cornwall    Edward P. of Wales D. of Cornwall and 2. of Chest

**Based on John Norden's travels**, this 1610 hand-coloured map, *Cornwall*, came from John Speed's *Theatre of the Empire of Great Britain* (1611) and features crests of former Earls of Cornwall along the base. A centre of fishing and tin mining, the county was connected to the rest of England by coastal trade. William Camden noted the practice of improving the soil by adding seaweed and sea-sand, though livestock production dominated farming. Tin mining was sophisticated: water power was essential, not least for powering the mills. **LEFT**

**Dover Harbour**, showing proposals for the enclosure of the harbour behind piers, 1552. Although made more expensive by the need for harbour works, Dover was the most important port for travel to France, and is mentioned in four Shakespeare plays: *King John*, *Henry VI, Parts One* and *Two*, and *King Lear*. In *Henry VI, Part One*, Dover is where Henry sends the jewel that is the pledge of his affection for Margaret of Anjou, thence to be taken to France. In *King Lear*, Gloucester sends Lear to Dover for his protection, while, once blinded, Gloucester himself attempts suicide there. In this busy locality, the French invade in *Lear* and the English assemble to oppose them. **OVERLEAF**

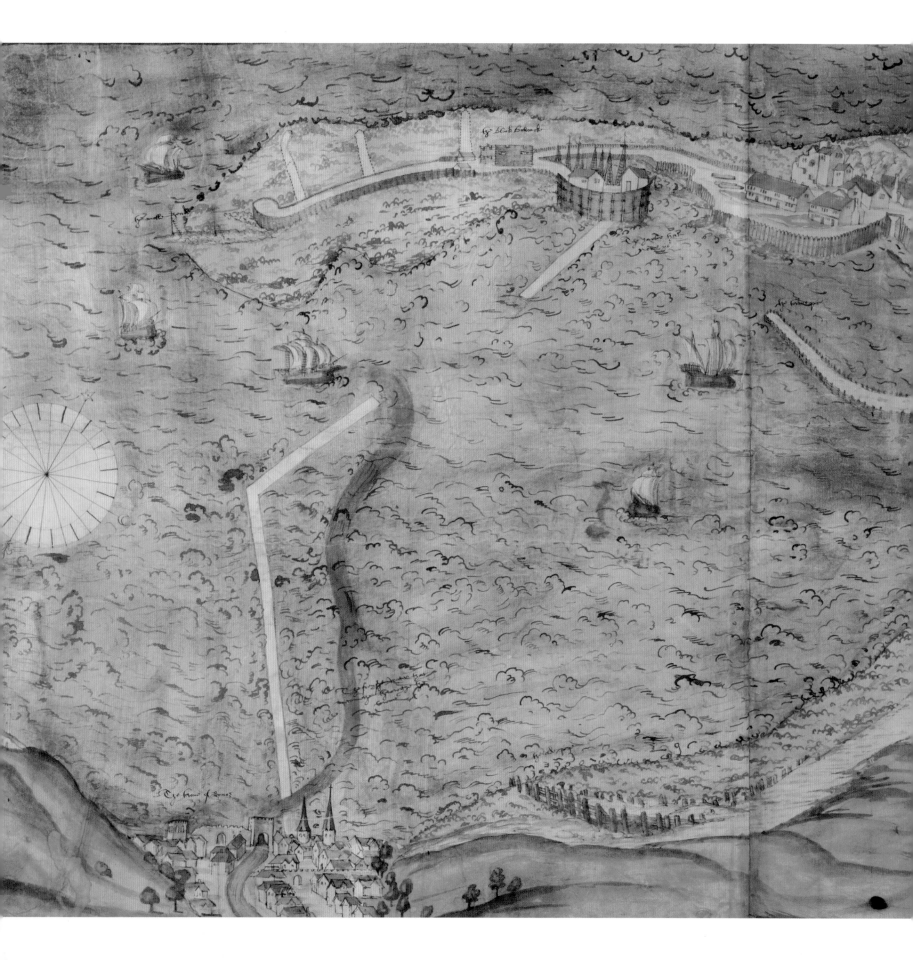

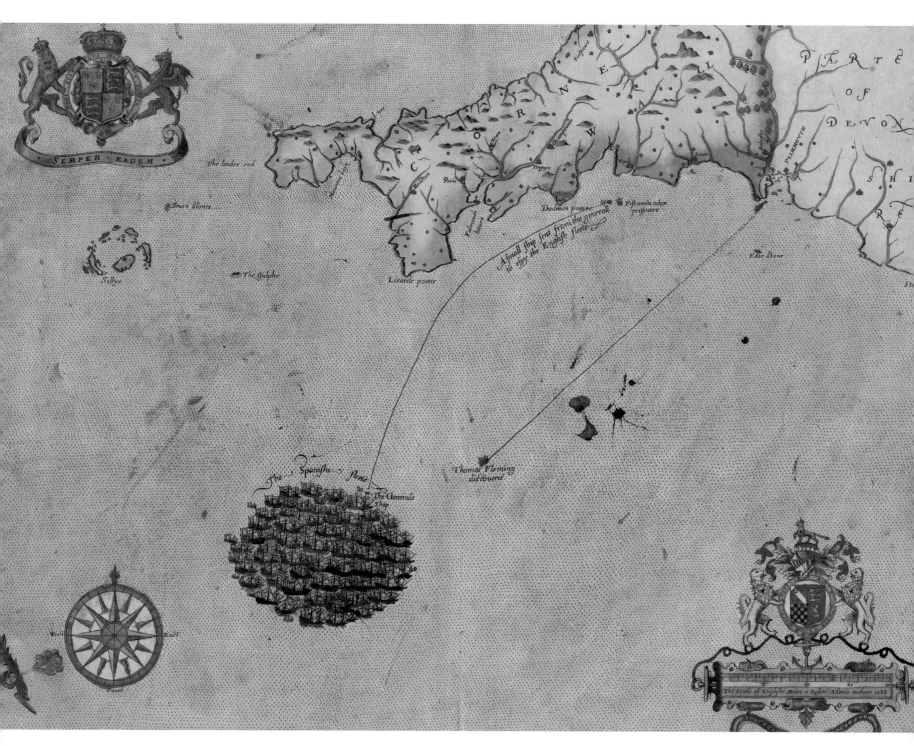

SEMPER·EADEM

PÆRTE OF DEVON SHIRE

C O R N E W A L L

PLIMMOUTH

The landes end

Scilly Stones

The Gulphe

Scillye

Lisarde pointe

A small ship sent from the generall to espy the English fleete

Fair Stone

Dodman pointe

Thomas Fleming discoverie

The Spanishe fleete

The Generals Ship

West

East

South

The Scale of Englishe Miles Rob: Adams authore 1588

*The Armada Maps* by Robert Adams, engraved by Augustine Ryther, were intended to accompany Petruccio Ubaldini's *A Discourse Concerning the Spanish Fleet invading England in the year 1588*. The Spanish Armada was an attempt to send a major fleet of 130 ships up the English Channel in order to cover an invasion of England from the Spanish Netherlands (modern Belgium) by the effective Spanish Army of Flanders, under the talented Alessandro Farnese, Duke of Parma. However, it was thwarted by a combination of poor planning, a skilful English naval response, and the weather – the latter fuelling the development of belief in a Providential sanction for English Protestantism; to contemporaries, the unassailable nature of divine approval was clear.

The Spanish fleet had sailed along the Channel, maintaining a tight formation to protect its more vulnerable vessels, while harried by long-range English gunnery. This did scant damage, and, during nine days of engagements, the Spaniards retained their formation. The English fleet, with the advantage of superior sailing qualities and compact four-wheeled gun-carriages, which permitted a high rate of fire (many of the Spanish guns were on cumbersome carriages designed for use on land), suffered even slighter damage, and was most endangered by a shortage of ammunition. When the Spanish fleet anchored off Calais, it found that Parma had been able to assemble the transport vessels necessary to embark his army for England, but that they could not come out from port until after the English and Dutch naval squadrons had been defeated.

Instead, the Spaniards lost the initiative. The formation of their fleet was disrupted by an English night attack using fireships, and the English fleet then inflicted considerable damage in a running battle off Gravelines. A strong south-westerly wind drove the Armada into the North Sea. With no clear tactical objective after Parma's failed embarkation, the Spanish commanders ordered a return to Spain via the hazardous north-about route around the British Isles. However, a succession of violent and unseasonable storms lashed the fleet as it passed north of Scotland and down the rocky west coast of Ireland; ship after ship was smashed or driven ashore, and only a remnant of the fleet and a portion of its crew reached Spain.

Elizabeth's reported speech to the troops assembled at Tilbury, east of London, in order to repel the likely invasion is well known. She stressed both her own dedication to, and her identification with, England, and her remarks were not idle ones: William of Orange, the other leading Protestant champion and opponent of Philip II, had been assassinated in the Netherlands in 1584:

*'I am come amongst you … not for my recreation and disport, but being resolved, in the midst and heat of battle, to live and die amongst you all, and to lay down for my God, and my kingdom and for my people, my honour and my blood, even in the dust. I know I have the body of a weak and feeble woman, but I have the heart and stomach of a king, and of a king of England too, and think foul scorn that [the Duke of] Parma or [the King of] Spain, or any Prince of Europe should dare to invade the borders of my realm.'*

This speech, the accuracy of which is controversial, would have sat well in a Shakespeare play. However, in a contrast also seen in Shakespeare's *Henry V*, with the depiction of Henry very different to that of some of his army – notably Bardolph (executed for looting), Nym (also hanged for looting) and Pistol (a fraud) – the situation might have been less happy had the Army of Flanders landed. The English defences in 1588 were inadequate, with poor fortifications, insufficient and mostly poorly trained troops, and scant supplies. In addition, the defensive coverage was patchy.

The Council was convinced that London was the key target, and there was particular concern about the Spaniards landing on the Essex bank of the Thames, and thus not needing to fight their way through Kent and across the Thames. It was, therefore, scarcely surprising that Providence was seen as being at work in England's survival. **OPPOSITE**

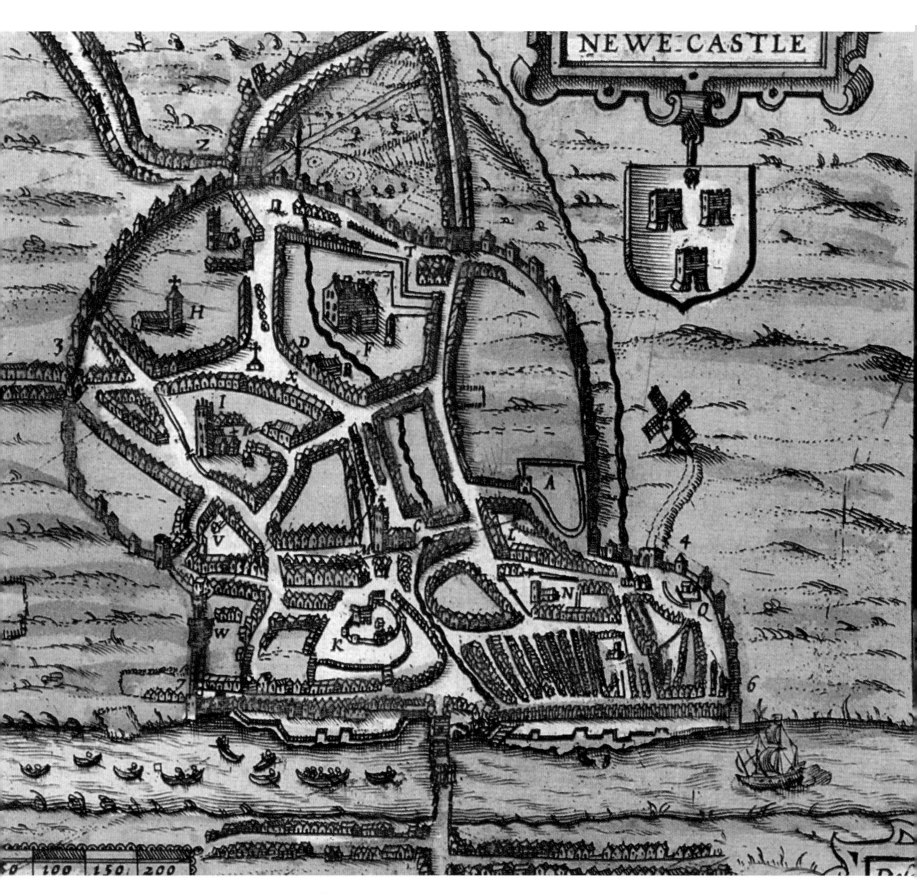

NEWE CASTLE

| | |
|---|---|
| A | Kings maner |
| B | Kings Lodgings |
| C | Grammer Schole |
| D | The manner |
| E | Newe house |
| H | Black friers |
| I | Saint Iohns |
| K | High Castle |
| L | Almese Houses |
| M | Saint Nicholas |
| N | Alhallowes |
| O | Trinitie House |
| P | Pandon Hall |
| Q | The wall Knoll |
| R | The Stone Hill |
| S | The maisen deeu |
| T | Almose Houses |
| V | West Spittle |
| W | White Friers |
| X | Scottish Inne |
| Z | Newe yate |
| 3 | West gate. |
| 4 | Pandon yate |
| 6 | Sandgate yate |
| 7 | Close gate |
| 8 | The Key |

*Newcastle*, 1610, John Speed. A major centre of the coal trade and of coal-based manufacturing, Newcastle remained a walled city and fortress – a major defensive site against Scottish invasion. The amount of coal shipped from the Tyne rose to 400,000 tons by 1625, much of it to London. When the Scots invaded England in 1644, one of their objectives was to secure coal supplies for their Parliamentary allies in London. Shakespeare did not mention the city. The bridge was built in the late twelfth century to replace one destroyed by fire in 1248. With frequent repairs it lasted until destroyed by flood in 1771. The bridge included towers, a drawbridge and a prison.

**Great Yarmouth** was a major port, important as the leading port for the prosperous region of East Anglia and also as a key centre for fishing – indeed, it was the site of a great Michaelmas fair where large quantities of herring and other fish were sold. Exports from Norwich and of Norfolk grain, especially barley, went out of Great Yarmouth, while coal from North-East England was imported here for East Anglia.

Greate Yarmowthe

The No

OCCIDENS

ORIENS

MERIDIES

ACADEMLÆ  OPPIDI

RIC. LYNE SCVLPSIT  A° DNI 1574

HOSPITIA ARCISTAR

A  Kinges Hall
B  Michaell houese
C  Physwicke Ostell
D  Gregoreye Ostell
E  Garett Ostell
F  St Marie Ostell
G  St Austines Ostell
H  Bernarde Ostell
I  St Thomas Ostell
K  Buttolph Ostell

HOSPITIA IVRISTARVM

L  Ovine Inn
M  Paules Inn
N  Clemens Ostell
O  Trinitie Ostell
P  St Nicholas Ostell
Q  Burden Ostell
R  Domus Pythagore
S  D St Beds
T  Cratee ferina ubi olim pons
Cantebir a Cantebrig unde Cantebrigia.

Cambridge was the site of one of England's only two universities and a major centre for the Protestantisation of the country during the sixteenth century. Indeed, major clerics took their degrees there. Under Edward VI (r. 1547–1553), Martin Bucer, a leading Continental Protestant, was Professor of Divinity. Engraved on copper, Richard Lyne's 1574 map *Cambridge* contained much that is recognisable today, in particular the magnificent Chapel of King's College. Unlike today, the castle is presented as a defensible structure. The river, with its different channels, plays a more significant part in the town than today, and this enhances the significance of 'The Bridge'. A domestic element is brought to the map by the animals shown grazing in nearby fields, and a man fishing in the river. The earlier Catholic nature of Cambridge is present with place names such as Grey Friars and White Friars. The city is not mentioned in Shakespeare. **LEFT**

*Mills on the River Trent*, *c.*1558. Water power was a key element in the agriculture and industry of Shakespeare's time, and was tapped by the waterwheels in mills. Particularly important for the production of flour, water power was also used for blast furnaces. Shakespeare refers to both the milling industry and the power of water: in *The Tempest*, Prospero refers to Ariel as 'vent[ing] thy groans as fast as 'mill-wheels strike' (1.2). The course of the river provides the basis for Hotspur's complaint when the division of the country is discussed by the conspirators in *Henry IV, Part One*. **BELOW**

**Map of the Parish of Smallburgh**, Norfolk, 1582, by John Darby. One of the first English local maps to be drawn to a consistent scale, this is in unusually good condition, probably due to its never having been displayed because of its unfinished state. There is no title, several field name panels are left blank, and some decoration is only in pencil. In addition to these omissions, there is no numerical or alphabetical key to the terrier – the written register of plots that, with the information it contained of acreages, tenants and leases, would have been indispensable for the practical management of the estate.

Fourteen miles north-east of Norwich, Smallburgh was a Saxon settlement where much common land was enclosed in the Tudor period, although much of such land remained unenclosed and can be seen on the map.

The map was made for Edward, Lord Morley who had regained possession of the lands in 1578. His Catholic father had lost them in 1572 when he was accused of treason.

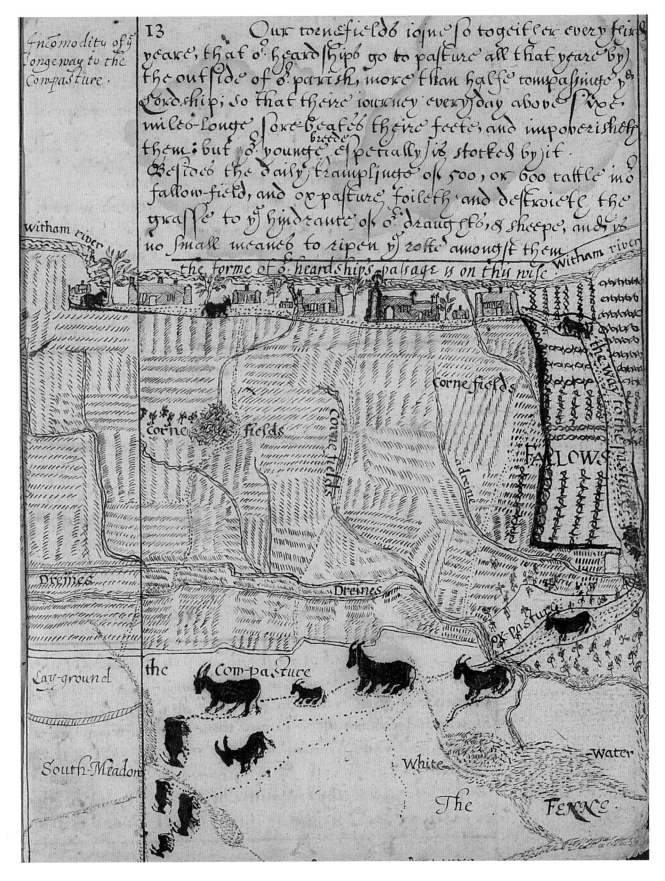

**Map of Chelmsford**, county town of Essex in 1591, by John Walker. This plan includes pictograms, most prominently of the Church, as well as the 'backsydes' of the dwellings, which provided them with land for planting and animals. The son of a carpenter, Walker described himself as an 'architector'. The basic layout of the town has not changed. **FAR LEFT**

**Petition by villagers of Bassingham**, south-west of Lincoln, 1629, complaining about their stock having to make a long six-mile walk around the parish boundary to the pasture because of the open fields. The inclusion of a map in the petition to the Countess of Warwick in favour of enclosure reflected the increasing carto-literacy of the period. Bassingham was eventually enclosed by Act of Parliament. **LEFT**

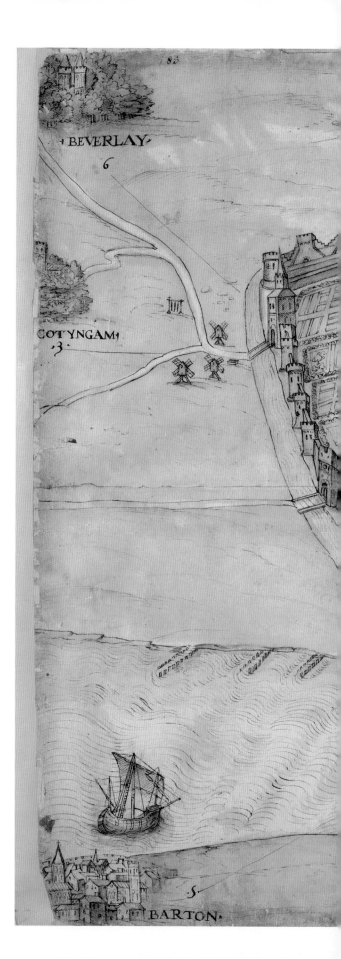

Map of Hull and the Humber estuary, sixteenth century. The fortified nature of this important seaport emerges clearly in this map. The region is not mentioned by Shakespeare, but nearby Ravenspur, where invaders did not have to face defences, is mentioned in *Richard II*, *Henry IV, Part One*, and *Henry VI, Part Three*.

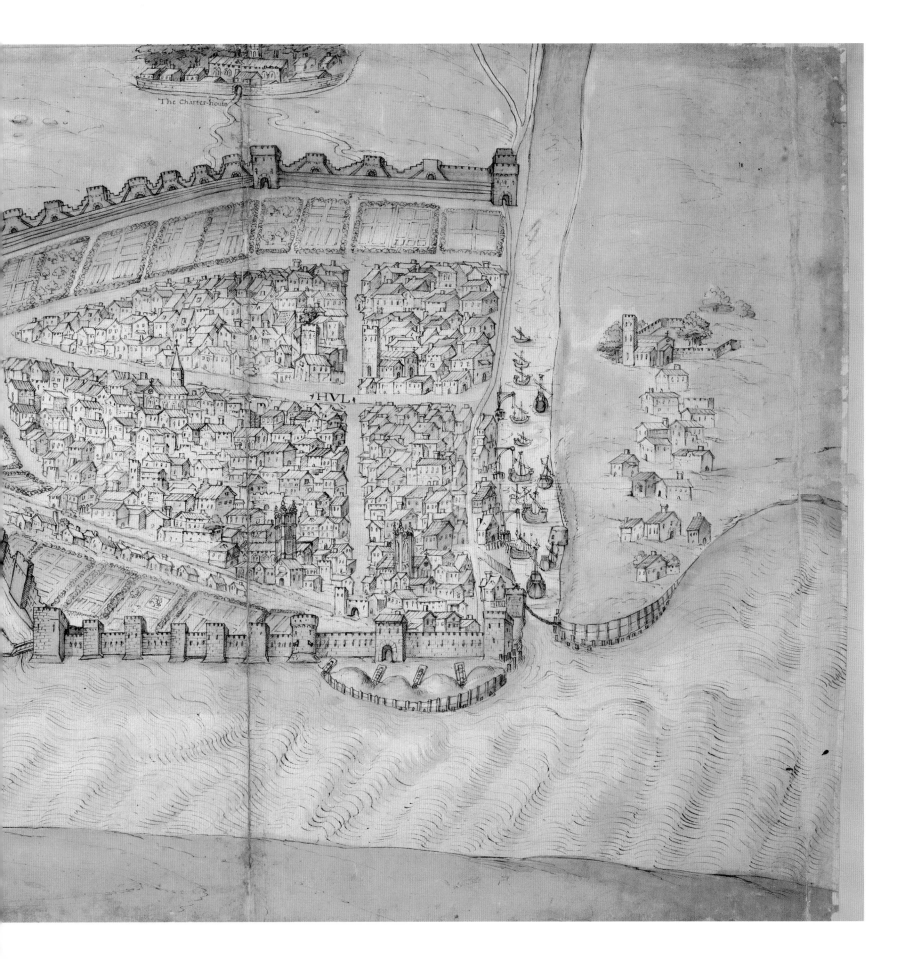

The Charter-house

HVL

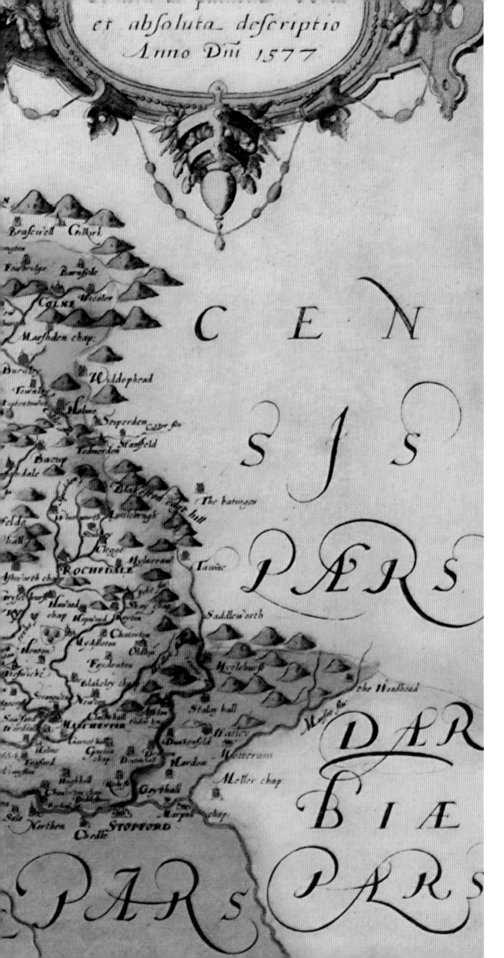

et absoluta descriptio
Anno Dñi 1577

**This map of Lancashire** by Christopher Saxton was owned by William, Lord Burghley, who was especially concerned about this county as it had a particular concentration of Catholics. Burghley's interest in maps greatly affected Saxton's career. No action is set there by Shakespeare, but the House of Lancaster, descended from Edward III's fourth son, John of Gaunt, plays a major role in the History Plays.

# Mapping London

Maps of London changed greatly in the sixteenth century, not least because there were more of them. They were also different to what had come earlier. The depiction of London by the St Albans monk Matthew Paris that dated from around 1250 was essentially a pictogram. It was drawn as part of what has become known as a 'road map' for pilgrims to Jerusalem, although few would actually have carried it with them on the journey, often using it instead, like other artistic accoutrements, as a devotional tool for pious contemplation at home. The journey began at London, where pilgrims could visit the shrine of Edward the Confessor at Westminster, which was shown on the pictogram. In the drawing, St Paul's Cathedral, with its distinctive spire (destroyed by lightning in 1561), was in the centre. Similarly, a woodcut image of London, with rooftops, church spires and city wall, appeared in the *Chronicle of England*, a work published by William Caxton in 1480, with a new edition by his successor, Wynkyn de Worde, appearing 11 years later. This image indicated that print could reproduce conventional forms.

The so-called Copperplate map depicting London in about 1559, the first known printed map of London, was very different. It offered a dense assemblage of pictures, including a real jumble of late-medieval wooden buildings, cramped streets and courtyards, with boats on the river. The buildings are shown in semi-perspective, with particular attention given to the more significant ones.

Published in 1572, but surveyed perhaps 20 years earlier, and possibly a single-sheet version of the larger original 'Copperplate' map, a map of London was included in the *Civitas Orbis Terrarum*, a major and still-impressive German atlas. The figures in the foreground provided the sense of a panorama, as did the three-dimensional boats and

buildings. Nevertheless, this was essentially a plan. The basic shape of the walled Roman and medieval city was unchanged, but suburban development was occurring on all sides. There were relatively small extra-urban pockets of development to the east and to the north as far as Charterhouse. Southwark, on the south bank of the Thames, was still modest in scale. A more detailed, hand-drawn map of Southwark of about 1542 is now preserved in the National Archives and this shows the many inns and churches there, as well as the manor house, pillory, stocks and bullring.

Of much greater significance were the extensive tracts west of the river Fleet between the City of London and the old Palace of Westminster, along Holborn, and especially along the Strand between Charing Cross and Whitehall – long an area of settlement. The City of Westminster reached from Temple Bar on the east to the old Palace of Westminster on the west.

London had burst out of the walls, which increased the issues involved in depicting it, as it also did for other cities. In contemporary European cities, walls provided the main way in which cities were both delimited and shaped, but when this process ceased because of large-scale extra-mural growth it led to new depictions of cities. Venice was another city that could not be depicted by means of fortifications.

The Agas map of 1591 reflects further growth in and of London, including the great activity on the river. The royal palace at Whitehall is shown as linked by two arches over the public road (Kinges Streate), giving access to the St James hunting grounds as well as the tiltyard for jousting. Two years later, a map drawn by Peter van den Keere, and usually referred to by the name of its publisher, John Norden, appeared. A scale was included, while the coats of arms around the map were those of the 12

This map of London appeared in Georg Braun and Frans Hogenberg's *Civitates Orbis Terrarum*, published in Cologne and Amsterdam in 1572, and was derived from the Copperplate map of about 1559. London featured frequently in Shakespeare's plays, both directly as a key site in the History Plays, notably for Richard III's seizure of power, and subliminally in the depiction of all cities across the plays. The bustle and 'low-life', as in the Eastcheap tavern that is Falstaff's kingdom in *Henry IV*, contrasts with the world of the royal court. As Shakespeare's plays were first produced in London, the audiences were also seeing themselves in the characters portrayed on the stage.

LONDINVM. FERACISSIMI AN
GLIAE REGNI METROPOLIS.

THE TOWRE

great livery companies. In Southwark, both 'the play house' and 'the beare houses' are shown. The map focused on the great houses along the river Thames. Appearing in 1616, Visscher's facsimile of London was essentially another highly detailed picture.

The emergence of a specialised trade in printed maps and atlases in London was a slow process. Although technical proficiency was achieved, the English failed to match the Dutch in creating a bespoke industry. In contrast, the production of books as a whole rose considerably during Elizabeth's reign, to nearly 3,000 titles in the 1590s, which contrasted with about 800 in the 1520s and about 1,800 in the 1560s.

London numbers put pressure on housing and employment, at the same time as they added to the vitality of the city. Migrants, from home and abroad, provided labour, unskilled and skilled, and the latter contributed to the development of new trades and products, for example in glass-making and brewing.

Meanwhile, much of the drama of the English Reformation was played out in London. So also with the drama of the Earl of Essex's coup attempt in 1601. This was a theatrical episode that matched much seen on the stage, although Essex's failure was followed by his execution.

Four years later, a small group of Catholic conspirators managed to smuggle gunpowder into the cellars under Parliament, planning to blow it up when James I opened the session on 5 November 1605. The conspirators hoped that the destruction of the royal family and the Protestant elite would ignite rebellion and lead to the overthrow of the Protestant establishment. The plot, however, was exposed because of an attempt to warn a Catholic peer. Captured in the cellars, Guy Fawkes was tortured to force him to reveal the names of his co-conspirators, and then executed.

**The 'Copperplate' map of London** is an early large-scale printed map of the City of London and its immediate environs, surveyed between 1553 and 1559, which survives only in part. It is the earliest true map of London, as opposed to panoramic views, such as those of Anton van den Wyngaerde. The original map was probably designed for hanging on a wall, and is believed to have measured approximately 3ft 8in (112cm) high by 7ft 5in (226cm) wide. No copies of the printed map itself are known to have survived, but between 1962 and 1997 three of the original engraved copper printing plates, from a probable total of 15, were identified. These three cover the greater part of the built-up heart of the City of London.

The map takes the form of a 'bird's-flight view': the street layout and other ground features are shown in plan, as if viewed directly from above, while buildings, people and other standing features are shown as if viewed from a great height to the south of the City, but without the foreshortening of more distant features that would be necessary for a true perspective view. **OPPOSITE**

CIVITAS LONDINV[M]

This antient and famous City of London, was first founded by Brute the Trojan, in the year of the World two thousand, eight hundred thirty & two, and before the Nativity of our Saviour Christ, one thousand, one hundred, and 30. So that since the first building, it is thousand 6 hundred 60 & 3 years. And sithence was repaired & enlarged by King Lud, but at this present so flourisheth, that it containeth in length from the East to the West about 3 English miles, from the North to the South about 2 English miles. It is also so plentifully peopled, that it is divided into a hundred and 18 Parishes within the Liberties, besides 16 Parishes that are in the suburbs. It is planted on a very good soyle: for on the one side it is compassed with corne & pasture ground, and on the other side it is indosed with the river of Thames, which not only aboundeth in all kind of fresh water-fish, but also is so navigable, that it as well bringeth abundance of commodities from all parts of the World, as also conveieth forth such commodities as the plentifulnesse of our Contry doth yeild us: which both augments the same thereof a broad, and also increaseth the riches thereof at home, so that as it is head and chief City of the whole Realm, so is it likewise head and chief Chamber of the whole Realm, as well for our outward as inward commodities. God prosper it at His pleasure Amen.

A bird's-eye view of London, first printed from woodblocks in about 1561. Widely known as the Agas map, from a spurious attribution to the surveyor Ralph Agas (c.1540–1621), the map offers a richly detailed view both of the buildings and streets of the city and of the environs. No copies survive from 1561, but a modified version, printed in 1633, shows the Stuart coat of arms replacing the Elizabethan one, and the Royal Exchange, which opened in 1571. Although smaller scale and cruder, the Agas map is related to the 'Copperplate' map.

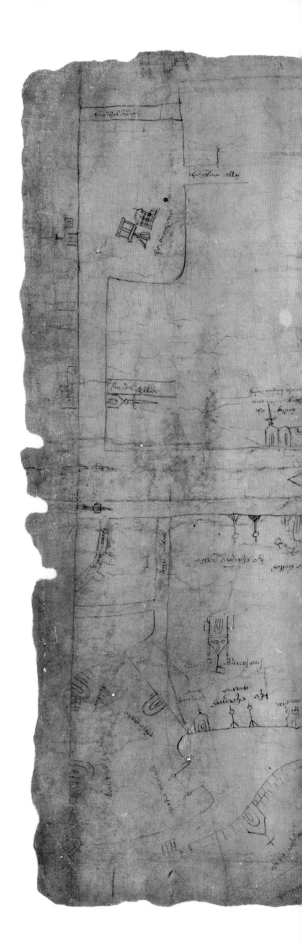

**Plan of Southwark**, c.1542. This map shows streets and named buildings: the manor place and liberty, churches, cross, bullring, market place, court house, prison, pillory, inns, gates, walls and hospital. No scale is included and the map is oriented to the east. It may have been produced to display the extent of the King's liberty and that of the liberty of the manor place, or to show areas of sanctuary as required by the Act of 1541. Outside the City of London, Southwark became the key area for locating playhouses, with the Rose (1587) joined by the Swan (1595) and the Globe (1599).

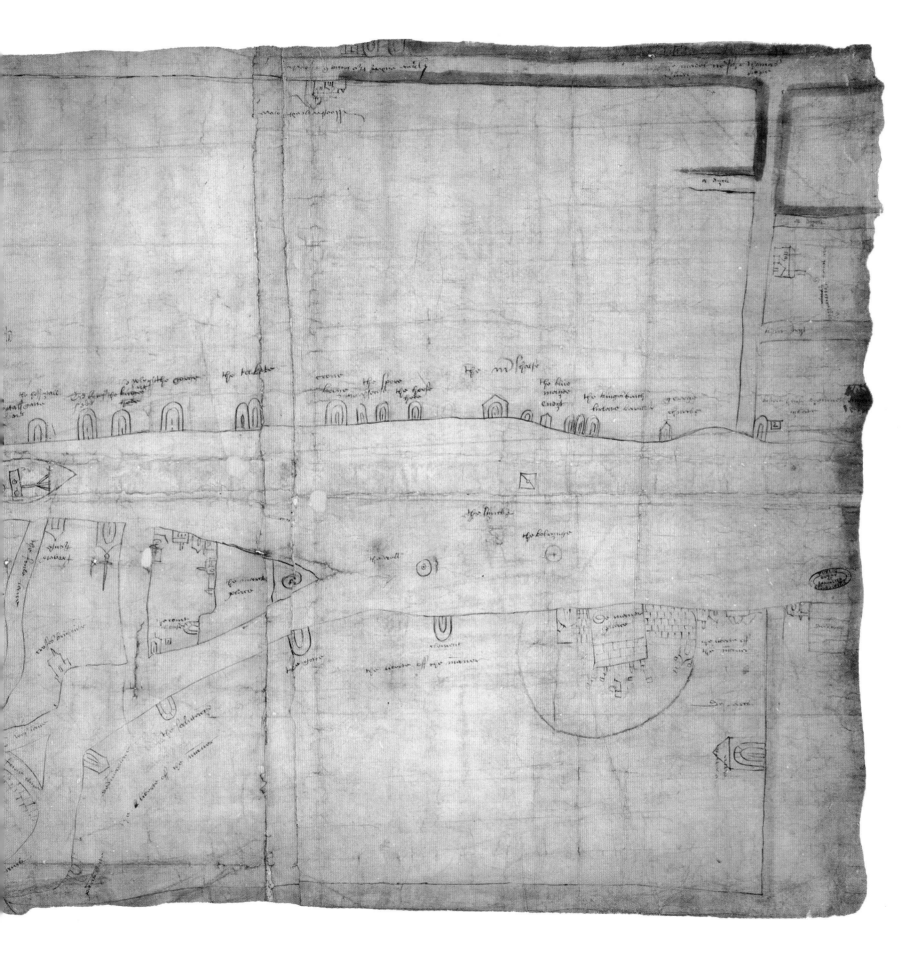

S. PAULES CHURCH

Hansted Mills
Hansted
S. Brides
Paulis Warf
Quene hythe
Three Cranes
The Water house
Cheap

The Eell Schipes
The Gally fuste

THAMESIS

The Bear Gardne
The Globe

**Engraving of a view of London** – a detail from the 1616 *Londinum Florentiss[i]ma Britanniae Urbs* by Claes Visscher (1586–1652). The artist may never have visited London. Indeed, the image could have derived from older printed views of the city as it would have been earlier. From a viewpoint on the south bank of the Thames, the image captures some of London's most important buildings, including St Paul's Cathedral and the Globe Theatre. The Thames is shown as disproportionately wide.

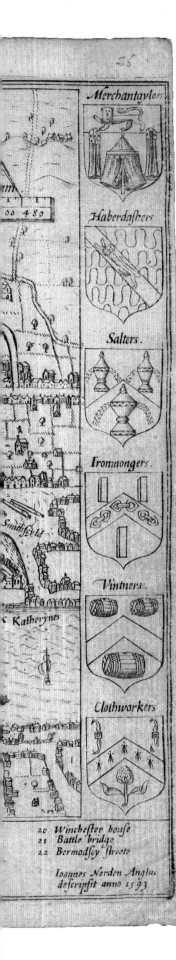

Map of London, 1593, by Pieter van den Keere. Born in Ghent, van den Keere (c.1571–1646) was an important map engraver. In 1584, he moved with his family to London in order to escape Catholic persecution. In 1583, he settled in Amsterdam, where he pursued his career. This is a precise map that uses a letter and number key and includes the coats of arms of the Guilds as well as a scale. The proximity of the countryside emerges clearly and the walled nature of the city is apparent – a factor that focuses attention on the gates. **LEFT**

The Globe Theatre was the major setting for the Chamberlain-King's Men from 1599 until it was burned down in 1613 during a performance of *Henry VIII*. The new theatre was built from the timbers used for the previous incarnation, this was an open-air amphitheatre that was close to circular. In *The Tempest*, Prospero foretells that the great Globe 'shall dissolve' like the play itself. **ABOVE**

# Mapping History

Shakespeare very much engaged with the past, notably of England, but also of Rome and of Scotland. What such an engagement meant in spatial terms, notably concerning an understanding of past geographies, was uncertain. However, there was an increasingly clear sense of the past as distinctive. This was linked to the emergence of a particular awareness of history, derived notably from the Renaissance typology and progression of historical eras (Classical – medieval – modern) and the related Protestant proposal of Christian periods: Early-Church – Medieval Church – Reformed Church. In part, this emergence was an aspect of the general impact of Humanism and, specifically, the emphasis that was placed on literal, rather than allegorical, interpretations of Scripture and the Classics, and also on the accuracy and clarity of the text.

There was an element of the Renaissance's focus on historical documents in the relationship between antiquarian studies and maps. Interest in post-Roman, pre-medieval England became more important in part as a distinctive English narrative of ecclesiastical history was advanced in order to justify the English Reformation, which supposedly reversed a medieval usurpation of the Early Church by the Papacy. The Anglo-Saxon scholar and cartographer Laurence Nowell (1530–c.1570), Dean of Lichfield Cathedral, in his 13-section manuscript and mid-sixteenth-century map of England and Wales, gave place names in Old English and used Old English letter forms. The Kent antiquarian, map-maker and Justice of the Peace William Lambarde (1536–1601), a pupil of Nowell who enjoyed Elizabeth's favour, not only produced the first English county history, *A Perambulation of Kent* (1576), but also drew a map of the Anglo-Saxon kingdoms.

A wish to relate time to place was becoming more common. There had been many remarks to the effect that geography was an important ancillary to history – a kind of second eye – but these were essentially rhetorical before about 1580, and possibly later. However, there are signs of important shifts in interest and perception, notably with an understanding of close relations between history and geography, as in *Microcosmus, or a Little Description of the Great World. A Treatise Historical, Geographical, Political, Theological* (1621).

The significance of time, the separation between past and present, came to be more strongly asserted and more readily understood and, in creating the past as a subject, made its depiction as different more of an issue. Historical maps, maps drawn to depict past events, were conscious historical statements dependent on a sense of the past as a separate sphere. John Speed's *Prospect of the Most Famous Parts of the World* (1627) was illustrated by a double-page black-and-white map of *The Invasions of England and Ireland with all their civil wars since the [Norman] Conquest*, a map first published in about 1601. This map had faults, particularly in its depiction of events greatly separate in time – from over half a millennium – as simultaneous. This was a traditional device characteristic of *mappae mundi*, but, in this case, it led to a work that was crowded and without apparent form or analysis. It is not surprising that the pictures of fleets arriving were impressionistic, but the map was arresting and illustrative, and definitely added visual interest to the book. Speed's county maps also included historical information, for example sites of battles. Some narrative histories, too, included maps. The translation of Thucydides by Thomas Hobbes, first published in 1629, for instance, contained maps that were clearly conceived to help illustrate the text, rather than being a simple adornment.

The first historical atlas appeared in Shakespeare's lifetime. It was the work of one of the

*Sacred Geography*, Jerusalem, 1584, Christian van Adrichem. This impressive plan of the city of Jerusalem at the time of Christ was created by Adrichem and first published in 1584. Adrichem used myriad sources to develop his plan, including Bernhard von Breitenbach's woodcut panorama of the city, Sebastian Munster's view, the texts of pilgrims Burchard of Mt Sion and William Wey, the Bible and Josephus. The plan is oriented to the north, with the camps of the historic city's invaders just outside the city walls, and the ancient City of David and Mt Sion in the south. There are more than 250 key locations identified and numbered, which are more fully described in Adrichem's text. One of the most important contributions of the plan is Adrichem's identification of the locations of the 14 sites of the Stations of the Cross, which are still accepted today. Adrichem's plan of

Jerusalem remained the definitive layout of the city until archaeological discoveries during the nineteenth century.

The *Theatrum Terrae Sanctae* was an atlas and history of the Holy Land and was Adrichem's most important and famous work. Born in Delft, Christian Kruik van Adrichem, or Christianus Crucius Adrichomius, was a Catholic priest and theologian. Adrichem worked for 30 years on his three-part history of the Holy Land, but only succeeded in publishing the first part, *Urbis Hierosolyma Depicta*, during his lifetime. The remaining two parts were published posthumously by Georg Braun in 1590, with subsequent editions in 1593, 1600, 1613, 1628 and 1682. *The Theatrum Terrae Sanctae* contained 12 maps and plans: one of the Holy Land, nine of territories of the Tribes of Israel, one of the Exodus, and a town plan of Jerusalem.

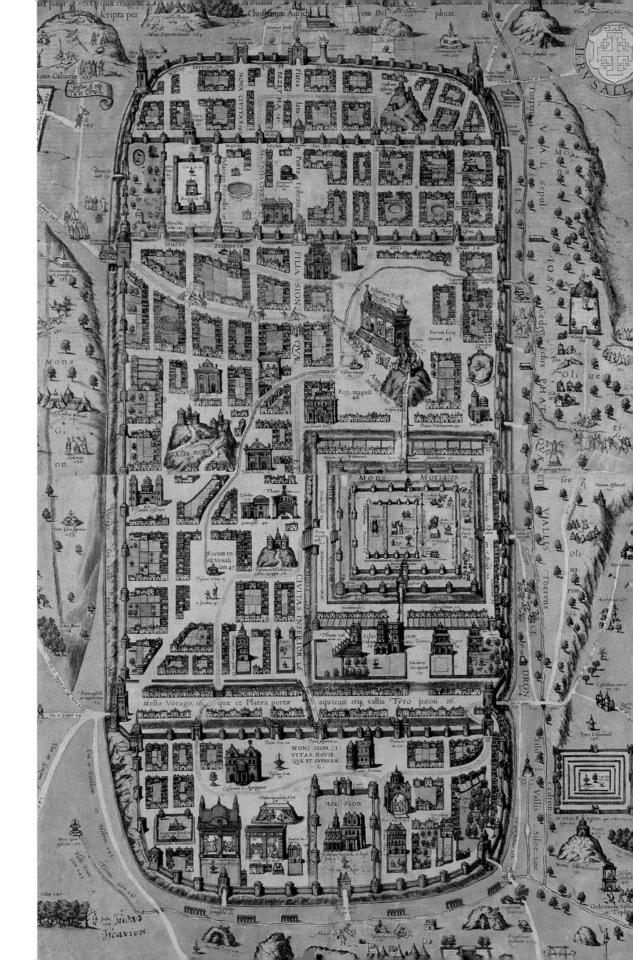

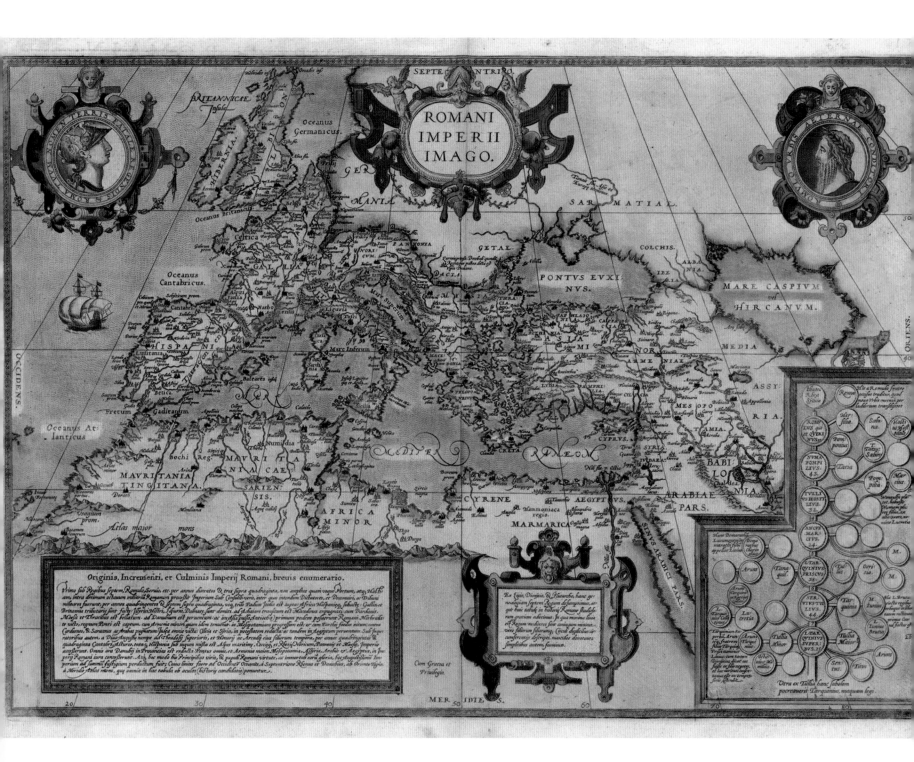

This fine and very interesting historical map of the Roman Empire is based on Ortelius' own two-sheet map of 1571. It is embellished by the portraits of Romulus and Remus and by a genealogical tree showing the lineage of the emperors. The panel explains the history of the Empire.

Ortelius' *Parergon* began as a companion to his *Theatrum*, but eventually it became an independent work. In fact, this collection of maps of the ancient world was so significant that it became the model for all historical atlases published throughout the seventeenth century. Unlike the *Theatrum*, which consisted of existing maps re-engraved by Ortelius, the maps in the *Parergon* were drawn by Ortelius himself. As a scholar of antiquity, a dealer in antiques and a visitor to ancient sites, he was well prepared to execute the maps, and all the maps from the *Parergon* reflect his passion for the Ancient world.

The city of Rome and the conflicts of its Empire are the setting of *Coriolanus, Julius Caesar, Antony and Cleopatra, Titus Andronicus* and, due to its consequences for Britain, *Cymbeline*. Ortelius visited England in 1577 and corresponded with leading English intellectual figures, including William Camden, John Dee and Humphrey Llwyd. Dee and Hakluyt ownded copies of the *Theatrum*.

leading European cartographers, Abraham Ortelius (1527–1598). Born in Antwerp, and well travelled in France, Italy and Germany, he turned to cartography in the early 1560s, creating an atlas, the *Theatrum Orbis Terrarum* (*Theatre of the World*), which was published in Antwerp in 1570 and of which about 40 editions had appeared by 1612.

Ortelius was also interested in the geography of the Ancient world, the period of Shakespeare's Roman world, and provided the most significant and accessible spatial depiction of them. He published a map, *Romani Imperii Imago* (1571), and the *Synonymia geographica sive populorum, regionum, insularum, urbium ... appellationes et nomia* (1578), a major repertorium of geographical names that provided an alphabetical list of place names mentioned by Classical authors with, against each, the names employed at other periods. The following year, Ortelius began to draw historical maps for the *Theatrum*. These maps of the Classical world – the *Parergon* – were his own work, unlike the copies of other maps that he used for the contemporary world in the *Theatrum*. Between 1579 and 1598, Ortelius drew 38 maps for the *Parergon*, and this section of the *Theatrum* grew from 12 plates in the 1584 Latin edition to 26 in 1591, 32 in 1595, and 38 in 1603. The accompanying text was also by Ortelius. That more plates were added after Ortelius' death reflected the value of the work.

The *Parergon* was translated into French, Italian, German and English, the English edition – containing 43 plates in the *Parergon* section – coming out in 1606. The 1595 *Parergon* appeared as a separate edition in Antwerp that year. Ortelius also had the Roman 'Peutinger' map (a fourth-century map known from a surviving eleventh-century copy) engraved and published in 1598, probably the first printed facsimile of a Classical map; it was subsequently included in several editions of the *Parergon*. Thus, the *Parergon* was a very successful work, its

impact spread by translations and new editions.

The *Parergon* began with 'Sacred Geography', as, according to the values of the time, the Bible took precedence over the world of the Classics. The journeys of the Patriarchs and of St Paul readily lent themselves to cartographic depiction, as did those of key secular figures, notably Aeneas and Alexander the Great; journeys were a major theme in cartography. The Classical world was presented in great detail, although the *Parergon*'s maps centred on Rome rather than Greece. The emphasis on Italy detracted even more from due attention being given to the Near and Middle East, notably Egypt and Mesopotamia (Iraq), and there was no sense of chronological progress in the organisation of the maps. Thus, the map of the campaigns of Alexander was followed by that of the travels of Ulysses: history succeeded by myth, and far earlier myth, in a mixture commonplace in this period.

Ortelius was affected by current concerns and present-day images, as Speed was to be, and, indeed, as Shakespeare was. Alexander's fleet was depicted as sixteenth-century boats, while the Low Countries, in Ortelius' map of them in the Roman period, consisted of the 17 provinces belonging to the Habsburgs in the mid-sixteenth century. This created a sense of territorial coherence that was misplaced for the earlier period. For example, the Low Countries had been divided at the time of the Roman Empire, with most of the region within the Empire, but much beyond it. Aside from maps and text, Ortelius also included a number of views, including two fantasy ones: 'Tempe' and 'Daphne'. The *Parergon* represented the significant shift from the single-sheet historical map to the atlas, as well as reflecting the degree to which knowledge of the worlds of the Bible and the Classics was seen by pedagogues and princes alike as a vital aspect of genteel education.

And so with Shakespeare's plays. Thus, *Pericles* is titled more fully *Pericles, Prince of Tyre*, and introduces, as the initial major characters, Pericles and the sinister, incestuous king Antiochus the Great, whose palace is in Antioch, which the prologue identifies as in Syria. Ephesus, Tharsus and Mytilene also feature as locations. The play, which ultimately derives from the Greek romance of Apollonius of Tyre, is located in the pre-Christian world, with Diana's temple playing a role. The Mediterranean is important not simply in the shape of the plot device of storms, but also because it serves as the way to link places, as is also the case with *Othello*, *The Comedy of Errors* and *Antony and Cleopatra*. Thus, Pericles alters his course to Tarsus because he is off its coast. His daughter, Marina, is kidnapped by pirates on the seashore and taken to Mytilene, where she is sold for prostitution. After being reunited with Pericles, they follow a vision sent by Diana and sail to the city of Ephesus on the Aegean coast of Anatolia, the setting of *The Comedy of Errors*, where Pericles finds his long-lost wife. Such references are made easier because the Mediterranean was not only the axis of the Ancient world known to the English, but also an important part of their contemporary world.

The geography of the Ancient world also plays a role in the other plays. Thus, in *Antony and Cleopatra*, the play is organised in terms of the contrast between Rome and Egypt. However, far more is involved in the geopolitics of the play. In the second scene, Mark Antony, who has been seduced by his interest in Cleopatra, is warned about the threat to the Roman Empire:

'... Labienus –
This is stiff news – hath with his Parthian force
Extended Asia; from Euphrates
His conquering banner shook, from Syria
To Lydia and to Ionia.' (1.2)

*The Invasions of England* and *Ireland with all their civil wars since the Norman Conquest*, c.1601, by John Speed. Speed's first printed map was an historical summary of England, Wales and Ireland, reflecting his own historical interests and, perhaps, intended as an illustration to be inserted into his *History of Great Britain*, which he published prior to the atlas volumes. The map shows the numerous battles from the Norman invasion in 1066 to the time of publication, and includes many textual annotations. Two blocks of text to the lower left-hand side of the map are devoted to Irish history. Sea battles are also described, including the relatively recent defeat of the Spanish Armada, whose progress, pursued by the English fleet, is clearly illustrated and recorded in panels of text, along the Channel and into the North Sea. The invasion most discussed by Shakespeare was that of French forces under the Dauphin, who landed in Kent in 1216 in an attempt to overthrow King John, an attempt defeated under the latter's infant son, Henry III.

The
INVASIONS
OF ENGLAND
And
IRELAND
with al their Ciuill
Wars Since the
Conquest.

DIEV ET MON DROIT

Performed by Iohn Speed, and ar to be solde in Popes head alley by George Humble.

The Spanish fleet first discried in their pretensed inuasion of England Iuly 19. 1588. reg. Eliz. 30.

The English fleet

The Spanish fleet

OF GALLIA

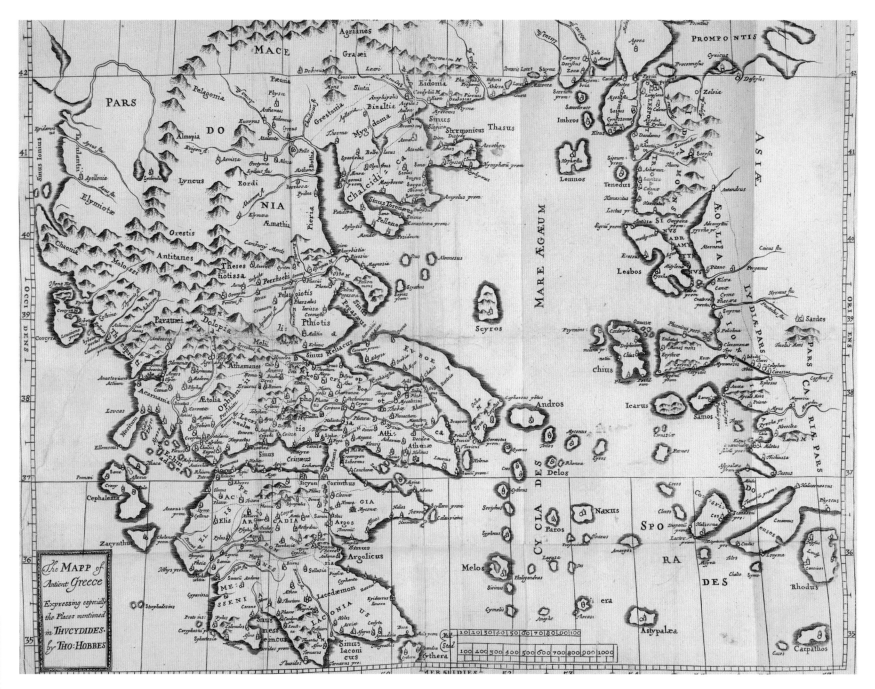

In 1629, Thomas Hobbes published
the first English translation, directly
from the Greek, of Thucydides'
*History of the Peloponnesian War*.
This edition included a map
representing Greece at the time
of Thucydides, which Hobbes
drew himself.

This was an exaggeration of the challenge from the Persian-based Parthians – who were not able to advance to Ionia, the Aegean province of Turkey – but, to contemporaries, it captured a sense of Oriental power as well as locating the geography in terms of the known landscape of the Classical world. In turn, Ventidius, the Roman victor over the Parthians in Syria, is described as having the option of chasing them through Medea and Mesopotamia. A sense of Oriental power was also captured in the description of Alexandria in the play.

However, this approach is less comfortable for the Italian city of Modena, where Antony, it is reported, was once beaten. It is mentioned without any explanation of its location; and the same is true of Mount Misenum, also in Italy, near where the pirates are based. A soldier assumes that listeners will understand a reference to 'the Phoenicians go a-ducking' (3.7) – in other words, preferring to fight at sea: Phoenicia was on the coast of modern Lebanon, with Tyre as its major city.

Geographical references that draw on the Classics are often to the fore. In *Othello*, when Iago tells the Moor that his mind may change, Othello replies:

'Never Iago. Like to the Pontic Sea,
Whose icy current and compulsive course
Ne'er keeps retiring ebb, but keeps due on
To the Propontic and the Hellespont,
Even so my bloody thoughts, with violent pace,
Shall ne'er look back, ne'er ebb to humble love,
Till that a capable and wide revenge swallow them up.'
(3.3)

This refers to the argument in Pliny the Elder's *Natural History* that, fed by the rivers that flow into it, such as the Danube, the Dnieper, the Dniester and the Don, the waters of the Black Sea (the Pontic Sea) always flow into the Sea of Marmora (the Propontic) and the Dardanelles (Hellespont), but never ebb back again.

These four maps from 1598 are Ortelius' version of the *Peutinger Table* – decorative maps, in a sequence of four plates, each with two strip maps, which depict the imperial roads and posts within the Roman Empire throughout Europe, North Africa and Asia as far as Toprobana (Sri Lanka). The format distorts the landmasses but provides an excellent view of the cities and roads, and includes distances between the posts. The three most important cities of the Roman Empire – Rome, Constantinople and Antioch – are represented by enlarged symbols including the emperor seated on a throne.

The *Peutinger Table*, as it is generally known, derived its name from Konrad Peutinger, who once owned the original, which is generally held to have derived directly or indirectly from a Roman prototype. Ortelius had manuscript copies made in 1598 from the original scroll and supervised the engraving, but did not live to see their publication. This is the *Parergon* edition with the Latin text on verso, printed by Balthasar Moretus and published in 1624. **RIGHT**

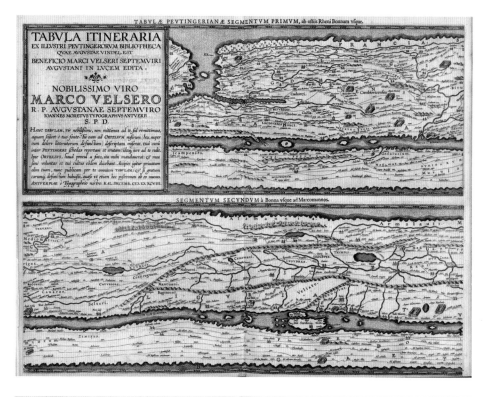

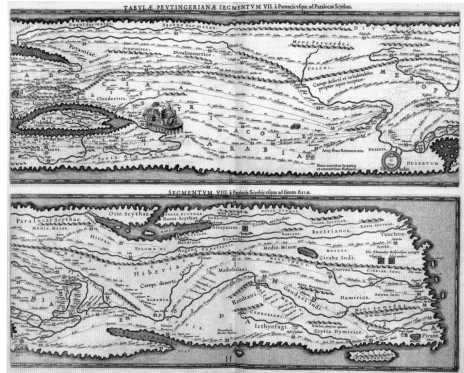

_Map of Britain_ by Laurence Nowell (1530–c.1570). A key figure in the development of Old English studies, Nowell graduated from Oxford in 1552 and then travelled, his journeys probably both inspiring and being inspired by his interest in cartography. The manuscript maps of Britain and Ireland that he produced in the mid-1560s were the most accurate of any similar maps to date. The ever-active William Cecil was the patron of Nowell, who produced a small, accurate pocket-sized map of England and Ireland for him. Nowell also made the first accurate cartographic survey of the east coasts of Ireland. His manuscript _Vocabularium Saxonicum_ was the first Old English to early-modern English dictionary. The map fits in a lot of place names, and marks major forests, rivers and mountains or hills, although Scotland is not handled as well as England. **LEFT**

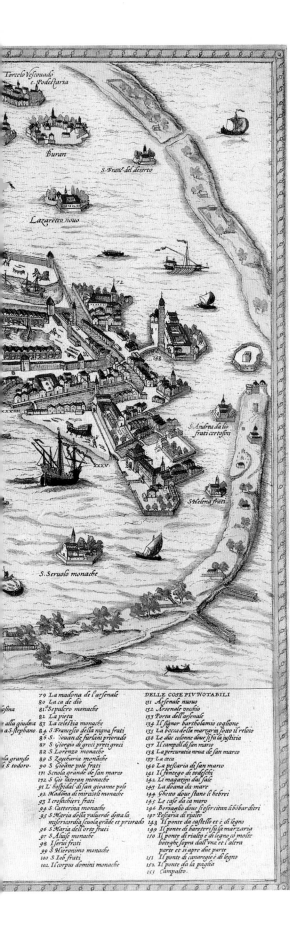

| 79 La madona de l'arfenale | DELLE COSE PIV NOTABILI |
| 80 La ca de dio | 151 Arfenale nuouo |
| 81.ᵗ Sepulcro monache | 152 Arfenale vecchio |
| 82 La pieta | 153 Porta dell'arfenale |
| 83 La celestia monache | 154 Il fignor bartholomio coglione |
| 84 S. Francefco della nigna frati | 155 La bocca della marzaria fotto il reloio |
| 85 S. iouan de furlani priorado | 156 Le due colonne doue fi fa la justitia |
| 87 S. giorgio di greci preti greci | 157 Il campali di fan marco |
| 88 S Lorenzo monache | 158 La percuratia noua de fan marco |
| 89 S Zacheria monache | 159 La ceca |
| 90 S Gioãne polo frati | 140 La pefcaria di fan marco |
| 171 S Gio lateran monache | 141 Il fontego di todefchi |
| 91 L' hoffidal di fan gioanne polo | 142 Li magazin dal fale |
| 92 Madona di miracoli monache | 143 La doana da mare |
| 93 I crofechieri frati | 144 Ghetto doue ftano li hebrei |
| 94 S Catterina monache | 145 Le cafe dà ca moro |
| 95 S Maria della valuerde detta la | 146 Bersaglio doue fi efercitan li bõbar dieri |
| miferieordia fcuola grãde et priorado | 147 Pefcaria di rialto |
| 96 S Maria dell'orto frati | 148 Il ponte da caftello et è di legno |
| 97 S Aluife monache | 149 Il ponte di bareteri fu la marzaria |
| 98 I ferui frati | 150 Il ponte di rialto è di legno cõ molte |
| 99 S Hieronimo monache | botteghe fopra dall'vna et l'altra |
| 100 S Iob frati | parte et si apre due parte |
| 101 Il corpus domini monache | 151 Il ponte di canaregio è di legno |
| | 152 Il ponte da la paglia |
| | 153 Campalto. |

**The mapping of Europe** developed during the sixteenth century, notably with more drawings to scale, but also with important publication enterprises. This was the case in particular with the six-volume *Civitates Orbis Terranum*, produced between 1572 and 1617 by Georg Braun, the editor, and Frans Hogenberg, the engraver. It provided the first atlas of towns in the shape of a selection of 546 distinctive bird's-eye views and map views of cities, including this one of Venice. Texts appeared on the obverse of the plates, with image and information complementing one another. The pair had dozens of contributors, most of whom relied on existing maps, though none were as important as the Antwerp-based Flemish painter Georg (Joris) Hoefnagel, who had produced many drawings of cities and towns during widespread travels round Europe.

# Shakespeare's Europe

State boundaries in the sixteenth century were not those of the present. To take 1564, Shakespeare's year of birth, and compare it to the present underlines the need for caution in readily applying modern names for countries or states as if there has been scant change. There are examples of much continuity: in terms of European frontiers, Portugal has remained largely unchanged, although an area east of the Guadiana River was gained by Spain in 1801. However, Spain was used in 1564 as a shorthand term for the far-flung territories of the King of Spain. The division of the inheritance of the Emperor Charles V (who was Charles I of Spain) ensured that, at Shakespeare's birth, these dominions – those then ruled by Charles' only son, Philip II of Spain – included not only Spain and its territories in the Americas and a number of bases on the coast of North Africa, but also half of Italy (Sicily, Sardinia, the Milanese and the Tuscan coastal *Presidi* – garrisons such as Porto Longone), as well as the Burgundian inheritance as enlarged by Charles. The latter covered Franche-Comté, the region around Besançon, now in France; and the Low Countries – essentially modern Belgium, Netherlands and Luxembourg, but including parts of modern France, especially Artois, while excluding the prince-bishopric of Liège. The last was one of the many ecclesiastical states that showed that the idea of rule by a cleric continued to seem a viable option to Catholics. Their rulers were not brought on stage as villains by Shakespeare, unlike in Marlowe's *Massacre at Paris* and Webster's *Duchess of Malfi*.

Spain's great rival in Shakespeare's lifetime might seem to the English to be England, not least in the immediate aftermath of the Spanish Armada in 1588, but was really France, as was readily apparent in the 1600s. Shortly before Shakespeare's birth, France had expanded through war, gaining the prince-bishoprics of Metz, Toul and Verdun in 1552, and Calais (from England) in 1558; Boulogne, lost to England in 1544, was regained in 1550. Nevertheless, France had not yet made the major advances that were considerably to change its eastern frontier: the independent duchy of Savoy (a composite state with Piedmont and Nice) still reached to the river Saône until 1601; Lorraine was an independent duchy until 1766 and ruled by hostile dukes until 1737; and France was only ceded Alsace (and not all of that) in 1648, Artois and Roussillon in 1659, and Franche-Comté in 1678.

Much of this expansion was into what had been part of the middle kingdom created in the ninth century from the Frankish inheritance. In the fifteenth century, the period of Shakespeare's History Plays, much of this middle kingdom had been given international vitality as an expanding state by the dukes of Burgundy. A large part of the Burgundian inheritance had later been acquired first by marriage by Charles V and, subsequently, by inheritance, by his son, Philip II. As a result, the struggle between Habsburg and Valois, Spain and France, was, in part, a long-established conflict between Burgundy and France.

In northern Europe, the collapse in 1523 of the Union of Calmar, which had joined Denmark, Sweden, Norway, Finland and their ancillary territories, had left two competing states: Finland was part of the kingdom of Sweden, which had rebelled and become independent under King Gustav I Vasa. The kings of Denmark also ruled Norway, Schleswig and Holstein, as well as parts of modern Sweden, especially Gotland and Scania. Poland was a large composite state that included Ukraine, much of Belarus and Lithuania, as well as holding suzerainty (overlordship) over the duchy of Prussia (East Prussia), which was ruled by a branch of the house of Hohenzollern. Russia was yet another state that

OCEANVS   GER   MANICVS.

The Princes   Battel:

The Arch-Dukes Battel.

English

English

English

PORT.

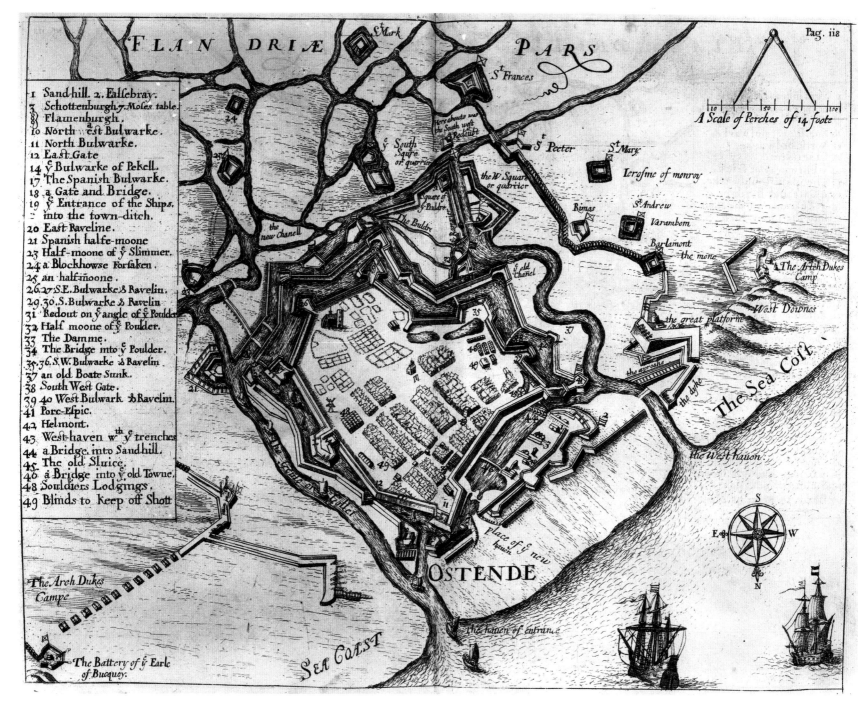

did not have the same borders as it does today. Under Ivan IV, the Terrible (r 1533–1584), it had just conquered the khanates of Kazan (1552) and Astrakhan (1556), and was to begin expansion across the Urals to the east, but it had not yet reached the Black Sea or the Pacific.

Germany, Italy and south-eastern Europe in 1564 were also very different from how they are today. The Balkans were ruled by the Ottoman (Turkish) Empire – an Islamic monarchy based, from 1453, at Constantinople (modern Istanbul), which also ruled Egypt (from 1517), much of South-West Asia (Syria from 1516), and the northern shores of the Black Sea, where the khanate of the Crimea was a dependent state. The Ottomans' conquest of much of Hungary after Süleyman the Magnificent's victory at Mohacs in 1526 had brought them into direct contact with Habsburg power, and dramatically so when the Ottomans unsuccessfully besieged Vienna in 1529.

Historical setting ensured that Othello, but not many of Shakespeare's other warriors, could fight the Turks. In *Richard II*, the fate of the future Henry IV's rival, Thomas, 1st Duke of Norfolk, in 1389–1398 is discussed. In practice, he certainly died in Venice, having gone on a pilgrimage to Jerusalem, but for the Bishop of Carlisle in Shakespeare's play:

> *'Many a time hath banish'd Norfolk fought*
> *For Jesu Christ in glorious Christian field,*
> *Streaming the ensign of the Christian cross*
> *Against black pagans, Turks, and Saracens;*
> *And toil'd with works of war, retired himself*
> *To Italy; and there at Venice gave*
> *His body to that pleasant country's earth,*
> *And his pure soul unto his captain Christ,*
> *Under whose colours he had fought so long.' (4.1)*

Earning Henry's wrath, Carlisle also predicts chaos in England if Richard is overthrown:

> *'The blood of English shall manure the ground*
> *And future ages groan for this foul act;*
> *Peace shall go sleep with Turks and infidels.' (4.1)*

The Habsburgs also benefited from Mohacs as the kingdoms of Bohemia and Hungary had been united under the same crown from 1490, and, with the death of the childless King Louis at Mohacs, the Habsburgs were able to acquire what the Ottomans did not need: Charles V's brother, Archduke Ferdinand of Austria, was the brother-in-law of Louis, and Ferdinand became King of Hungary. As a result, the Habsburg position in most of what is now Austria and Slovenia was enhanced by the acquisition not only of what became Habsburg Hungary (much of modern Slovakia, and parts of modern Croatia and Hungary), but also of Bohemia and Moravia (the modern Czech Republic), as well as Silesia (south-west modern Poland) and Lusatia (to the south-east of Berlin).

Since 1438, the Habsburg ruler had been elected Holy Roman Emperor, which provided him with a measure of authority, although less power, in the Empire – an area roughly coterminous with (matching the outline of) modern Germany, Austria, the Netherlands, Belgium, Switzerland, the Czech Republic and much of northern Italy. In these areas, sovereignty was divided and a large number of territorial princes, mostly lay but some ecclesiastical, as well as imperial free cities, such as Cologne, Frankfurt and Hamburg, exercised effective power, within the loose bounds of an imperial constitution. The emperor was the most prestigious lay figure in Christendom.

Most of Europe was ruled by hereditary monarchs, and its politics were therefore affected by

**_The Siege of Ostend_ by Francis Vere.** As so often with war, particular places took on significance because they became the focus of campaigning. This was especially so with Ostend which, from 1601 to 1604, played a key role in the Dutch Revolt – a struggle with Spain in which England was involved as the main ally of the Dutch from 1585, when Robert, Earl of Leicester was sent with an expeditionary force to help. With its extensive modern fortifications, Ostend was different to Harfleur, which Henry V had besieged in 1415. However, in both sieges, the willingness of the besiegers to storm positions was crucial to the outcome.

what has been termed 'proprietary dynasticism'. The most important Christian dynasty, in their own eyes, and in those of most other commentators, was the Habsburg one, and Charles V saw himself as the natural foe of Süleyman the Magnificent. His brother succeeded him as emperor, a position then held continually by Austrian Habsburgs until 1740. During Shakespeare's lifetime, the Valois and then, with the accession of Henry IV in 1589, the Bourbons ruled France; the Tudors, and then the Stuarts, England; the Vasas Sweden; the Stuarts Scotland; the Hohenzollerns Brandenburg; the Wettins Saxony; the Wittelsbachs Bavaria; the Medici

Tuscany; and so on down to small principalities in Germany and Italy. These principalities might not confer much power, but the families that ruled them, for example the Gonzaga of Mantua and the Farnese of Parma, followed dynastic goals of their own with the same ambition as their more prominent counterparts; as indeed did aristocratic families that lacked sovereign power.

The Empire and the Papacy were the most prominent of the elective monarchies, a group that included Bohemia, Hungary and, from the 1570s, Poland. The Papacy ruled a broad swathe of central Italy. The Swiss Confederation, Venice and Genoa

were the leading republics. Venice ruled an extensive empire that, in 1564, included Cyprus, Crete, the Ionian Islands, Dalmatia and much of north-eastern Italy, notably Brescia, Cremona, Padua and Vicenza – an empire, however, that was vulnerable to attack, especially from the Turks. Genoa ruled the surrounding area on the Italian mainland, as well as the island of Corsica. It was driven from the Aegean by the Turks.

Monarchs helped provide unity and direction to policy, but royal and other courts and ministries were factious, and this undermined attempts to provide a unitary account of states and to give pol-

***Cadiz,* from *Civitates Orbis Terrarum*** by Ortelius, based on the original by Joris Hoefnagel. Cadiz was prominent for English readers due to the English attacks on the city in 1587 and 1596 – attacks that reflected the use of forward assault on enemy ports in order to disrupt their preparations. There was no prospect of gaining a base, but these attacks could be

highly disruptive. In 1596, the Spanish fleet was supported by the guns of the city, while the ably commanded Anglo-Dutch force fought its way into the defended anchorage and conducted a successful opposed landing followed by the storming of the city which lacked adequate defences.

ENVÆ PICTVRA
FERE CONSVMPTA
ILLIVS VETVSTATIS
ES COMMVNIS
T ANNO MDXLVII

icies consistency. Particular difficulties arose over the succession, which served as a question mark against the consistency of policies and the stability of ministries, and very obviously so with England from the 1540s to 1603 and with the Denmark of *Hamlet* and the Scotland of *Macbeth*. Dynastic monarchy was also confronted by the problems of weak or inadequate or unpopular monarchs, as in France in the 1560s–1580s with Francis II (r 1559–1560), Charles IX (r 1560–1574) and Henry III (r 1574–1589). All of these were unable to control the factionalism of the leading nobility, as their predecessors had done – by refusing to surrender the means and fruits of patronage to any one faction and thus remaining the focus of authority and power. In *The Tempest*, Prospero's lack of commitment to his rule as Duke of Milan permits his brother Antonio to overthrow him:

> 'The government I cast upon my brother,
> And to my state grew stranger, being transported
> And rapt in secret studies.' (1.2)

Lear, John, Richard II and Henry VI are all depicted as inadequate rulers, while Julius Caesar, who was not a monarch, is too vain.

Other than in the cities, wealth and prestige across Europe were based on the possession of land, most of which was owned by a hereditary nobility, whose most powerful members constituted an aristocracy. The legal status of the nobility, and the extent to which there was a clearly differentiated aristocracy, varied greatly by country.

Although they sought to further their will, the rulers of Christian Europe also compromised with existing interests and ruled by virtue of, and through, systems of privilege, rights and law that protected others as well as themselves. Monarchs presented themselves as powerful. However, in

*Genoa*, 1481, copied by Cristoforo de Grassi in 1597 from a now-lost drawing celebrating the departure of the fleet in response to a call by Pope Sixtus IV to drive the Ottomans (Turks) from the Italian city of Otranto. The Ottomans had seized Otranto with an amphibious expedition the previous year in what was a major show of force as they were also besieging Rhodes. However, Mehmed II's successor, Bayezid II (r.1481–1512), who faced opposition from his brother Jem, abandoned Otranto in 1481. Lacking the visual appeal of Venice, Genoa nevertheless was also an important Mediterranean naval power, usually supporting Spain. However, it never engaged the imagination – and certainly of the English – as Venice did, most notably through Shakespeare's dramas set in the whole of the city (*The Merchant of Venice*) or part of it (*Othello*).

**OPPOSITE**

practice, 'states' were not only weak but also subject to outside pressures, which the rulers had only a limited ability to mould, let alone determine. The crucial political question became that of the Crown issuing orders that it knew would meet with a ready response, in large part because it was reacting to élite views. This formulation may seem over-optimistic as well as glib, as co-operation was often limited, and that was the case from both directions. Nevertheless, this approach was accurate not only for 'state' authority, but also for aspects of social control and religious authority.

In part, however, the notion of sides is misplaced. A culture that stressed the ideal of a Christian community, and the model of good kingship and willing obedience, was matched by the reality of the politics of patronage – a social and political relationship that placed obligations on both parties and, thus, cut across any notion of government and subjects. This was especially true at the level of the aristocracy, but it was the case not only at that level. Shakespeare depicts this politics of patronage in his presentation of royal courts.

Similarly, the nature of aristocratic society ensured that the social gap between monarch and subjects should not be exaggerated; rulers and greater aristocrats shared glorious lineages and a similar lifestyle. This encouraged the aristocrats to expect that they would not be dealt with like other subjects. Many of the leading aristocratic families, for example the Condé in France, were cadet branches of royal houses. This could ensure a bridge between Crown and nobility, but could also serve to provide leadership and legitimation for aristocratic opposition to royal policies. A particular dynamic was presented by royal bastards.

Aristocratic opposition could focus, as in England, France and Spain in the early seventeenth century, on royal favour for ministers who lacked support from other aristocrats and who breached

*Seville,* from Ortelius' *Civitates Orbis Terrarum,* which gave map accounts of many leading cities throughout Europe. In *Love's Labour's Lost,* the Spaniard Don Adriano de Armado is presented as a comic figure, at once bombastic and ridiculous. **BELOW**

**A centre of Spanish commercial power,** Seville also contained a royal palace, but Philip II preferred the Escurial near Madrid. Like most cities, Seville was on a major river, in its case, the Guadalquivir. **RIGHT**

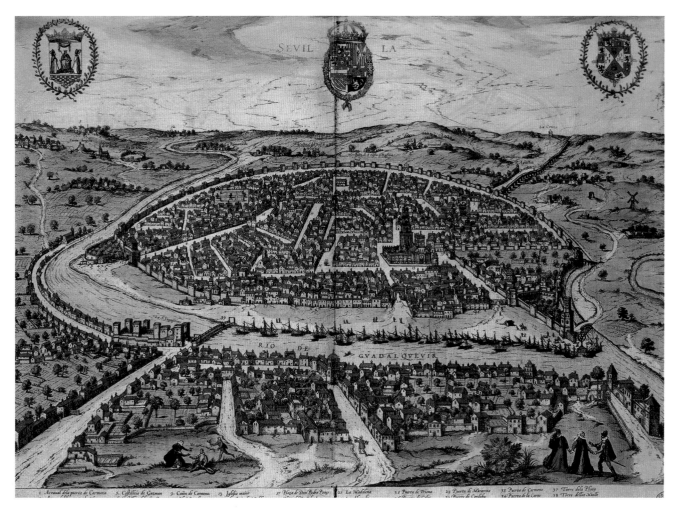

SEVIL LA

SEVILLA

Iglesia maior    Las Casa de la contrac-    Torre de la    Torre del oro    El Castillo    Xaunierra
                 tacion de las    El alcaçar    plata                Triana
                 Indias                La Puerta de    Las    El muelle    Las Sierras
                              Xeres    ataraças    S. Elmo    de Ronda

El arenal    Puente di triana

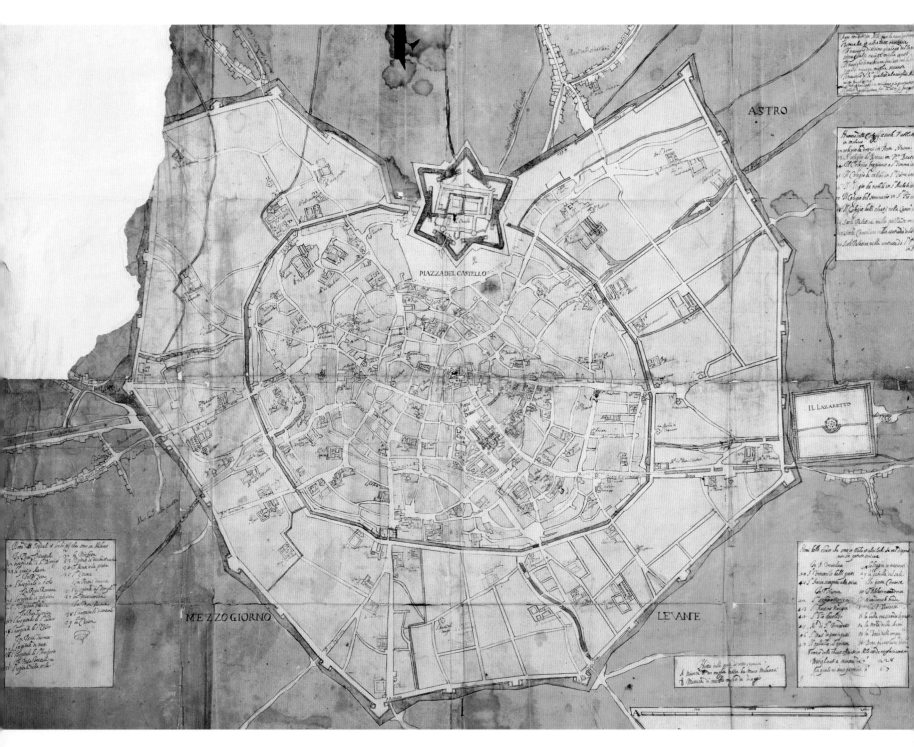

ASTRO

PIAZZA DEL CASTELLO

IL LAZARETTO

MEZZO GIORNO

LEVANTE

the conventions of aristocratic political society. The continual importance of informal channels of authority in political and governmental systems in which bureaucracy played only a limited role focused attention on such ministers, and also ensured that the role and skill of monarchs were important.

These relationships cannot be covered adequately in maps, and more generally it is necessary to appreciate that the geographical character of power was very different to the situation today. Prior to the urbanisation of the nineteenth and twentieth centuries, when a large percentage of the rural population of Europe moved to the major urban areas, the bulk of the population lived in the countryside. As a result, they were essentially under the authority of their landlords, such as Justice Swallow in *Henry IV, Part Two*, while the agencies of central government were weak. Maps need to be understood, in terms of appreciating the central problem and issues of distance, when considering and assessing both strategies of rule and governance, and, therefore, political capability and stability.

Cultural and institutional practices were part of the equation. The habit of obedience towards authority was matched by a stubborn, and largely successful, determination to preserve local privileges. This helped to ensure that the focus of authority was often a local institution or a sense of locality, rather than a distant ruler. This determination was exacerbated by the weakness in many states of what might be considered proto-nationalism, a situation, however, that did not extend to England where such proto-nationalism was clearly seen in Elizabeth's reign.

In contrast, on the Continent, provincial Estates (representative bodies), for example in parts of France, played a potent political role as a signifier of identity, irrespective of their constitutional powers. On the Continent, whether or not such Estates existed, rulers had to take note of the strength of regional and local feelings. These owed something to the roles of distance and proximity in defining senses of identity.

Irrespective of this factor, the agencies of central government tended to be weak and to be limited by clientage, factionalism and corruption. Privilege was not simply an obstacle to government, but was often essential to its operation and effectiveness. In addition, a habit of regarding society in terms of distinct groups with different rights and functions, as opposed to the modern concept of a uniform citizenry, led to a corporate approach to privilege, as with aristocratic tax exemption and legal rights.

During Shakespeare's lifetime, accounts of war came from Europe, from both near and far. He was born in the decade in which both the French Wars of Religion and the Dutch Revolt broke out, and died just before the outbreak in Bohemia in 1618 of the Thirty Years' War. A new wave of Wars of Religion came to affect much of Europe in the 1560s, notably in France, the Low Countries and the British Isles. In each, rebellion was linked to religious disaffection, although other factors also played a role, especially tensions within the elite. In addition, as an instance of an apparent Islamic threat, a rising in Granada in 1568 was brutally suppressed, with large numbers of the Moriscos (apparent Moorish converts from Islam) slaughtered. In 1609, the Moriscos were expelled from Spain.

In the Low Countries (modern Belgium and the Netherlands), the unpopular religious and fiscal policies of the ruler, Philip II of Spain (brother-in-law to Elizabeth as husband of her predecessor, Mary I) and his neglect of the Dutch nobility led to riots in 1566–1567 and then to the re-imposition of order by a powerful Spanish army under the Duke of Alba. Ideas of ensuring peace through concilia-

*Milan and its Canals.* The centre of power in Lombardy, the walled city of Milan was dominated by a star-shaped citadel. Long under local rulers – notably the Visconti and then, after a brief republican interlude in 1447–1450, the Sforza – Milan changed hands frequently during the Italian Wars (1494–1559), with repeated French attempts to gain control, and important battles nearby as a result, notably Pavia (1525). However, the Habsburgs were left dominant, ensuring that they were the leading power in northern Italy. The city appears a few times in Shakespeare: in *The Two Gentlemen of Verona*, Valentine falls in love with the Duke of Milan's daughter, Silvia; and in *The Tempest*, Prospero, the rightful Duke of Milan, is displaced by his brother Antonio, who, at midnight, opens the gates to 'a treacherous army' (1.2).
**OPPOSITE**

tion and limited religious toleration, as advocated by the *politiques* in France, by Elizabeth I in England, and by the Warsaw Confederation of 1573 in Poland, were unacceptable to Philip II – a ruler who saw his orthodoxy as simultaneously a providential, dynastic, political and personal necessity. To the English, this re-imposition became a potent image and reality of tyrannical military power, and of misrule at its most brutal. More than 1,000 people were executed and about 60,000 went into exile. There was scant concession to the local political culture and the role of consent.

The sense of Catholic cruelty was taken further by the killing of the Huguenot (Protestant) leaders in France in the St Bartholomew's Day Massacre on the night of 23/24 August 1572 as King Charles IX, the brother-in-law to Mary, Queen of Scots, turned against them. This gave Marlowe a subject in his *The Massacre at Paris*, a play printed in about 1594.

Moreover, this event provided an instance of a plot point frequently made by Shakespeare – the relationship of developments in different countries: freed from the risk of French intervention, Alba suppressed a fresh wave of Dutch rebel activity. He did so in a brutal fashion. The slaughter of many people – for example cutting the throats of the garrison of the town of Zutphen in 1572, and the killing of all bar 60 people in Naarden that year – led many other towns to surrender. In 1573, the surrender of the fortified city of Haarlem was followed by the cutting of the throats of about 2,000 members of the garrison. Yet, the Spaniards failed to crush the rebellion, in part because of the customary difficulty in moving from output, in the shape of military achievements, to outcome, in the form of political settlement.

War involved not just fighting on the battlefield, but also a broader range of activities, some of which captured the darker side of human interaction. Religious activity, education, publications, censorship, marriage, the household and poor relief were battlefields. The conflict was as much about soft power as it was about hard power, and it is no accident that the Society of Jesus, or Jesuits, was established by Ignatius of Loyola in 1534 as a quasi-military Cath-olic order. Nor is it surprising that clerics were slaughtered by both sides in the Low Countries and France, or that worshippers were intimidated, if not killed. Image-breaking was important to the process by which Protestants seized control of churches. Crucial to all religious conflict was a degree of popular engagement, including in the form of riots and massacres. Concern about popular action led governments to erect fortifications. Shakespeare's engagement with such rioting in his plays, as in *Henry VI, Part Two* and *Julius Caesar*, related to political, and not religious, violence.

The Dutch Revolt led, in the long term, to the overthrow of Philip II's rule in the northern provinces, which became the Dutch Republic (modern Netherlands), but, in the more populous and economically advanced south (modern Belgium), it proved possible for him to regain control. This owed much to the achievements of the Army of Flanders from 1579 under its brilliant commander Alexander Farnese, Duke of Parma. However, it was also necessary for Philip's representatives to make concessions, producing a settlement acceptable to the influential Walloon nobility. In contrast, the Dutch state was dominated economically by the towns of the Province of Holland, especially Amsterdam, and this dominance led to a different social politics to that in the southern provinces.

Meanwhile, the root causes of dissension in France persisted, notably religious division, aristocratic factionalism and royal weakness. Particularly in the towns, but not only there, there was a high

*Tunis, 1535,* by Braun and Hogenberg. Portugal and Spain devoted much effort in the fifteenth and sixteenth centuries to gaining control over North Africa, but were hit by both a Moroccan and an Ottoman resurgence. Positions that had been held or dominated, such as Algiers, Biserta, Bona, Bougie, Tripoli and Tunis, were lost – Tunis falling to the Ottomans in 1574, although, in 1600, Tangier, Ceuta, Melilla and Oran were all still under Philip III of Spain. This map shows his grandfather, Charles V, seizing Tunis in 1535. In *The Tempest*, the villains are shipwrecked in the Mediterranean by Prospero as they return from the marriage of Claribel, the daughter of Alonso, King of Naples, to the King of Tunis.

AFRICA,
olim APHRO-
DISI-
VM.

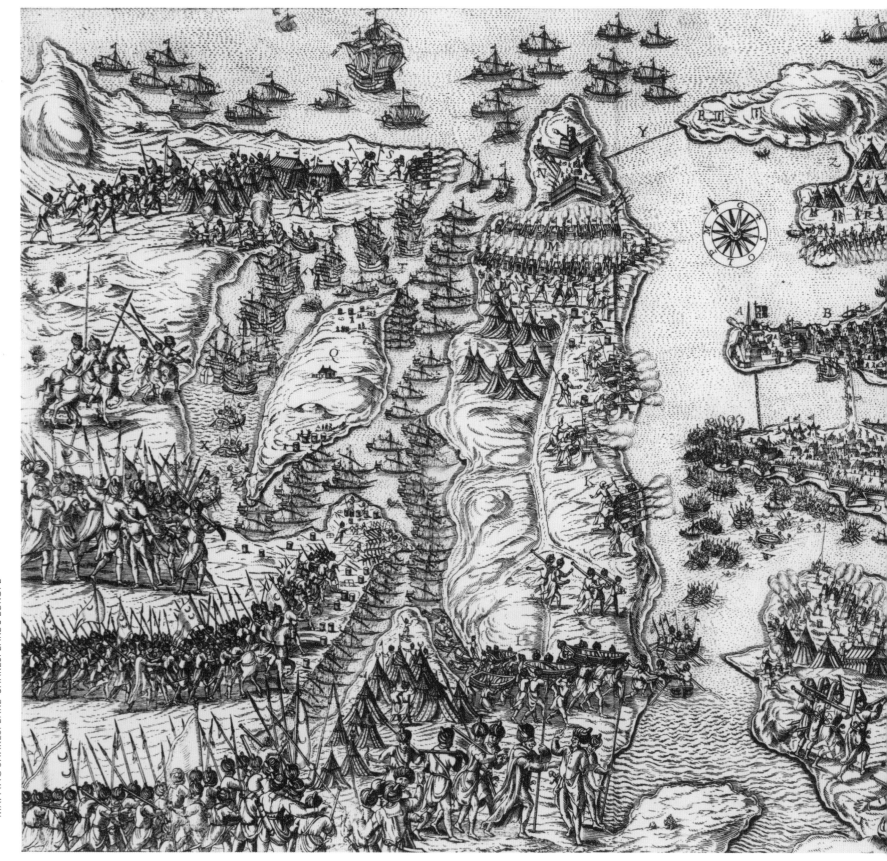

*Siege of Malta,* **1565,** Italian School. While limited in its precision, this engraving captured the major pressure the Ottomans (Turks) brought to bear on Malta. This situation was a background to the crisis affecting Cyprus in the early stages of Shakespeare's *Othello,* and Christopher Marlowe made reference to Malta in the title of his play *The Jew of Malta.* The siege was an epic worthy of celebration across Christian Europe in part because the defenders were not Spaniards.

level of popular engagement with the confessional struggle. This engagement led to outbursts of mass violence, as well as to a degree of independence from aristocratic leadership. Royal power and authority collapsed in the 1580s, reaching a nadir in 1589 when the childless Henry III (another brother-in-law to Mary, Queen of Scots), the Catholic king, was assassinated by a Catholic zealot while unsuccessfully besieging Paris, from which he had been driven by the more radical urban elements of the Catholic League. Spain and England then intervened on opposite sides in the war in France.

However, having converted to Catholicism, Henry of Navarre consolidated power and was crowned, as Henry IV, in 1594. Although it is disputed by modern scholars whether he actually used the phrase 'Paris is worth a Mass', the sentiment it expressed was a reflection of his political pragmatism. Buying off the major Catholic aristocrats with a recognition of their provincial power bases, and the Huguenots with concessions to Protestant worship by the Edict of Nantes (1598), Henry achieved domestic peace, although the condition of peace with Spain (the Peace of Vervins, 1598) was an acceptance of Spanish hegemony. The latter threatened England anew and ensured that pressure could be brought to bear on the Dutch in the continuing war, but Spain's financial burdens helped lead to the negotiation of the Twelve Years Truce with the Dutch in 1609.

To a degree, there was a change in the second half of Shakespeare's life, with the end of both the French Wars of Religion and the war between France and Spain in 1598, the war between England and Spain in 1604, the war between Austria and the Turks in 1606, and the war between the Dutch and Spain in 1609. England was not engaged in war after 1604 during Shakespeare's lifetime, while the beating of drums was subdued on the Continent.

Yet 'alarums' continued, and, indeed, Henry IV was a great patron of map-making for military purposes. Jean de Beins, who became Royal Engineer in France in 1607, produced plans for fortresses in the Dauphiné – a province vulnerable to attack from northern Italy, but also the means of attacking it – as well as preparing maps of the valleys and towns there – maps from which more general maps were prepared. Sensitivity about the stability of Henry's position had led the French ambassador to complain about a production of George Chapman's *The Conspiracy and Tragedy of Charles, Duke of Byron*, a play based on the Biron Conspiracy of 1600–1602. As a result, performances were banned in 1605, and when in 1608 the play was revived, the company that performed it was hit by arrests.

In 1610, the Jülich-Cleves succession crisis in the Rhineland appeared to presage large-scale conflict between France and Spain, which was only averted when Henry IV of France was assassinated by a fanatical Catholic in a scene that would have done credit to a Shakespeare play. Even so, there was campaigning in this crisis involving Dutch, French and Imperial forces as well as those of the Protestant Union of German princes. James I, however, remained neutral; he saw himself as a pacific figure.

Moreover, prior to the outbreak of the Thirty Years' War, there was instability in the Holy Roman Empire (Germany and the Habsburg lands), northern Italy and France. Venice fought Austria in 1613–1616; Charles Emmanuel I of Savoy-Piedmont invaded the Monferrato in northern Italy in 1613; in 1611 the Estates of Bohemia clashed with an army raised by Archduke Leopold, a Habsburg prince; and in 1614 Dutch and Spanish forces confronted each other in the Rhineland. James I again remained neutral.

Also in 1614, Louis XIII of France marched south with his army to impose his authority on

*Siege of Calais*, 1558. The loss of Calais by Mary was unpopular with her successor Elizabeth I, who made ineffective diplomatic efforts to regain the town, which had been a possession of the English Crown since 1347. In 1558, failure to flood the surrounding lowlands by the defenders under Thomas Wentworth, the Lord Deputy of Calais, enabled François, Duke of Guise, to capture the city after a siege of only seven days. Control over the city would have been very useful in the invasion crisis caused by the Spanish Armada in 1588. In Shakespeare's history plays, Calais is mentioned as a place of transit, where both Henry V and Henry VI embark. In *Richard II*, Bolingbroke accuses Mowbray of corruption while he governed the city.

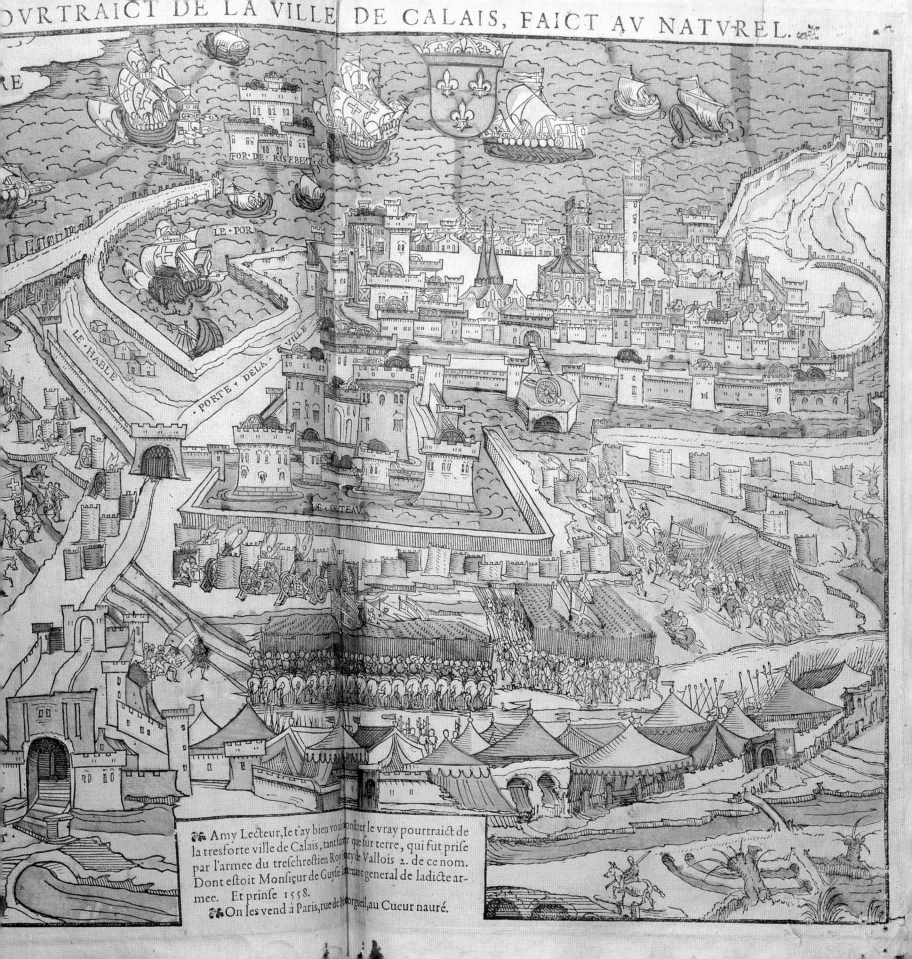

POVRTRAICT DE LA VILLE DE CALAIS, FAICT AV NATVREL.

FOR DE RISEBE

LE POR

LE HABLE

PORTE DE LA VILLE

LE CHTEAV

Amy Lecteur, Ie t'ay bien voulu monstrer le vray pourtraict de la tresforte ville de Calais, tant sur mer que sur terre, qui fut prise par l'armee du treschrestien Roy Henry de Vallois 2. de ce nom. Dont estoit Monsieur de Guyse lieutenant general de ladicte armee. Et prinse 1558.
On les vend à Paris, rue de Montorgueil, au Cueur nauré.

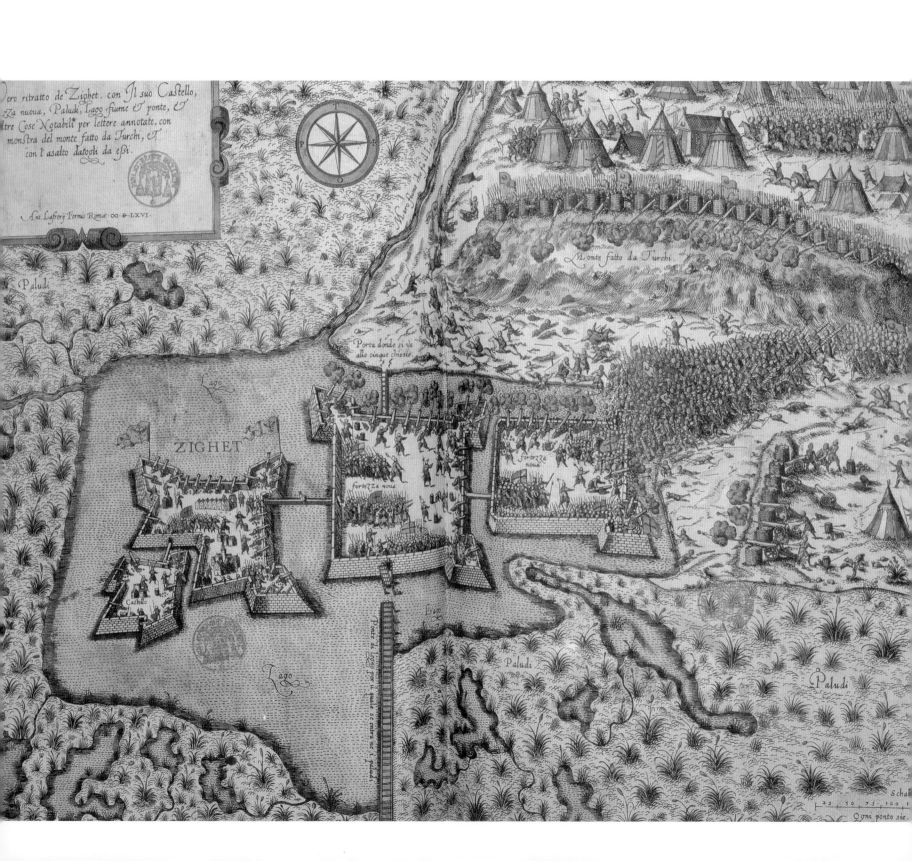

Vero ritratto de Zighet, con Il suo Castello,
Za nuoua, Paludi, Lago fiume et ponte, et
ltre Cose Notabili per lettere annotate, con
monstra del monte fatto da Turchi, et
con l'asalto datooli da essi.

Ant. Lafreij Formis Romae ꝏ D LXVI

Paludi

Paludi

Monte fatto da Turchi.

Lago fiume da foil Lago et Paludi

Porta donde si va
alle cinque chiesie.

Lago

ZIGHET

Castello

fortezza nuoue

fortezza
nuoue

Lago

Ponte di Legno per il quale se entra ... paludi

Lago

Paludi

Paludi

Paludi

Scha...

Ogni ponto sie...

Béarn, an independent territory in southern France that was a royal fief, but one where Catholic worship was not permitted. Opposition was overawed and Béarn was formally annexed. It had a common border with one territory mentioned by Shakespeare, Navarre, and was close to another, Roussillon.

In light of all of this, it is easy to understand why Shakespeare's contemporaries would have seen the wider world as troubled, with violence an ever-present prospect, and why this situation was a context for the pursuit of other aspects of life, such as romance and trade.

Further afield, Russia was expansionist under Ivan the Terrible, but he failed to win a dominant position on the Baltic. In *The Winter's Tale*, Hermione is supposedly the daughter of the Emperor of Russia, who, for Shakespeare's audience, was generally Ivan – a man who had a reputation for letting bears loose among the people, something that is echoed by the bear's entry in the play. Ivan's attempt to annex Livonia (much of modern Latvia) was thwarted by Stephan Báthory, the dynamic king of Poland, who campaigned successfully from 1578 and forced Ivan to peace in 1582. Russia also failed to defeat the Swedes.

In turn, civil war began in Sweden in 1597 when opposition to the Catholicism of Sigismund Vasa (Sigismund III of Poland, r 1587–1632), who had become King of Sweden in 1592, helped his uncle, Duke Charles of Södermanland, to organise opposition to him. In 1598, Sigismund arrived in Sweden with an army, but his half-heartedness led him to return to Poland that year. Sigismund was deposed by the *Riksdag* (parliament) in 1599 at the behest of Charles, who became Charles IX in 1604. The situation demonstrated a classic instance of an uncle seizing power.

Sigismund appeared initially to have more success in Russia, where he intervened in the Time

of Troubles (1604–1613) and had his eldest son proclaimed Tsar, only for the Poles to be driven out by the new Romanov dynasty, who took a role in ending strife that was analogous to that of the Tudors and Bourbons. Meanwhile, Charles IX of Sweden had also intervened, clashing with Poland. In addition, in 1611–1613, the Danes fought Sweden.

Given this confusion, it is scarcely surprising that in *Hamlet* Shakespeare displays a troubled power politics, with Fortinbras, the nephew of the King of Norway (then in fact not an independent kingdom but part of Denmark), obliged by his uncle not to attack Denmark but, instead, encouraged to turn against the Poles. Hamlet questions a captain in Fortinbras' army as to the goal, to be told:

> 'We go to gain a little patch of ground
> That hath in it no profit but the name:
> To pay five ducats, five I would not farm it'.
> (4.4)

Fortinbras returns victorious, 'with conquest ... from the Polack wars' (5.2), at the close of the play.

In 1593, war broke out between the Turks and Austria, and this Thirteen Years' War continued during much of Shakespeare's writing career, creating a state and sense of flux in international relations, as well as perception of a war that might broaden out. The Austrians initially did well, only for the Turks to put them under pressure in 1594. In 1595, the Turks suffered a collapse of their alliance system as former protégés – the rulers of Moldavia, Wallachia and Transylvania – all came out in support of the Austrians. The presence of the new Sultan, Mehmed III, with the army in Hungary in 1596 testified to a sense of crisis. Turkish victory at Mezö-Kerésstés, however, was hard won; neither side was able to display clear military superiority. Instead, the war, which ended in 1606 with a peace

that essentially returned the situation to the pre-war situation, repeatedly indicated the significance of a form of coalition warfare, in the shape of the importance, yet unpredictability, of the subordinate parts of imperial systems. Thus, the Transylvanians changed sides to back the Turks in 1599, only to be defeated by the Wallachians. The politics of re-alignment, or, rather, betrayal, made the propensity of political players in Shakespeare's plays to consider and enact betrayal appear highly credible.

*Siege of Szigetvár,* 1566. This painting depicts the last campaign of Süleyman the Magnificent. Szigetvár in Hungary, the fortress of Count Nikola Zrinski, surrendered two days after Suleyman died. His death was kept secret until after the final assault. Conflict with the Ottomans was part of the context of Christendom, but, in opposition to Philip II, Elizabeth was eager to recruit Muslim help. In *The Merchant of Venice*, there is reference to the Prince of Morocco fighting on behalf of Süleyman against the Safavids of Persia. **OPPOSITE**

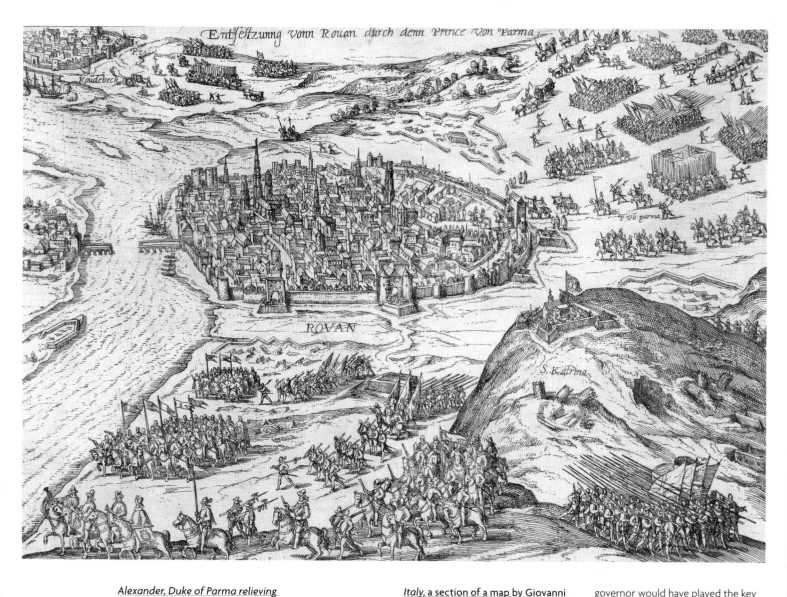

_Entſetzunng vonn Rouan durch denn Prince Von Parma_

ROVAN

S. Katrina

*Alexander, Duke of Parma relieving Paris*, 1590, by Franz Hogenberg. With the royal succession in France contested from 1589, much of the Spanish Army of Flanders under Parma was committed by Philip II in support of the Catholic League, in an eventually unsuccessful attempt to prevent the Protestant Henry of Navarre from triumphing as Henry IV. The Spaniards relieved Paris from siege in 1590 and Rouen in 1592. Many civilians died from starvation during the siege of Paris. **ABOVE**

*Italy*, a section of a map by Giovanni Battista Ramusio from the *Sala dello Scudo* – a reception room in the Doge's Palace, Venice. The *terraferma*, the mainland under Venetian control, had been extended westwards to benefit from the collapse of the Visconti Dukes of Milan after the unexpected death of Duke Gian Galeazzo in 1402. Between 1404 and 1441, Venice took Belluno, Vicenza, Padua, Verona, Bergamo, Brescia and Ravenna. In Shakespeare's lifetime, Venice retained this presence despite Habsburg hostility, and the Venetian

governor would have played the key role in controlling strife in Verona, where *Romeo and Juliet* is set. Due to Venetian control, strife within Verona was far less than in, for example, Bologna or Florence. The kings of Spain ruled Milan to the west, and to the north and north-east were the dominions of the Austrian Habsburgs. **RIGHT**

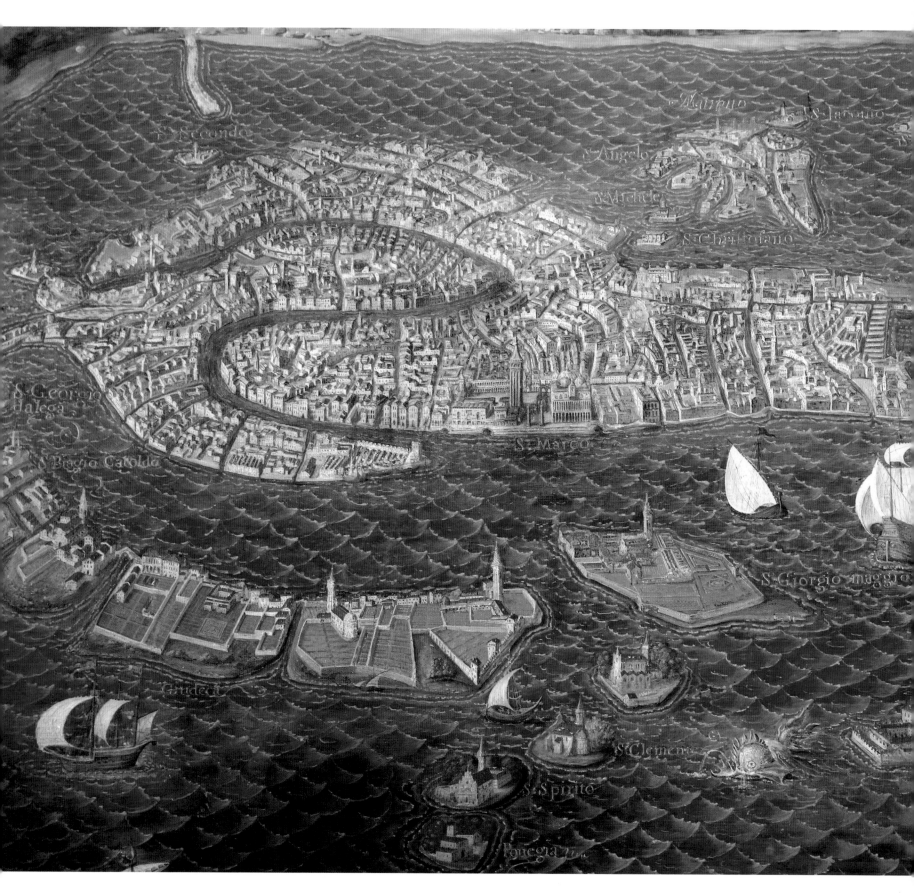

S. Matruio

S. Iacomo

S. Secondo

S. Angelo

S. Michele

S. Christofano

S. Georgio dalega

S. Marco

S. Biagio Catoldo

S. Georgio maggio

Giudeca

S. Clemene

S. Spirito

Pouegia

144

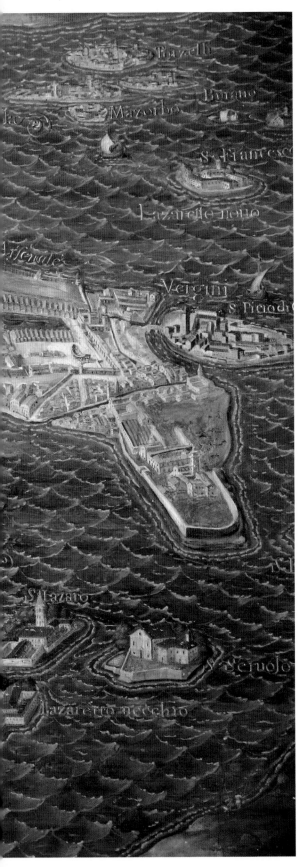

**_Venice_, from the Vatican Gallery of Maps.** The depiction of Venice classically presented maritime themes. In Shakespeare, the city was significant not only as the setting for _The Merchant of Venice_, but also as the source of authority and power in _Othello_. Venice was also a major territorial power in northern Italy, as well as a prominent opponent of the Habsburgs. **LEFT**

**_Italy_, from** the Vatican Gallery of Maps by Ignazio Danti, c.1536–86. Both decorative and useful, these maps, produced in 1580–81, provided an effective account of the geography of Italy, although there were errors in shape and alignment. The centrality of Rome appeared clearly in this map, as did the role of the Apennine Mountains. Commissioned by Pope Gregory XIII, the cycle of 40 maps was positioned in order to create the impression of strolling through Italy from north to south. The cycle begins with two maps of Italy as a whole – one of ancient Italy and one of its modern counterpart. Danti (1536–1586) – painter, astronomer and map-maker – was made Pontifical Mathematician by Pope Gregory XIII. Italy was the setting for many of Shakespeare's plays. **BELOW**

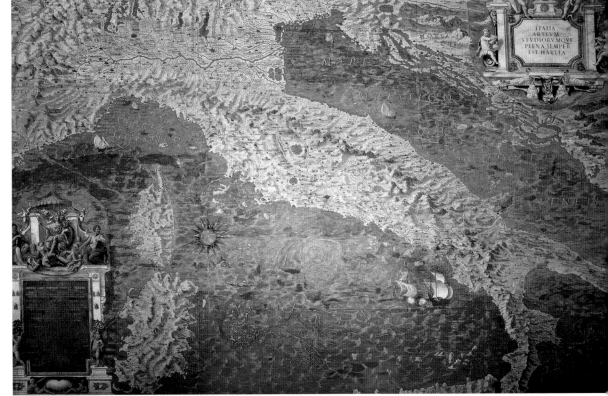

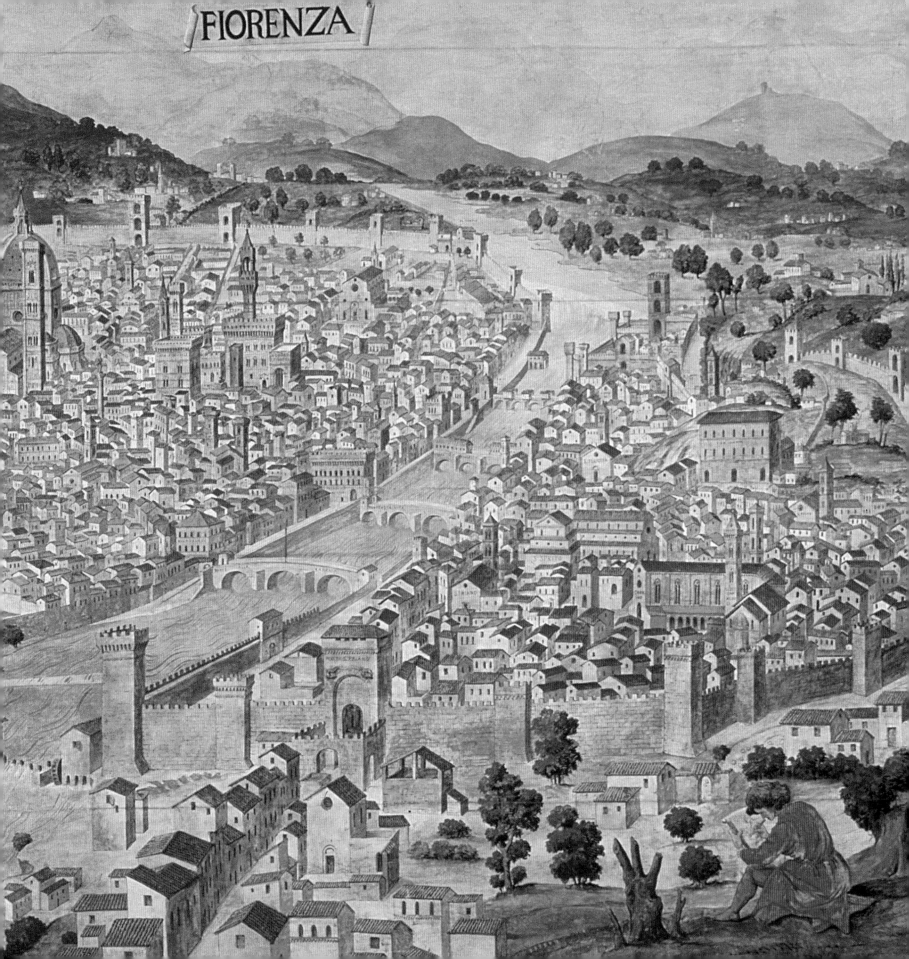

*Florence*, based on Francesco Rosselli's woodcut *Pianta della Catena*. Rosselli (1447–1513) used perspective to offer this complete view of the city and its context, and included himself on a vantage point outside the city. Fishing and ferrying are shown, as are birds feeding on a dead animal outside the wall, a pack-donkey, and construction techniques that make much use of wood. Florence was the setting for much of *All's Well That Ends Well*, the plot of which was largely based on Giovanni Boccaccio's *Decameron* (*c.*1353). **PREVIOUS PAGES**

*Augsburg*, 1521. This map reveals a less attractive total view than that of Florence, but one that captures the well-defended nature of this important and prosperous Imperial Free City, which was founded by the Romans and was the basis of the commercial empire of the Fugger family of bankers. The earliest-known plan view from north of the Alps, this map was dedicated to the Emperor Charles V, the nephew of Katherine of Aragon. **RIGHT**

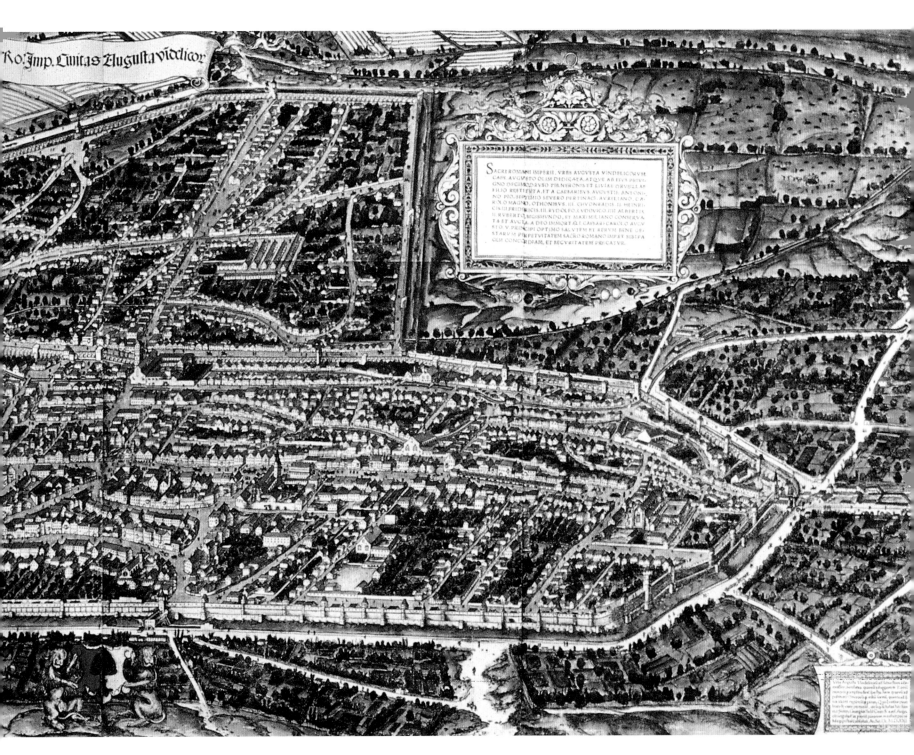

Ro. Imp. Cuitas Augusta videlicor

SACRI ROMANI IMPERII, VRBS AVGVSTA VINDELICORVM,
CAPS. AVGVSTO OLIM DEDICATA, ATQVE AB EIVS PRIVI-
GNO DECIMO RVSO TI. NERONIS ET LIVIAE ORVELLAE
FILIO RESTITVTA, ET A CAESARIBVS AVGVSTIS, ANTONI-
NO PIO, SEPTIMIO SEVERO, PERTINACI, AVRELIANO, CA-
RIXO MAGNO, OTHONIBVS, III. CHVONRADIS, II. HEINRI-
CIS III FRIDERICIS, III. RVDOLFO, LVDOVICO, IIII. ALBERTIS
II. RVBERTO, SIGISMVNDO, ET MAXIMILIANO CONSERVA-
TA ET AVCTA, A DEO IMMORT. ET CAISARI CAROLO AVG-
STO, V. PRINCIPI OPTIMO SALVTEM ET RERVM BENE GE-
STARVM PERPETVITATEM SACRO ROMANO IMPE. SIBI PA-
QVE CONCORDIAM, ET SECVRITATEM PRECATVR.

149

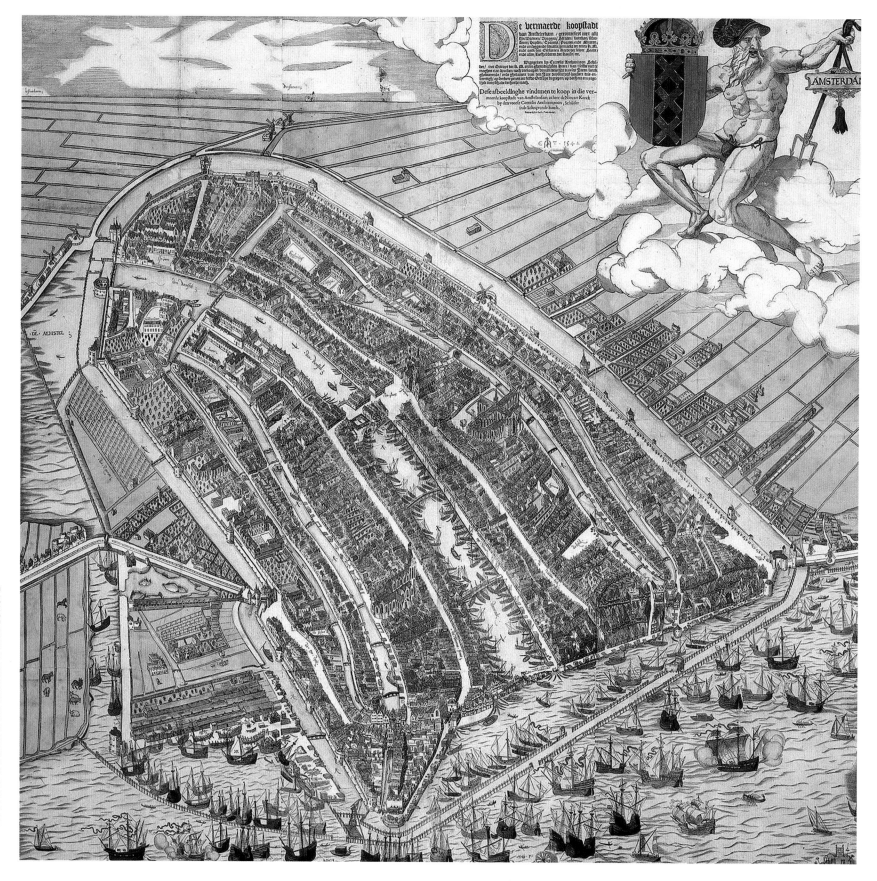

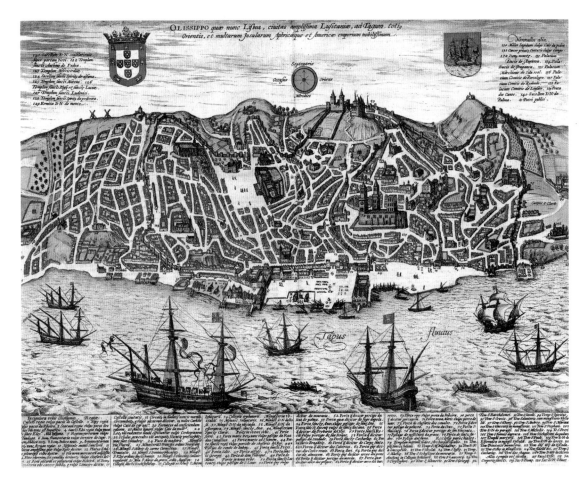

*Amsterdam*, 1544, by Amsterdam-born Cornelis Anthonisz (*c*.1505–1553). The northern equivalent of Venice, Amsterdam did not comparably grasp the imagination of Shakespeare's contemporaries, in part because of the longer-established significance of nearby Antwerp. This coloured print of a fine woodcut made from a painting by Anthonisz in 1538, when the city had a population of about 12,000, is the oldest surviving plan of Amsterdam and very much captures the significance of shipping. The 1538 painting was commissioned by the city as a gift to its ruler, Charles V. **FAR LEFT**

*Lisbon*, 1598, from *Volume V of Civitates Orbis Terrarum*, by Braun and Hogenberg. Portugal had become newly important to the English in the late sixteenth century as a result of the takeover of Portugal as a result of its conquest in 1580 by Philip II of Spain. The English unsuccessfully supported Don Antonio, a pretender to the throne, and in 1589 launched an attack on Lisbon, which was a key anchorage
for any preparations for an invasion of England. The attack failed to match Philip II's success there in 1580. With its excellent anchorage in the Tagus estuary, Lisbon was a key centre of trade with the Indies and Brazil. The nautical significance of the country is seen in *As You Like It*, when Rosalind tells Celia that her love for Orlando is boundless: 'my affection hath an unknown bottom, like the bay of Portugal' (4.1). **LEFT**

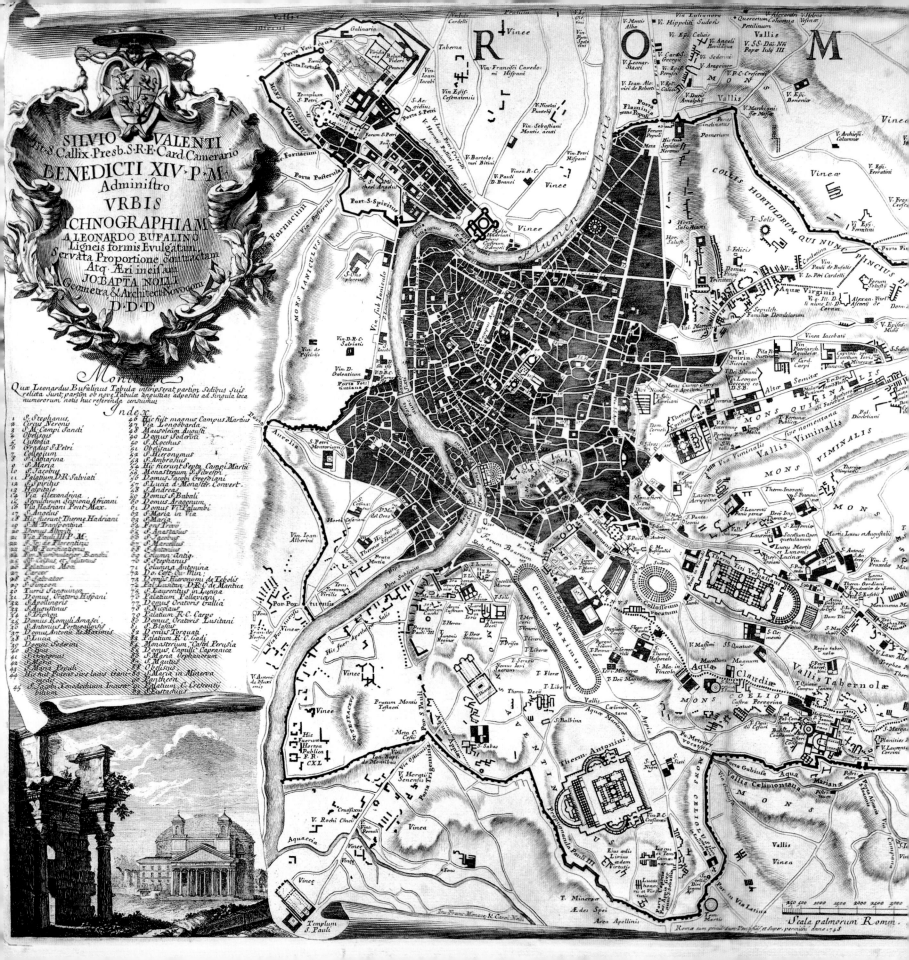

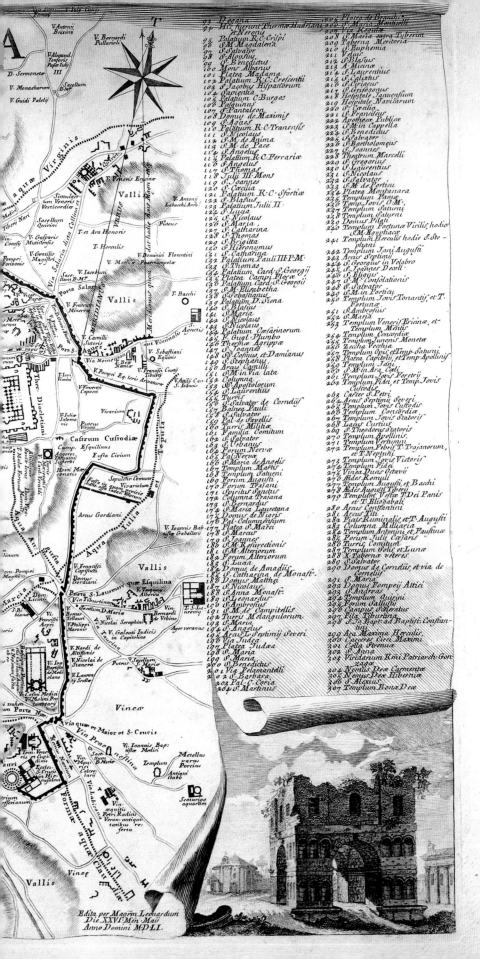

*Rome,* by Leonardo Bufalini, 1549.
Rome had been a symbolic centre surpassed only by Jerusalem, but this was greatly compromised by the Reformation. The traditional presentation of Rome was captured in this map, since it showed a combination of religious and Classical sites, which were explained by means of an alphabetical key. The city, however, had been badly battered when it was stormed and sacked in 1527 by mercenaries who were out of control.

Paul III, Pope from 1534 to 1549, was an important patron of Michelangelo, but in 1549–1550 a Papal conclave (meeting) was held in Rome that led to the election of Julius III after bitter disputes between the French and Imperialist factions, including accusations that the death of one of the candidates was due to poisoning. During the Counter-Reformation, Rome was enhanced, notably by Pope Sixtus V (r 1585–1590), with Baroque architecture and street planning. In his plays, Shakespeare does not offer any particular knowledge of Rome's geography.

**Moscow**, from **Civitates Orbis Terrarum,** 1617, by Braun and Hogenberg. The foundation of the Muscovy Company and the development of trade links in the 1550s ensured that English interest in, and knowledge about, Russia increased. This was encouraged by the role of Ivan IV, the Terrible, in Baltic power politics in the late sixteenth century, although his attempt to annex Livonia was thwarted by the Poles in 1578–1582. After Ivan's death, Russia, however, faced internal disorder and foreign invasion in the serious Time of Troubles during which the Poles seized Moscow in 1610, their besieged garrison surrendering in 1612. The Tsar had been overthrown and murdered in a riot in Moscow in 1605. A pretender, the False Dmitrii, was then proclaimed Tsar, only to be overthrown and killed in 1606. He was replaced by Prince Vasilii Shuiskii, who was overthrown in 1610, again in a conspiracy involving noble leadership and mob action.

Russia appears in Shakespeare in *Measure for Measure*, when the lengthy case involving Elbow, Froth and Pompey leads Angelo to remark: 'This will last out a night in Russia,/ When nights are longest there' (2.1), as well as in In *Love's Labour's Lost*, in which Ferdinand, King of Navarre, and his three lords are 'Disguised like Muscovites, in shapeless gear' and described as 'a mess of Russians' (5.2).

METROPOLIS TO.
Albæ.

pars vrbis dicta Kitaigorod

vrbis, suo circumdata muro, dicta Bielgorod

Tertia pars vrbis versus Septentrionem vocata Skorodum.

Chasteau de vincenes

Picpuce    S. Antoine de champ    Conflan    Charenton

Porte S. Antoine

La Bastille    Isle Louuier

La place
Royalle    R. S.ᵗᵉ
Antoine    P.S. Paul    P. S.ᵗ Bernard

Morets du Temple    S. Iean    P. au foin    Notre
Dame    Place M.

Rue du Temple    P. de Greue

Faux bourg S. Martin    P. S. Martin    S. Martin    R. au Champs    R. S.ᵗ Martin    R. S.ᵗ Denis    Pont Notre
Dame

H. S. Louis    La Trinit    Le pont

La Mare    P. S. Denis    Le Bonseau    R.    S.ᵗ Denis    les Halles

Les marets    R. Mont-orgueil    Mont-Marthe    R. Coquillere    R. S.ᵗ Honore    Le pont    Le pont

Portici    R. Coquillere    LA RIVIE

La grange Batellere    le Palmail    S. Roch    LA RIVIER

Faubourg    Les Capucins

Faubourg S. Henri

Matheus Merian Basiliensæ Fecit

AVEC LA DESCRIPTION DE SON ANTIQVITE

*Paris*, Matthäus Merian, 1615. The walled nature of cities was clear in this map, and rightly so as Paris had been besieged during the French Wars of Religion, notably after Henry III lost control to the Catholic League, in the Day of the Barricades and was duly assassinated while besieging the city in 1589. Henry IV (*r.*1589–1610), a consummate pragmatist who allegedly said 'Paris is worth a Mass', gained control of the city in 1593 and brought recovery and eventual stability. However, his assassination in Paris in 1610 was followed by a revival of unrest, although not at the level seen in the early 1590s.

The St Bartholomew's Day Massacre of Protestants in 1572 gave Christopher Marlowe the subject for his *Massacre at Paris*, a play printed in about 1594, but Shakespeare never engaged with the city in this fashion.

*Vienna,* **1529,** by Niklas Meldeman (1518–1552). The Turkish siege of 1529 was not the subject in Shakespeare's *Measure for Measure*, which was set in the city, and the area was again the site of major conflict in the Thirteen Years' War between Austria and the Turks in 1593–1606. Meldeman's map was characteristic in presenting all aspects of the siege in one image even though they were spread over a month. Turkish atrocities are shown, including men tied to wheels, impaled on pikes and hung. Meldeman worked in Nuremberg. **LEFT**

*Elsinore* (**Kronberg Castle**) – the setting for *Hamlet* – c.1588, by Braun and Hogenberg. On the east coast of the Danish island of Zealand, this fortress protected passage through the Sound into and from the Baltic. The tolls levied there were a major source of revenue for Denmark. **ABOVE**

# 'An Ethiop's ear'
## Beyond Europe in the Age of Shakespeare

## AFRICA

Exploration was opening up to Europeans' eyes a world beyond Europe, but most of this world was obscure and the stuff of vague report. To take as an example Ethiopia, otherwise known as Abyssinia, there had been direct contact in 1541 when the Portuguese sent 400 musketeers to help against the Turks and their local allies. The Ethiopians rewarded these musketeers with land in the 1540s in order to retain their services, and these musketeers (and their descendants) continued to play an important military role into the following century. Developments subsequently, however, were scarcely well known in Europe, let alone England. Under serious pressure from the local Islamic sultanate of Adal and from its Turkish supporter, Ethiopia was also affected by the expansion northwards of the Oromo peoples, nomadic pastoralists who made effective use of horses, which increased their mobility. This helped them live off the land, out-manoeuvring the more cumbersome Ethiopian forces.

However, in confronting these problems, Ethiopia benefited from vigorous leadership by Serse-Dingil, the Emperor from 1562 to 1597. Compared with Elizabeth I of England, he serves as a reminder of the variety of effective forms of rulership in the period. Commanding in person, Serse-Dingil defeated Adal in 1576, followed, three years later, by victory over an alliance of Turkish forces with Bahr Nagash Ishaq of Tigre and the ruler of Harar. This ended Turkish attempts to overrun Ethiopia from the Red Sea. Serse-Dingil then also expanded Ethiopia to the west, while he defeated the Oromo in 1572 and 1586. He also changed Ethiopia's military system, complementing the traditional reliance on the private forces of provincial governors and other regional potentates with an extension of the troops directly under royal control – a policy that was also to be followed in Persia (Iran) by Shah Abbas. Susenyos (r.1607–1632) continued the expansion to the west. He also incorporated many of the Oromo into his army and settled many in his dominions. However, Susenyos' conversion to Catholicism led to serious rebellions and he duly abdicated.

Ethiopia was not the only part of Africa vaguely familiar to Shakespeare's audiences or at least mentioned in his plays. Morocco, too, was known. In 1578, one of the most significant battles in Shakespeare's lifetime occurred at al-Qasr-al-Kabir/Alcazarquivir, when the Moroccans crushed a Portuguese invasion. King Sebastian led a poorly prepared army of 18,000–20,000 men, crucially short of cavalry, into the interior in order to challenge the sharif, Abd al-Malik, and his force of about 70,000 men. As so often with Shakespearean plays, rifts within a ruling family were a key issue. Sebastian sought to benefit from division within Morocco by helping Muhammad al-Mutawakhil, the former sharif, who had appealed for Sebastian's assistance, having been deposed by his Turkish-backed uncle, Abd al-Malik. Sebastian hoped to establish a client ruler; in short, reality reflected the politics of England during the Wars of the Roses as depicted by Shakespeare.

Sebastian sought battle, believing that his infantry would successfully resist the Moroccan cavalry. In the event, the skilful, well-disciplined Moroccan force claimed a crushing victory thanks to superior leadership and discipline, more flexible units and tactics, and the contingent events of the battle. The entire Portuguese army was either killed or captured, and Sebastian was killed, although legends about his survival in secret circulated long afterwards, as did the belief that he might come forth to save Portugal.

As a result of the battle, Philip II of Spain, the

*Map of Africa*, 1564, by Giacomo Gastaldi. Gastaldi (1500–1566) worked in Venice and this map reflected the information available in Europe, notably in its inaccurate depiction of the route of the river Niger. His maps of Africa and Asia were frescoed on the walls of a room in the Doge's Palace in Venice and then proved the basis for printed versions. Shakespeare makes reference to various parts of Africa, including Morocco, Tunis, Egypt and Ethiopia, as well as to the more mysterious world described by Othello:

'... deserts idle,
rough quarries, rocks and hills
    whose heads touch heaven,
........
of the Cannibals that each
    other eat,
The Anthropophagi, and men
    whose heads
Do grow beneath their shoulders.'
(1.3)

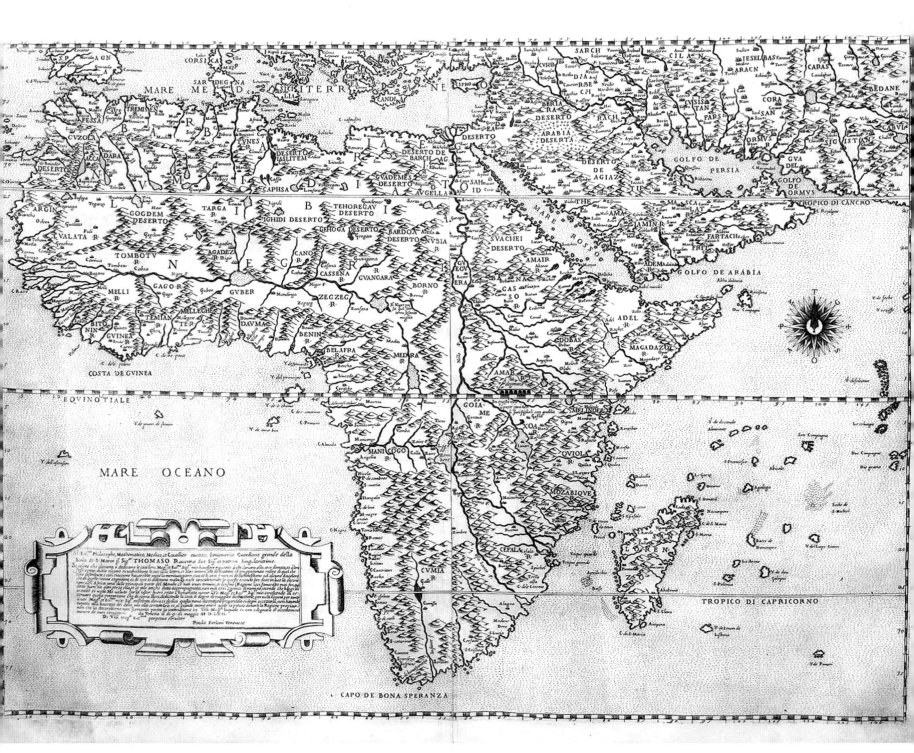

uncle of the childless Sebastian, seized Portugal in 1580, while the English came to back a pretender to Portugal and to seek the support of Morocco against Spain. English traders sold cast-iron artillery to Morocco, buying saltpetre, a crucial constituent of gunpowder.

Morocco itself staged a near-legendary campaign. Only about half of the 4,000 troops sent south in 1590 across the vast dry expanse of the Sahara Desert by Mūlāy Ahmad al Mansūr of Morocco survived the crossing. Mansūr's aim had been to secure gold from the Songhai Empire, as well as recognition for his claim to be caliph, the Muslim chief civil and spiritual ruler. The Moroccans benefited from the Portuguese arms seized in 1578, while many of the troops sent were renegades: Christians who had become Muslims, notably 2,000 musketeers. The English defeat of the Spanish Armada in 1588 had lessened the chance of Spanish intervention in Morocco, which, in turn, encouraged the Moroccan expedition across the Sahara.

The resulting Moroccan victory, under Judar Pasha, at Tondibi on the river Niger in 1591 led to the collapse of the Songhai Empire. In this battle, Moroccan musketry defeated the 12,500-strong Songhai cavalry and about 30,000 infantry, an army equipped with spears and bows, and lacking firearms. The Moroccans also benefited from the poor leadership of their opponents. The flight of the Songhai emperor, Ishāq II, helped lead to a collapse of his army, and the Moroccans soon after captured the cities of Gao and Timbuktu without resistance. It was no wonder that Morocco appeared potent and fabulous to the audience of Shakespeare's period.

Most of Africa did not have this resonance. The slave trade was developing from West Africa but, as yet, English participation was far smaller than it was to become by the late seventeenth century. That said, the English did make an attempt, from the 1550s, to break into Portugal's trade with West Africa and the profitable slave trade from there to the Spanish New World. Plymouth-born John Hawkins, for example, obtained his slaves in West Africa on the coast of modern Sierra Leone by raiding rather than through purchase, losing men in the process to poison arrows and other hazards, as well as by piracy against Portuguese ships. He then shipped the slaves across the Atlantic in 1562 and 1564 and sold them to the Spaniards at considerable profit – one means of gaining access to the Spanish-controlled bullion of the New World. Thus, the slaves were not sold to England, where, indeed, there were increasing (albeit small) numbers of free black people, and some in service. Henry VII, for instance, was one of many prominent Europeans who kept some black domestic servants, but the lack of evidence of many others would suggest that black slaves were not at all common in England. The few exceptions were probably gifts and were not sold on.

Hawkins' slaving voyages were stopped by the Spaniards in 1568 on his third attempt, one authorised by Elizabeth despite Spanish complaints, though in the late sixteenth century, the English commitment to the slave trade was limited. Most English voyages to West Africa were for pepper, hides, wax and ivory, and in search of gold rather than slaves – English trade with West Africa did not focus on slaves until the mid-seventeenth century. The English met with firm resistance in this trade from the Portuguese.

As far as West Africa was concerned, relatively little was known in England. Rule there was segmented, and most polities (a polity is a form of state) were not far-flung. This segmentation helped encourage widespread conflict, conflict that was to feed the slave trade both within the continent and also to the Atlantic and Islamic worlds. There was a major flow of slaves northwards across the Sahara, with cities such as Tripoli and Alexandria acting as major slave markets. There was also a considerable slave flow from East Africa to the Middle East, both across the Red Sea and via the Indian Ocean.

As *Othello* indicated, slavery did not prevent the existence of a range of attitudes towards Africans. Moors were particularly problematic as they were associated with North Africa, a Muslim area. In *Titus Andronicus*, Moorish Aaron, the black servant and lover of Tamora, the Queen of the Goths and new Empress of Rome, suggests the rape of Lavinia and the murder of Bassianus, and wrongly blames Titus' sons for the murder. The play closes with the new emperor resolving that justice be meted out to Aaron, 'that dam'd Moor', and the cause of all the mishap (5.3). Earlier, cruelty of a different type is revealed when Tamora seeks the death of the baby she has had by Aaron, although, no Lady Macbeth, she is unwilling to do the deed herself. The nurse declares the baby is:

*'Our empress' shame, and stately Rome's disgrace!*
*... A joyless, dismal, black, and sorrowful issue:*
*Here is the babe, as loathsome as a toad*
*Amongst the fairest breeders of our clime:*
*The empress sends it thee, thy stamp, thy seal,*
*And bids thee christen it with thy dagger's point.'* (4.2)

Aaron refuses, and declares:

*'Coal-black is better than another hue,*
*In that it scorns to bear another hue;*
*For all the water in the ocean*
*Can never turn the swan's black legs to white,*
*Although she leave them hourly in the flood.'*
(4.2)

*The East Indies*, 1592, by Petrus Plancius, published in Jan Huygen van Linschoten's book *Itinerario* (1590). India and the Indies provided images of wealth, as in *Henry VIII*, in which Thomas, 2nd Duke of Norfolk, describes the Field of the Cloth of Gold (1521) and reports on the wealth shown by the English in response to French competition: 'they made Britain India: every man that stood show'd like a mine' (1.1); while later, newly married to Anne Boleyn, Henry is described as having 'all the Indies in his arms.' (4.1). This map shows the spices that traders sought – nutmeg, sandalwood and cloves – and uses rhumb lines. The far-flung mapping is of limited accuracy, and includes sea monsters. Plancius (1552–1622), a Dutch-Flemish cartographer, was active in support of the Dutch East India Company. **RIGHT**

*Map of the World*, 1602, by Matteo Ricci. The large southern continent believed to balance the landmass in the northern hemisphere is clearly depicted in this map. Ricci, an Italian-born Jesuit priest who lived in China from 1582 until his death in 1610, was commissioned by the Emperor Wanli in 1602 to produce this map, which was carved into six wood blocks before being printed on rice paper. China is at the centre of the map, which was intended to impress the Chinese with Western knowledge and values. **FOLLOWING PAGES**

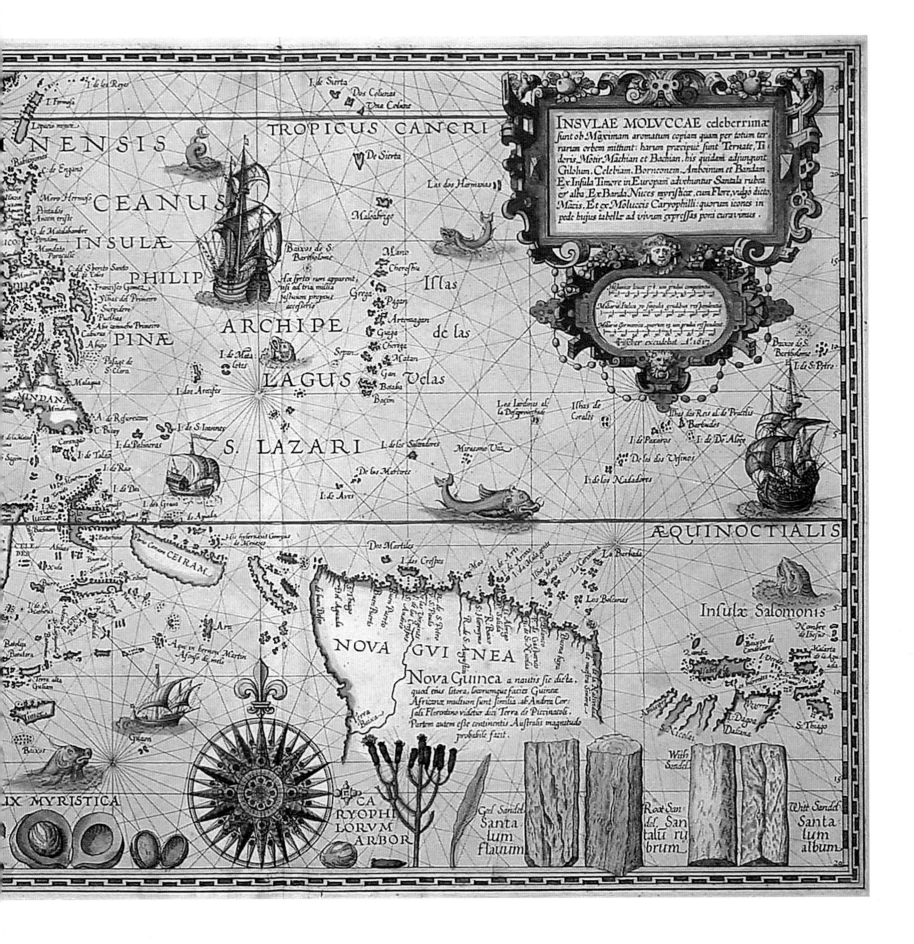

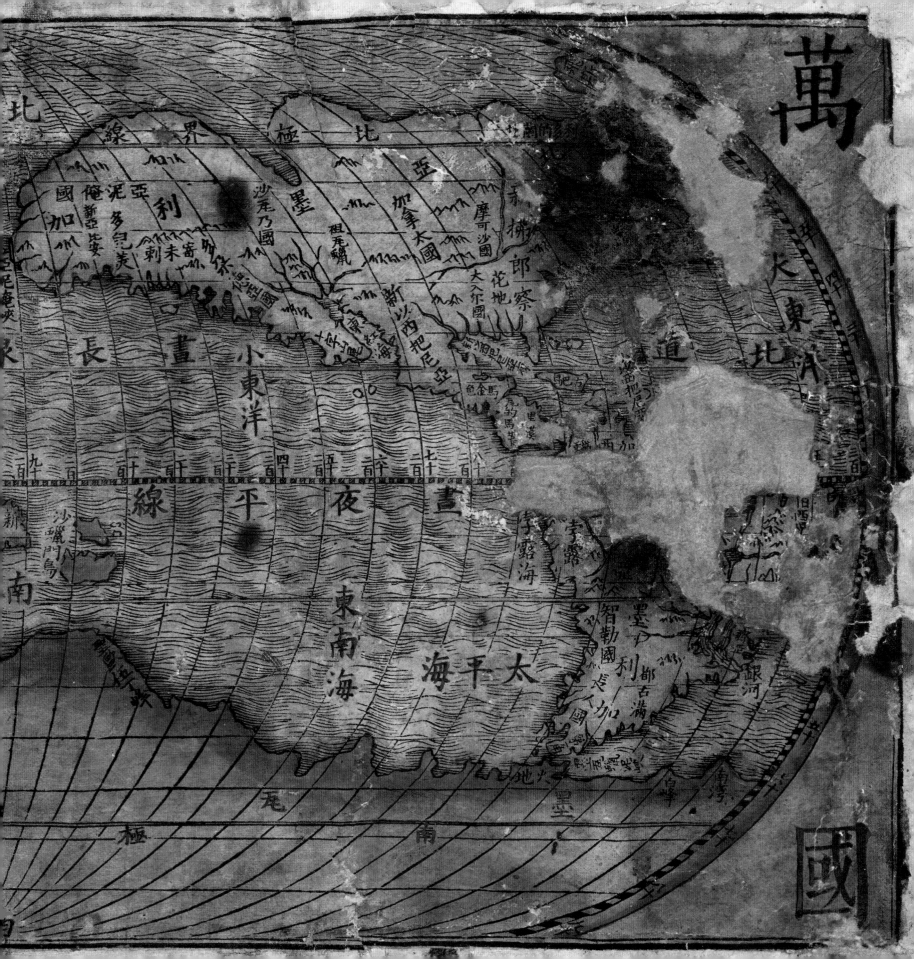

He instead kills the nurse, the killing being almost casual, as so often in Shakespeare.

Many came to stereotype black Africans, and many African cultural practices were misunderstood and recast in a negative light. Denigration of them as inferior and uncivilised was related to associating Africans with occupations linked to physical prowess, thus making slavery appear appropriate.

## ASIA

The drama of Christopher Marlowe's play *Tamburlaine the Great* (c.1587) offered London audiences an account of Asian power politics in which the rise and fall of empires was brought vividly to the stage – an account that provided a challenge to other playwrights. A contemporary of Richard II and Henry IV, and based in Central Asia, Tamburlaine's triumphs had taken him from northern India to the Aegean, from the conquest of Delhi to a victory over the Turks in 1402 near Ankara that led to the capture of the Sultan. He had died in 1405 when planning to invade China. Tamburlaine's achievements appeared to link the conquests of Alexander the Great with more recent dramas, such as the rise of the Ottoman (Turkish), Safavid (Persian) and Mughal (Indian) Empires. Marlowe has the dying Tamburlaine call for a map, not so he can contemplate his former successes, but, rather, so he can consider what more there is to seize:

'Give me a map, then let me see how much
Is left for me to conquer all the world,
That these my boys [sons] may finish all my wants.'
(Part 2 5.3)

In reality, there was no map available for Tamburlaine to use, but the audiences of Shakespeare's days could have found maps that enabled readers to follow his successes. The dying Tamburlaine reflects on his inability to compass all of the world: 'And shall I die and this unconquered?' (Part 2 5.3)

Shakespeare did not focus on a comparable figure, but preferred to anchor his conquerors in the Classical inheritance, notably with Julius Caesar and (very differently) Octavius/Augustus. The battles he depicted or described – Philippi and Actium – were located in a known and datable history. At Philippi, Brutus and Crassus were defeated, and at Actium, Mark Antony. There was a limit to the other figures he could have readily considered. Tamburlaine had been done, and little was known of Chinggis (Genghis) Khan, the great Mongol conqueror. Nevertheless, Ottoman (Turkish) history offered several fascinating figures, notably Süleyman the Magnificent (r. 1520–1566).

In Shakespeare's lifetime, the Turks had fought a major war with the Safavids of Persia (Iran) from 1578 to 1590. The eventual peace treaty gave the Turks under Sultan Murad III what they had conquered in Azerbaijan, the Caucasus and western Persia. As a result, the Turkish Empire reached its greatest extent territorially at the same time that Spain's reconquest of much of the Low Countries, its initially successful intervention in the French Wars of Religion, its ability to thwart the English attacks on Portugal and the Spanish New World, and its dominance of Italy all suggested that it was also approaching an apex of power.

There was a developing Turkish practice of acquiring geographical information and mapping. The most impressive Turkish work was the *Kitab-i Bahriya* (*The Book of Seafaring*) by the Turkish admiral Piri Reis, who, in this treatise on marine navigation, mapped and described the coastlines and cities of

*Selden Map.* One of the first Chinese maps to reach Europe, it is named after the London lawyer John Selden and in 1659 came from his estate into the Bodleian Library in Oxford. It shows not only China but also South-East Asia, Sumatra, Java, Borneo, the Philippines and Japan, as well as shipping routes from Quanzhou. An example of a reference to Asia can be found in Sonnet 7, which Shakespeare begins:

'Lo! in the orient when the gracious light
Lifts up his burning head...' (1–2)

_Kyoto, 1616–1624._ The image depicts an idyllic view of Kyoto near the imperial palace but, in practice, power in Japan was shifting. In 1603, Nijo Castle was begun as the official residence in the city of Ieyasu, of the first Tokugawa shogun, the key political and governmental figure who, based in Edo (Tokyo), had gained control of Japan in 1600 by secretly winning over some of his opponents. Finished in 1626, the castle overawed Kyoto, the imperial residence, and thus demonstrated the new power-relationship that the largely honorific emperor had had to accept. Although the English were aware of Japan, it is not mentioned by Shakespeare.

170

the Mediterranean. Reis created two versions of his book, in 1521 and 1525, with a third, and more richly decorated version, produced in the latter part of the seventeenth century. Without the institutional and other traditions of the Chinese, the Turks used frontier surveys to provide information on key areas of their porous frontiers. The first survey, of the province of Buda, was compiled in 1546 and reflected the acute military and political sensitivity of the Turkish–Austrian frontier in Hungary. Maps, including siege maps, also served the Turks as tools of military reconnaissance and intelligence.

Persia itself was affected by a level of division that would have done credit to the Shakespearean pen. The Qizilbash tribal confederation, on which Safavid power rested, was affected by a civil war that was related to disputes in the ruling dynasty. Isma'il II, who became shah in 1576, was slaughtered by his brothers, and his weak successor, Muhammad Khudabanda (r. 1578–1587), was overthrown by Abbas I (r. 1587–1629). A redoubtable warrior, Abbas brought stability and eventual victory.

Accounts of Abbas' battles were of interest in Christian Europe notably due to the knock-on impact of the threatening Turks. Thus, in 1592, Pope Clement VIII sent a mission to Abbas urging him to oppose the Turks, and, in 1602, another mission seeking to convert Abbas to Christianity with the promise of Western military assistance against the Turks. Relations between Abbas and the Christians, however, collapsed in 1606 when Austria negotiated peace with the Turks, which ensured that the latter would only have to fight a one-front war against Abbas. In turn, Abbas both offered Jerusalem (if he seized it from the Turks) to the Christians in 1609, and pressed Spain (and thus Portugal also) to declare war on the Turks, in order to avoid his making peace with them. Abbas' victories included defeating the Uzbeks in 1598 at

Rabát-Pariyán, a battle decided by a charge by Abbas' mounted bodyguard, led by the Shah himself; and the Turks at Sufian in 1605; and also captured Bahrain (1602), Kandahar (1622), Hormuz (1622) and Baghdad (1623), the last from the Turks.

In the Turkish Empire, meanwhile, there were large-scale rebellions from 1596 until 1609, albeit without the dynastic dynamic of the Wars of the Roses in England. There was a politics of rebellion, success, the buying-off of rebels, and the crushing of rebellion – sometimes, as in 1608, by turning against the rebels who had been bought off. For example, Kalenderoghlu Mehmed, the victorious rebel leader in Anatolia from the mid-1600s, was made governor of Ankara in 1607, only for the Grand Vizier to turn against him in 1608 and defeat him. Such politics could make those depicted by Shakespeare, most clearly in *Titus Andronicus*, and indeed by the revenge dramatists as a whole, appear normal. The killing of siblings was frequent in Turkish history as rulers sought to establish their position. Süleyman the Magnificent, for example, had his rebellious eldest son, Bayezid, killed in 1562: Bayezid had taken refuge with Shah Tahmasp I of Persia in 1559, but the latter allowed a Turkish executioner to kill him; and Süleyman's father, Selim I, the 'Grim' (r 1512–1520), had overthrown his own father and killed his own brothers in 1512.

In the Far East, Japan was unified by a major commander, Toyotomi Hideyoshi, in the 1580s and early 1590s. As with Shakespeare's depiction of suicides among the figures of Antiquity – notably Brutus, Crassus, Mark Antony and Cleopatra – Japanese commanders, such as Akechi Mitsuhide in 1582 and Shibata Katsuie in 1583, committed suicide when unsuccessful. Losing any sense of limits, Hideyoshi pressed for equal status with the Ming Emperor of China and planned to conquer

India. He had exceeded his grasp, and his large-scale invasions of Korea in 1592 and 1597 were thwarted by Chinese intervention. Hideyoshi died in 1598, and Tokugawa Ieyasu gained power in Japan in 1600 by secretly winning over some of his opponents, which was a key adjunct of warfare. Japanese invasion plans against the Philippines (where the Spaniards had established themselves from 1564) between 1593 and 1637 were not brought to fruition, and Japanese attempts on Taiwan in 1609 and 1616 failed. After a Christian rebellion in 1637 was suppressed, Japanese contact with Catholic Europe was cut off by the Sakoku Edict of 1639, while the Dutch traders were restricted to the artificial island of Deshima in Nagasaki Bay. Much of the politics of the world was as lurid as the politics of any Shakespearean play, or more so.

In Asia, there was a lengthy cartographic tradition, notably in China, where maps were used frequently in administrative works, particularly gazetteers of provinces. These local gazetteers gave travelling distances as well as including maps. China was central to the Chinese world view, and other peoples were very much on the fringe – a situation captured in Chinese maps.

In Oriental cultures, maps formed an aspect of the understanding and use of space, both of which had a spiritual character in the shape of geomancy, or *feng shui*. The specific positioning of buildings was important to their effectiveness and was an aspect in their propriety. For example, fortifications could take the place of missing hills in order to produce a pattern that was believed effective in defence. The enhancement of the environment for defence and to harm opponents was regarded as a key component of both *feng shui* and martial arts. Mountains and water were essential elements to ensure the proper martial positioning and circulation of energy to help achieve success.

Religious culture, especially Hinduism and Jainism, was the dominant theme in Indian mapping, which was linked to astronomy and required the development of astrolabes and celestial globes. Research on Indian mapping is still limited, but, as yet, the reproduction of landscape with geometric exactitude does not appear to have been the goal of Indian map-making.

Shakespeare played for the safety of clear sources by seeking Classical and English backgrounds, rather than the current-day drama of developments elsewhere. The exciting stories of the sixteenth century – the overthrow of the Aztecs and Incas, the Turkish advance in Europe, the unification of Japan, and Hideyoshi's invasion of Korea – were put to one side. The doings of Julius Caesar, Mark Antony and Cleopatra, in contrast, were known and resonated with the audience, and the plots of their stories were easier to construct and explain. The geographical context was also far better understood.

*Map of Alexandria,* by Braun and Hogenberg. The city is the setting for much of *Antony and Cleopatra,* including the start and the close, with Cleopatra's palace the centre of the action. In Rome, reports from Alexandria are brought to Octavius Caesar, who uses Mark Antony's public disposal of the East 'I' [in] the marketplace, on a tribunal 'silver'd', to condemn his former ally.

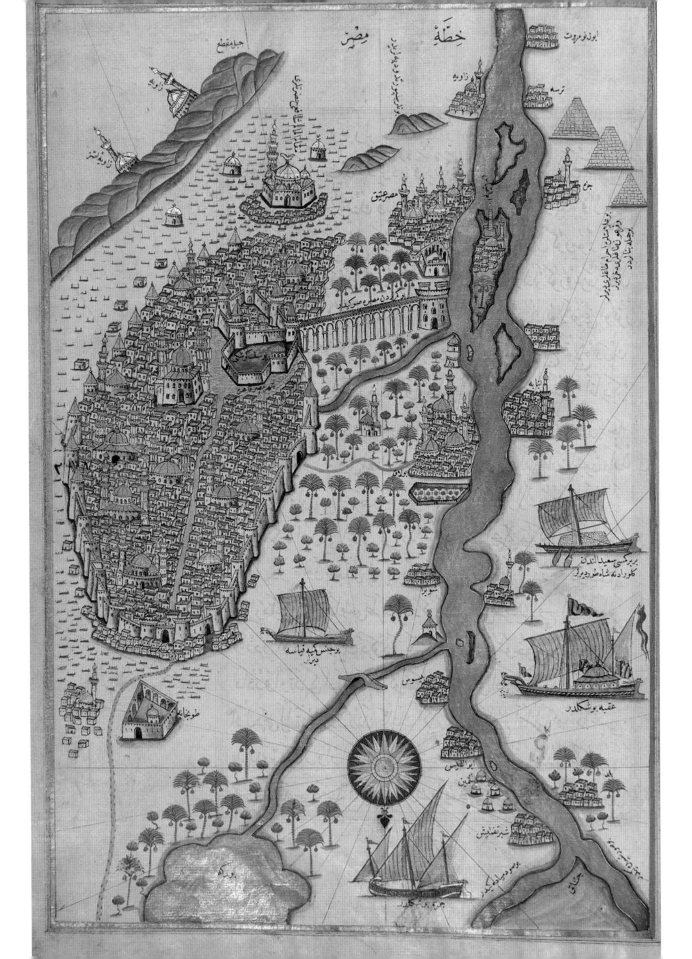

*Santo Domingo*, 1589, by Giovanni Battista Boazio, showing the English forces seizing the major Spanish position in Hispaniola. Although Shakespeare's History Plays focused on earlier opposition to France, England under Elizabeth was involved in a bitter struggle with Spain. Alongside successes, there were many failures and difficulties, and the theatre was an important aspect of escapism. Boazio worked in England and his maps included one of the capture of Cadiz. **FAR LEFT**

*Cairo*, 1521–1526, by Piri Reis. Whereas Alexandria, Cleopatra's capital in *Antony and Cleopatra*, engaged Shakespeare's interest as a city of Antiquity, Cairo – the capital of Islamic Egypt under the Fatimids and Mamluks and, from 1517, the Ottomans – did not. In 1517, Tumanbay, the last Mamluk sultan, was executed at the al-Zuwaylah gate in Cairo, having been defeated at nearby Raydaniyya by Selim I, the Grim, the Ottoman sultan. The rebel heads rolled around Cairo in 1522 by Mustafa Pasha, and the executions ordered there in 1525 by Ibrahim Pasha, the Grand Vizier, demonstrated the reliance of the Ottoman regime on force, its use in an exemplary fashion, and the extent to which it had to be turned to repeatedly. **LEFT**

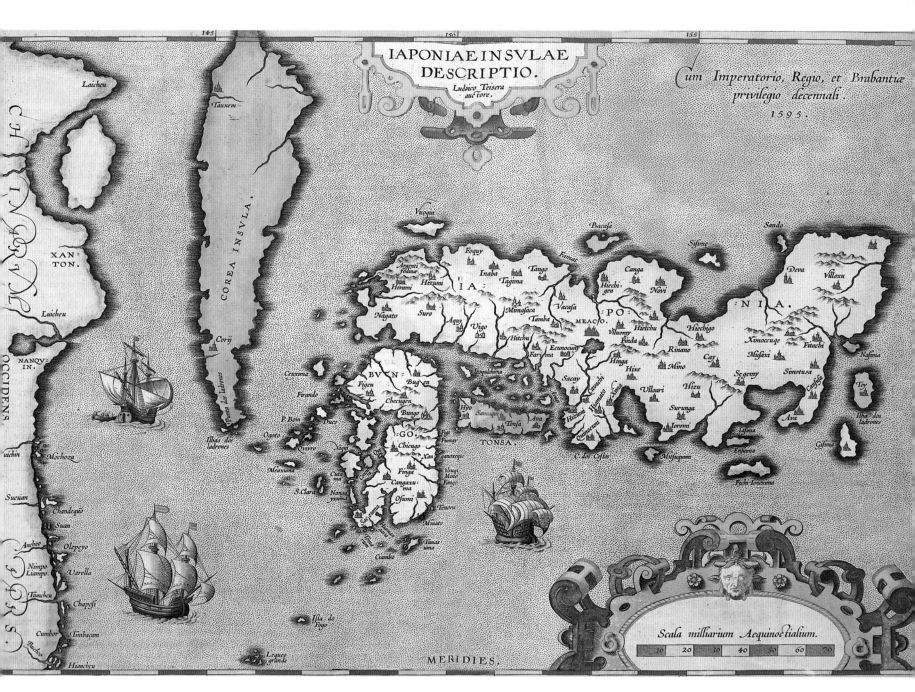

## IAPONIAE INSVLAE DESCRIPTIO.

Ludovico Teisera auctore.

Cum Imperatorio, Regio, et Brabantiæ privilegio decennali.
1595.

Scala milliarium Aequinoctialium.

*Map of Japan,* 1595, Ortelius, from the *Theatrum Orbis Terrarum.* Knowledge of Japan, Korea and the Chinese coast was limited, although European links were greater than they were to be in the seventeenth and eighteenth centuries.

The first Westerners to visit Japan were two Portuguese merchants in 1543. Some 60 years later in 1600, William Adams, a Pilot-Master on a Dutch East India Company ship, was the first Englishman to visit the country, landing on Kyushu. Most of the crew had died on the voyage. In 1611, the English East India Company

sent the *Clove* under the command of Captain John Saris to establish trading links with Japan, which Saris did by establishing a trading post at Hirado in 1613. These links proved precarious and the post was abandoned in 1623. **ABOVE**

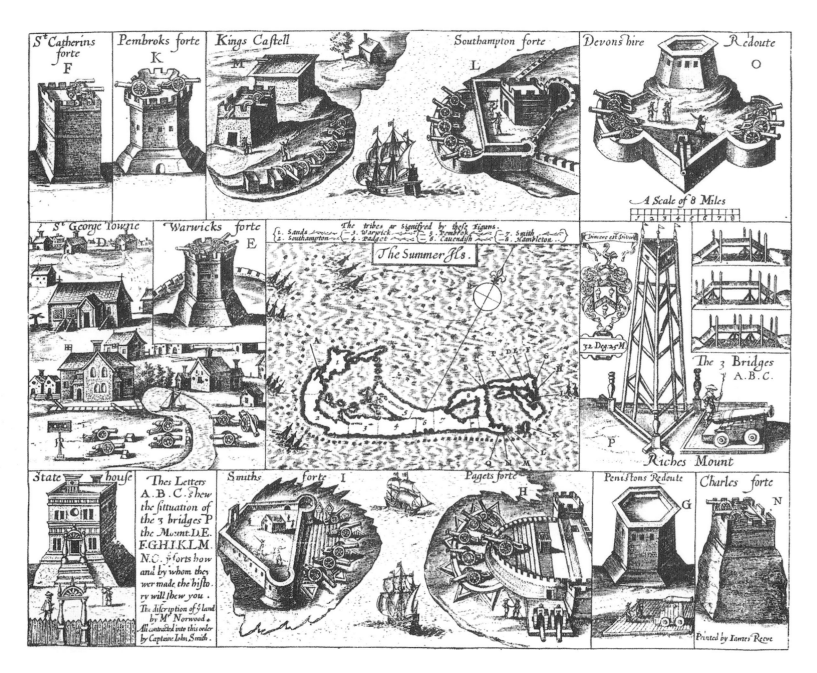

Captain John Smith's map of Bermuda, 1624. Once claimed and settled by the English, Bermuda was rapidly fortified in order to provide protection against possible attack, whether by Spain, France or pirates. Bermuda was the probable basis for the description of Prospero's island in *The Tempest*. **ABOVE**

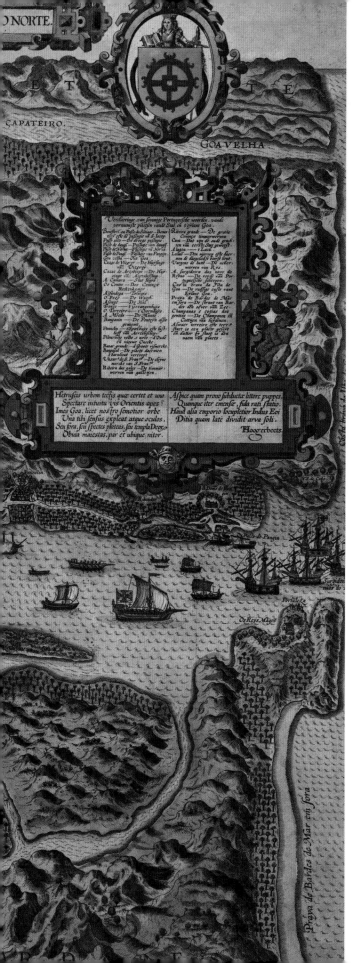

*Goa*, 1595, by Johannes Baptista van Doetichum the Younger. Captured by the Portuguese in 1510, Goa had become the key centre for European power and activity in the Indian Ocean, notably as the capital of the Portuguese *Estado da India*. Mercator had a correspondent in Goa, and English knowledge of India increased greatly in Shakespeare's later years in part as a consequence of the development of the English East India Company, established in 1600. In *Macbeth*, Shakespeare refers to 'the rich East' (4.3), while elsewhere Falstaff wants to exploit the merry wives of Windsor: 'They shall be my East and West Indies, and I will trade to them both' (1.3).

# Ideas of Space

Maps scarcely exhaust the human range of spatial awareness and expression. Indeed, the basic forms of awareness were reiterated weekly, both in church and at market day. The former ensured that the geography of a world view that spanned Heaven and Hell was fully expressed. In *King John*, Philip the Bastard enters during a battle carrying a head and saying:

> '... this day grows wondrous hot;
> Some airy devil hovers in the sky
> and pours down mischief.' (3.2)

So also with a wider confessional geography that included the placing of the Islamic world, not least Algiers and Jerusalem, as well as a Protestantism that offered a span from an allegedly Papist Antichrist to Protestant co-religionists. Venice brought in interaction with Jews in *The Merchant of Venice*, and *Othello* is set in Cyprus while it was a Venetian colony – before the Turkish conquest of 1570–1571. Indeed, the plot comes from the *Hecatommithi* (1565), a collection of tales by the Italian writer Giam battista Giraldi Cinzio. The plot of *Othello* brings in another aspect of difference, in the shape of the protagonist Othello: a Moor who has converted to Christianity.

Market days offered a very different and far more specific geography, focusing on the local understanding of spatial links, notably between towns, such as Stratford, and their hinterlands. These links could then be supplemented by ones between the towns themselves, and both complemented county divisions and clashed with them.

At a higher level, there was the question of regional identity. The end of the Council of the North meant that there was no specific institutional formulation in England, comparable for example to an area covered by an individual French *Parlement* or an Imperial (German) Circle. Nevertheless, there could still be an idea of a region, for example in East Anglia, the West Country or 'the North', at the same time that there were many divisions within these areas – whether economic, governmental, political, social and/or religious.

The links within, and between, regions were not affected by developments in transportation, because there was nothing that matched the situation in the century after Shakespeare's death when, after the Restoration of the Stuarts in 1660, the turnpiking of roads tentatively began while river improvements were pressed forward. In contrast, during Shakespeare's lifetime, road links remained particularly poor, and distance set a ready bound to certainty and confidence. Shakespeare's plays thus often depicted journeys as dangerous, and especially so if by sea. Indeed, storms played a frequent role in the plots, providing abrupt changes in fortune, as with the openings of *Twelfth Night* and *The Tempest* and Aegeon's account at the outset of *The Comedy of Errors*.

Another idea of space, one that was very different to that provided by physical movement, was provided by kinship groups. This was an aspect of the dynasticism that was repeatedly discussed in Shakespeare's plays with reference to lineage, parentage and marriage. These links had a spatial dimension as well, with figures from different areas brought into a relationship. As such, space and time were related.

Overall, there was the assumption on Shakespeare's part that his audience was familiar with geography. Shylock says of Antonio, the merchant of Venice: 'He hath an argosy bound to Tripolis, another to the Indies; I understand, moreover, upon the Rialto [in Venice], he hath a third at Mexico, a fourth for England' (1.3). Tripolis is Tripoli in Libya. The assumption is that these references are understood, as is also the case with the reference,

Allegorical portrait of *Sir John Luttrell* emerging from the sea, 1550, by Hans Eworth. This is a vivid depiction of effort and thankfulness after a shipwreck in the Bristol Channel. In *The Tempest*, an apparent shipwreck begins the action: Miranda, from the shore, observes what appears to be 'a brave vessel ... Dash'd all to pieces' (1.1). Shipwrecks also play a key role in other plays, including *Twelfth Night* and *Pericles*.

concerning the Prince of Morocco, to his complexion and to his fighting on behalf of Sultan Süleyman the Magnificent against the Safavids of Persia (Iran).

Possibly the details were less significant than the sense of distance and difference. So also for other references, as at the beginning of *The Winter's Tale*, where there is mention of 'great difference betwixt our Bohemia and your Sicilia' (1.1), which, today, would be the Czech Republic and Sicily. In *Measure For Measure*, the lengthy and ridiculous case involving Elbow, Froth and Pompey leads Angelo to remark:

> *'This will last out a night in Russia,*
> *When nights are longest there.' (2.1)*

The sense of distance is sometimes given poetic effect, as when Richard II banishes his cousin Bolingbroke, the future Henry IV, and also the latter's opponent, Thomas Mowbray, 1st Duke of Norfolk. Bolingbroke discusses this banishment with his father, John of Gaunt, Duke of Lancaster, who urges him to take it as a travel for pleasure, adding:

> *'All places that the eye of heaven visits*
> *Are to a wise man ports and happy havens.' (1.3)*

He also encourages him to experience places in part by reimagining them. Bolingbroke replies:

> *'who can hold a fire in his hand*
> *By thinking on the frosty Caucasus?' (1.3)*

The tone is lighter in *The Comedy of Errors* when Dromio of Syracuse describes Nell the 'kitchen-wench' being so greasy: 'I warrant her rags and the tallow in them will burn a Poland winter' (3.2) – in other words, a very cold winter for which more fuel would be required. Comparing the spherical Nell to a globe, Dromio cruelly claims, in a humour that now seems highly unpleasant:

> *'Dromio: ... I could find out countries in her.*
> *Antipholus: In what part of her body stands Ireland?*
> *Dromio: Marry, Sir, in her buttocks: I found it out by the bogs.*
> *Antipholus: Where Scotland?*
> *Dromio: I found it by the barrenness; hard in the palm of the hand.*
> *Antipholus: Where France?*
> *Dromio: In her forehead; armed and reverted, making war against her heir.*
> *Antipholus: Where England?*
> *Dromio: I looked for the chalky cliffs, but I could find no whiteness in them: but I guess it stood in her chin, by the salt rheum that ran between France and it.*
> *Antipholus: Where Spain?*
> *Dromio: Faith, I saw not; but I felt it hot in her breath.*
> *Antipholus: Where America, the Indies?*
> *Dromio: O, sir! Upon her nose, all o'er embellished with rubies, carbuncles, sapphires, declining their rich aspect to the hot breath of Spain, who sent whole armadoes of caracks to be ballast at her nose.*
> *Antipholus: Where stood Belgia, the Netherlands?*
> *Dromio: O, sir! I did not look, so low.'*
> (3.2)

Ephesus (*The Comedy of Errors*), Messina (*Much Ado*), Verona (*Romeo and Juliet*) and Vienna (*Measure for Measure*) are scarcely crucial locations for particular plays and, instead, are sketched in with economy. For Ephesus, this is notably so as it is drawn as a city where the occult allegedly plays a role, rather than as a detailed townscape:

> *'They say this town is full of cozenage;*
> *As, nimble jugglers that deceive the eye,*

*Dark-working sorcerers that change the mind,*
*Soul-killing witches that deform the body,*
*Disguised cheaters, prating mountebanks,*
*And many such-like liberties of sin.'* (1.2)

At the same time, there is, for Ephesus, as for locations for other plays, a setting described that is necessary both for the action and for the particular dynamics of characterisation, description and drama; for example:

*'The place of death and sorry execution,*
*Behind the ditches of the abbey here.'* (5.1)

At times, the departure from geography is readily apparent, even if such departure does not disrupt the plot. In *The Two Gentlemen of Verona*, there is a marked lack of specificity as to place, and, indeed, as to the identity of a ruler, as duke or emperor. In practice, however, there was confusion: the Duchy of Milan had become a Habsburg territory in 1540, with some dissension as to whether it was part of the inheritance of the Spanish or Austrian branches. There was also the case of much of northern Italy being part of the Holy Roman Empire.

Repeatedly, the places in question in the setting are courts, quays and marketplaces, rather than cities as a whole. The first, in particular, permits a disengagement from context, one also seen when rulers are exiled, as with *As You Like It* and *The Tempest*. That the last is set on a largely deserted island – its location lost in a storm conjured up by magic that affects a boat en route from Tunis to Naples – while *Much Ado About Nothing* is set in Messina in Sicily, is far less consequential than the fact that they both address types of court, and both show the courtly societies under great pressure. So also with *Hamlet*, a revenge tragedy that could have been set in Italy, where most are set, or anywhere else, rather than having to be in Denmark.

There are other geographical references that lack precision. In *Henry VI, Part One*, for example, the list of losses in France that is announced to Henry V's funeral party is designed to impress, and to establish a context of failure:

'Guinne, Champaigne, Rheims, Orleans
Paris, Guysors, Poitiers, are all quite lost.' (1.1)

This was a serious exaggeration, indeed misrepresentation, at that stage and also a major foreshortening. Henry died in 1422, but the second messenger brings news of the crowning of Charles VII at Rheims which, in fact, occurred in 1429, as did Talbot's defeat at Patay reported by the third messenger. The account made no reference to English gains in 1422–28, nor to English victories then such as Verneuil (1424). The English did not lose Paris till 1436.

This does not mean, however, that there is a placelessness to Shakespeare's plays, notably the non-History Plays, but rather, as is normal with the theatre, it means that the spectators did not have to bring too much to the occasion. Yet, that point directs attention to what they did bring: an awareness (and degree of knowledge) of a world that was changing rapidly, as exploration revealed more of the transoceanic world, while the politics of Europe were also in flux, testing, confirming or overcoming traditional assumptions about countries and peoples. Geography, history and politics came together to provide the setting for human dramas that were at once fictional and factual.

In this process, the mapping and remapping of the world reflected and encouraged this sense of change, and with it a lack of fixity that could encourage doubt and scepticism. It offered spatial location and meaning, but as part of a world that was modern in its acceptance of this very doubt, an acceptance most brilliantly conveyed by Shakespeare in *Hamlet*.

**Hardwick Hall.** An Elizabethan pleasure palace notable for its lack of fortification, this was one of the most impressive examples of surviving Elizabethan 'prodigy' houses, which was built with a royal visit in mind. The layout takes account of the needs of the travelling court. Hardwick Hall lacks the medieval castellated background of Kenilworth. It was built between 1587 and 1597 and designed by Robert Smythson, who drew on Italian Renaissance architectural innovations. **RIGHT**

**The only contemporary image** of a Shakespeare play in performance, the 'Longleat manuscript' is a pen-and-ink drawing attributed to Henry Peachman (*c.*1576–*c*1643), dated 1595. Its depiction of a scene from *Titus Andronicus* is confusing since the images appear to conflate two episodes, but that may well reflect the difficulty of the task and the striking nature of what is shown. The stage direction 'Enter Tamora pleadings for her sonnes going to execution' is not in any printed text. Moreover, in the text in Act 1, she pleads for just her eldest son. **LEFT**

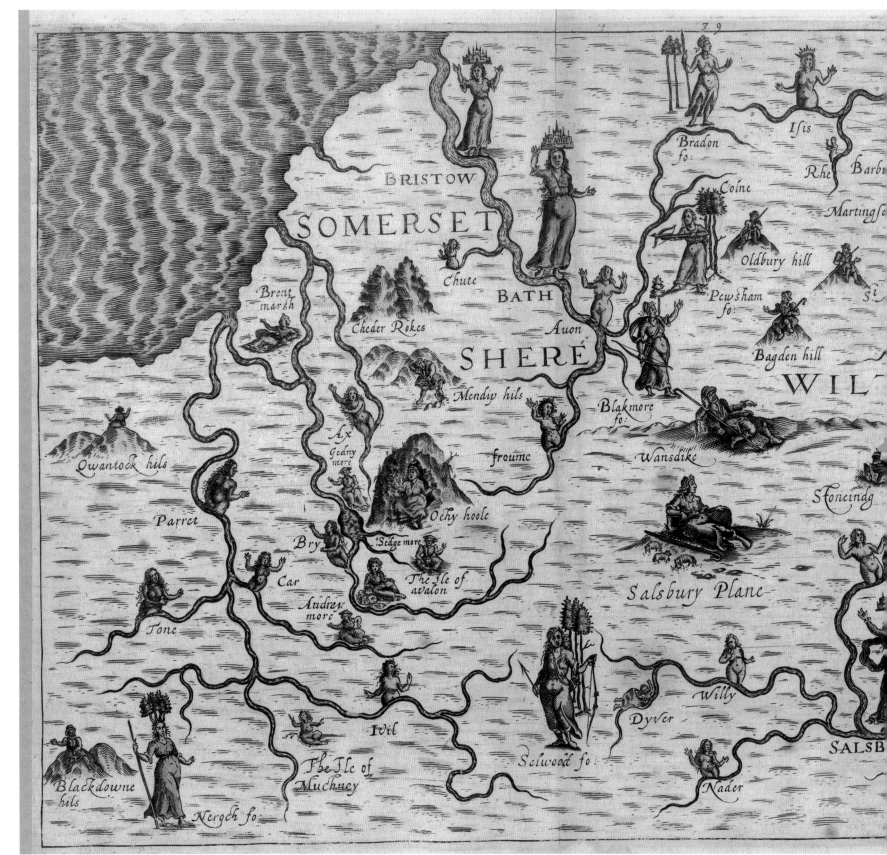

BRISTOW

SOMERSET

Bradon
fo:

Isis

Rhe

Barbi

Colne

Martingso

BATH

Chute

Oldbury hill

Pewsham
fo:

S.

Brent
marsh

Auon

SHERE

Bagden hill

WILT

Cheder Rokes

Mendip hils

Blakmore
fo:

froume

Wansdike

Qwantock hils

Ax
Gedny
more

Stoneindg

Parret

Ochy hoole

Salsbury Plane

Bry

Sedge more

Car

The Ile of
avalon

Audrey
more

Tone

Iuil

Willy

Dyver

SALSB

Blackdowne
hils

The Ile of
Muchney

Selwood fo:

Nader

Nergch fo:

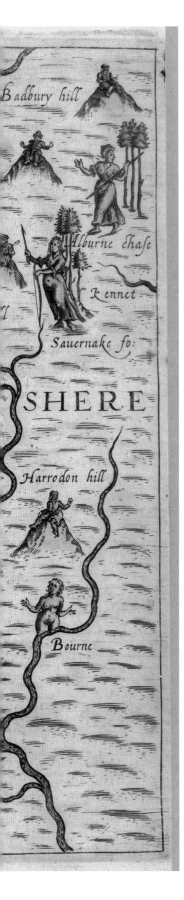

Map of Somerset and Wiltshire used to illustrate *Poly-Olbion*. This was a verse-epic that mythologised British history, written in 1612 by Michael Drayton (1563–1631) – a proficient poet who also wrote plays for the Admiral's Men, including the co-written *Sir John Oldcastle* (1600). According to John Ward, vicar of Stratford, writing in the early 1660s, Shakespeare died after contracting a fever in a heavy drinking session with Drayton and Ben Jonson. **FAR LEFT**

A 1596 sketch of a performance in the Swan Theatre, taken from *A Short History of the English People* by John Richard Green (1874). Built in 1595 in Southwark, the theatre was visited in 1596 by Johannes de Witt, a Dutch scholar who drew a picture that was copied by his friend Aernout van Buchel. Only the copy still exists, and it is the sole surviving interior view of an open-air theatre of the period. The stage projects into the yard, with the stage cover resting on two neoclassical columns. **LEFT**

# Index

*A Defence of Judicial Astrology* (1603) 45

*A Midsummer Night's Dream* 38, 52, 75, 183

*A New Description of Kent* 58, 59

*A Perambulation of Kent* 58, 110

*A Regiment of the Sea (etc)* (1573) 60

Abd al-Malik 160

Abyssinia [Ethiopia] 12, 160

Actium 168

Adal 163

Adams, William 176

Addison, Thomas 42

Aegean Sea 28, 127

Africa 12, 16, 26, 160–68

Africanicus, Leo 25

Agas map 98, 102–103

Agas, Ralph 103

Agnese, Battista 36

Alexandria 16, 25, 164, 172, 175

Algiers 134, 180

*All's Well That Ends Well* 6, 55, 148

*Almagestum Novum* 45

Alsace 122

Álvaras Cabral, Pedro 20

America 30

Amsterdam 109, 133, 151

Anatolia 114, 171

Angers 60, 67

Anjou 67

Ankara 171

Anne Boleyn 164

Anthonisz, Cornelius 151

*Anthony and Cleopatra* 175

Antilla 12

Antioch 118

Antipodes 19

*Antony and Cleopatra* 16, 41, 114

Antwerp 34, 60, 151

Apianus, Petrus 30

Arctic 30, 34

Aristotle 42, 52

*Arithmetical Navigation* 42

*Arte of Shooting in Great Ordnance* (1587)

Artois 122

*As You Like It* 75, 151, 163, 183

Asia 34

*Astronomia Nova* (1609) 42, 47

Atlantic Ocean 22, 34

*Atlas Major* 65

*Atlas Novus* (1655) 65

*Atlas of England and Wales* 71

Augsberg 148–149

Austria 125, 137, 159

Avon, river 75

Azerbaijan 168

Azores 34

Bacon, Francis 60

Bahr Nagash Ishaq 160

Bahrain 171

Bangor 65, 67

Barentsz, William 19, 20, 22, 33

Bartlett, Richard 60

Bassingham 93

Báthory, Stephan 141

Battista Ramusio, Giovanni 142

Bayezid II 129

Bearn 141

Bedfordshire 60, 71

Bedwell, William 34

Behaim, Martin 12

Beijing 12

Belgium 122, 125

Belluno 142

Bergamo 142

Bering, Vitus 34

Berkeley Castle 67

Bermuda 6, 177

Besançon 122

Biserta 134

Black Sea 26, 117, 125

Blaeu, Joan 65

Boccaccio, Giovanni 148

Bohemia 36, 125, 126

Bona 134

*Book of Prophecies* 20

Borneo 168

Bosworth, battle of 58, 75

Bougie 134

Boulogne 122

Bourne, William 60

Brahe, Tycho 41, 42, 47, 51

Braun, Georg 98, 111, 121, 134, 151, 154, 172

Brazil 20, 21

Breckland 63

Brecon 60

Brescia 127, 142

Bristol 6, 22

Bristol Castle 67

Britain 119

*Britannia* (1586)

Browne, John 60

Bucer, Martin 89

Buda 171

Bufalini, Leonardo 153

Burghley, Lord 60, 62, 97

Cadiz 127, 175

Cairo 175

Calais 83, 138

California 34

Cambridgeshire 60, 71, 89

Camden, William 62, 75, 76, 79, 113

Canada 34

*Cantino Planisphere* 21

Cantino, Alberto 21

Caribbean 20

Carleton, George 45

Cathay (*see* China)

Catholic League 142, 157

Cavendish, Henry 26, 30

Caxton, William 98

Cebu 20

Cecil, William, Lord Burghley 58, 68, 97, 119

Central America 25

Ceuta 134

Chamber, John 45

Chapman, George 138

Charing Cross 98

Charles Emanuel 1 (Savoy-Piedmont) 138

Charles IX (France) 129, 141

Charles V 30, 122, 126, 148

Charles VII 184

Charterhouse 98

Chelmsford 93

China 12, 21, 22, 168, 171, 172

Chinggis (Ghengis) Khan 12, 168

Christian IV 42

*Chronicles of England, Scotland and Ireland* (1577) 6, 56

Cinzio, Giambattista Geraldi 180

*Civitates Orbis Terrarum* 98, 113, 127

Clough, Sir Richard 60

Cologne 125

Columbus, Christopher 6, 20

*Comedy of Errors, The* 20, 34, 114, 180, 182

compass 12

Constantinople 118, 125

Copernicus, Nicolaus 42, 51

Copperplate map 98, 100, 101

*Coriolanus* 113

Cornwall 60, 62, 79

Coron 28

Corsica 127

Corte-Real, Gaspar 21

*Cosmographical Glasse, The* (1559) 37

Counter-Reformation 153

Cremona 127

Crete 28

Cuningham, William 37

*Cymbeline* 41, 42, 60, 67, 113

Cyprus 6, 34, 127, 137

d'Este, Ercole, Duke of Ferrara 21

Danti, Ignazio 145

Danube 117

Darby, John 91

Dardanelles (Hellespont) 117

Dartmoor 75

Dartmouth 75

Davis, John 26, 33

Day of the Barricades 157

de Castro, João 26

*De Fluminibus seu Tiberidis* (1355) 12

de Gama, Vasco 6

de Grassi, Cristoforo 129

de Kremer, Gerald (*see* Mercator) 30

*De Magnete, Magneticisque Corporibus, et de Magno Magnete Tellure (On the Magnet and Magnetic Bodies, and on the Great Magnet the Earth)* (1600) 48

*De Prospectiva Pingendi (On Painting Perspective)* 16

*De Revolutionibus Orbium Coelestium (On the Revolution of Heavenly Spheres),* (1543) 42

de Sassoferrato, Bartolo 12

de Verrazano, Gerolamo 34
de Verrazano, Giovanni de 34
de Wit, Frederik 55
de Worde, Wynkyn 98
de' Barbari, Jacopo 23
Deal Castle 58, 60
*Decameron* 148
Dee, John 33, 41, 58, 113
della Francesca, Piero 16
Denbigh 60
Denmark 159
*Description of the Earth for Use in Navigation* (1569) 30
Devon 60, 75
*Dialogo sopra i due massimi sistemi del mondo (Dialogue on the Two Principal World Systems* (1632) 42
Digges, Leonard 60
Digges, Thomas 60
*Discourse Concerning the Spanish Fleet Invading England in the year 1588* 83
*Discovery of the Large, Rich and Beautiful Empire of Guiana* (1596) 26, 27
*Divers Voyages* (1582) 22
Dnieper 117
Doge's Palace, Venice 28, 142, 160
Dorset 60
Dover 6, 13, 58, 79
Dover Castle 58
Drake, Francis 6, 26, 30
Drayton, Michael 187
*Duchess of Malfi* 122
Duisburg 30
Dürer, Albrecht 48
Dutch East India Company 36, 164
Dutch Revolt 125, 133
Dutch West India Company 36

East Anglia 72, 86, 180
East Indies 25, 26, 164
Edict of Nantes 137
Edo (Tokyo) 170
Edward III 97
Edward the Confessor 98
Edward VI 89
Egypt 12, 113, 160
Elder, John 65
Elizabeth I 6, 41, 48, 58, 60, 65, 71, 101, 133, 134, 141, 175

Elsinore (Kronberg Castle) 159
England 6, 10, 58, 60, 63, 85, 129, 130, 133
English Channel 60, 62, 83, 114
English Company of Merchant Adventurers 33
English East India Company 176, 179
Ephesus 28, 114, 182, 183
Equator 30
Escorial 28
Essex 93
Ethiopia 19, 26
Euboea 28
Eworth, Hans 180
Exeter 75

Farnese, Alessandro, Duke of Parma 83
Faroe Islands 33
Fens 63
Finland 122
Fleet, river 98
Flint Castle 60, 67
Florence 142, 145, 146-7, 148
Forest of Arden 75
France 10, 58, 67, 113, 130, 133, 134, 137, 138
Franche-Comté 122
Francis I (France) 34
Francis II (France) 129
Frankfurt 125
French Wars of Religion 133, 137, 168
Frisland 33
Frobisher, Martin 6, 26, 33

Galilei, Galileo 42, 45, 52
Gao 163
Gastaldi, Giacomo 34, 160-161
Gelibolu (Gallipoli) 16
*General and Rare Memorials Pertaining to the Perfect Art of Navigation* (1577) 41
Genoa 126, 129
*Geographica* (Ptolemy) 16, 25
*Geographica Sacra* 26
Georgia 34
Germany 10, 113, 125

Gheeraerts the Younger, Marcus 62, 67
Ghent 109
Gilbert, William 48
Globe Theatre 107, 109
Goa 36, 179
Godwin, Francis 42, 47
*Gough Map* 10, 15
Gough, Richard 15
Granada 133
Gravelines 83
Great Yarmouth 86
Greece 28
Greene, Robert 34, 36
Guaiana River 122
Guiana 26
Gustav I Vasa 122
Gutiérrez, Diego 25

Haarlem 134
Hadrian 10
Hadrian's Wall 10
Hakluyt, Richard 22, 28, 34, 113
Hall, Edward 6
Hamburg 125
*Hamlet* 141, 159, 184
Hampton Court 62
Harar 163
Hardwick Hall 184-85
Harfleur 125
Harlech 60
*Harmonice Mundi* (Harmonies of the World, 1619) 42
Harriot, Thomas 28
Hatton, Sir Christopher 71
Haverfordwest 60
Hawkins, John 163
*Hecatommithi* (1565) 180
Henry II (France) 129
Henry III (France) 137
Henry IV (England) 58, 65
Henry IV (France) 157, 168
*Henry IV* 20, 41, 60, 65, 68, 72, 75, 76, 79, 89, 94, 98, 133, 184
Henry the Navigator 20
*Henry V* 60, 83, 125
*Henry VI* 94, 134
Henry VII 163
*Henry VIII* 109

Henry VIII 22, 30, 58, 60, 164
*Hereford Mappa Mundi* (World Map) 8, 9
Hertfordshire 62, 68
Hevelius, Johannes 45, 47
Heydon, Sir Christopher 45
Hispaniola 175
*History of the Peleponnesian War* 116
Hobbes, Thomas 110, 116
Hoefnagel, Georg (Joris) 121, 127
Hogenberg, Frans 98, 121, 134, 142, 151, 155, 172
Holborn 98
Holinshed, Raphael 6, 56
Holy Land 12, 20, 111
Hondius, Jodocus 65
Hooke, Robert 45
Hormuz 12, 171
Horrocks, Jeremiah 42
Hudson Bay 30
Hudson, Henry 6, 26
Hugo Willoughbes land 33
Hull 58, 94
Humber 58, 94
Humphrey Llwyd 60, 62, 113
Hungary 125, 126, 141, 171
Huntingdonshire 60, 71
Hurado, 176

Iberia 16
India 6, 20, 36
Indian Ocean 16, 25, 30, 34, 36, 164, 179
Inquisition 42, 45
Ionian Islands 28, 127
Ireland 60, 119
Ishāq II 163
Isle of Man 63, 65
Italian Wars 133
Italy 6, 10, 113, 117, 142
Ivan IV, the Terrible 6, 125, 141, 154

James I 28, 34, 48, 76, 101
Japan 6, 34, 170, 171, 172, 176
Jerusalem 8, 16, 21, 110, 111, 171, 180
Jesuits 26
John Davis 37

John of Gaunt 97
Judar Pasha 163
*Julius Caesar* 41, 113, 134

Kandahar 171
Karakorum 12
Katherine of Aragon 30, 148
Kenilworth 75
Kent 60
Kepler, Johannes 42, 47
*King John* 13, 41, 58, 60, 67, 71, 79
*King Lear* 8, 13, 41, 55, 58, 65, 79
King Solomon's Mines 26
King's Lynn 72
*Kitab i-Bahriye* (Book of the Sea) 16, 168
Korea 172, 176
Kyoto 170
Kyushu 176

*La Descrittione dell'Africa* (1550) 25
Lambarde, William 58, 110
Lancashire 97
latitude 30, 33
*Le Operazioni del compass geometrico e militaire* 42
Lea, Philip 62
Leicestershire 75
Liège 122
Lincoln 93
Lincolnshire 72
Lisbon 21, 25, 151
Livonia 141, 154
Lizard Peninsula 62
*Londinium Florentiss[i]ma Britanniae Urbs* (1616) 107
London 6, 98, 107, 109
longitude 30, 33
Longleat manuscript 185
Lopez, Sebastião 25
Lorraine 122
Louis IX of France 12
Louis XIII (France) 138
*Love's Labour's Lost* 130, 154, 163
loxodrome 30
Luttrell, Sir John 180-181
Luxembourg 122
Lyne, Richard 89

Lythe, Robert 60

*Macbeth* 41, 56, 129, 179
Madrid 130
Magellan, Ferdinand 6, 20, 25, 30
Maine 67
Malta, siege of 1565 137
Mamluks 12
*Map of Europe* by Mercator 1554, 34
*Mappae mundi* 8, 10, 110
*Mariner's Mirrour, The* (1588) 37
Marlowe, Christopher 19, 28, 36, 137, 157, 168
Mary I (England) 133
Mary, Queen of Scots 67, 71, 137
*Massacre at Paris* 122, 134, 157
Matthew Paris 10
Matthew Paris' *Itinerary from London to Jerusalem* 13
Matthew Paris' *map of Great Britain* 10, 11
*Measure for Measure* 6, 154, 159, 182
Medea 117
Medina, Pedro 18
Mediterranean 6, 12, 16, 26, 34, 171
Mehmed II 129
Meldeman, Niklas 159
Melilla 134
Mercator, Gerald 30, 33, 36, 179
Mercator, Rumold 33
*Merchant of Venice* 6, 23, 129, 145, 151, 180
Merian, Matthäus 157
*Merry Wives of Windsor, The* 26
Mesopotamia 113, 117
Messina 19
*Metamorphoses* (Ovid) 38
Metz 122
Michaelangelo 153
*Micrographia* (1655) 45
*Microsmus* 110
Middlesex 60, 62, 68
*Midsummer Night's Dream* 18, 20, 67
Milan 133, 142
Milford Haven 60
Milo, Antonio 26
Mitylene 28
Modena 117

Mohacs, battle of 125
Mondon 28
Möngke (Mongol khan) 12
Moravia 125
Moretus, Balthasar 118
Morocco 160, 163
Moscow 154-5
Mount Misenum 117
Mount Snowdon [Snauden] 10
Mountains of the Moon 26
*Much Ado About Nothing* 19, 38, 55, 182, 184
Mughal Empire 168
Munster, Sebastian 110
Murad II 168
Murmansk 33
Muscovy Company 22, 154

Naarden 134
Nagasaki Bay 172
*Natural History* 117
Navarre 141
Netherlands 83, 122, 125
New Spain 36
New World 26
Newcastle 65, 85
Nice 122
Nieuport 122
Niger, river 160, 163
Nijo Castle 170
Nile 26
Norden, John 62, 68, 79
Norfolk 60, 72, 86, 91
North Africa 122
North America 22, 34
North Carolina 34
North Pole 30, 33
North Sea 83
North-East Passage 33
North-West Passage 22, 33
Northampton Castle 71
Northamptonshire 60, 71
Northumberland 60, 76
Norton, John 34
Norway 122
Norwich 72, 86, 91
Nova Scotia 34
*Nova Scotia Inventa* (1537)
Novaya Zemlya 33

Nowell, Laurence 58, 65, 110, 119
Nunes, Pedro 33

Ophir 26
Oran 134
Orinoco Valley 28
Ortelius, Abraham 25, 34, 60, 113, 130, 163, 176
Ostend 122, 125
*Othello* 6, 8, 114, 125, 129, 137, 160, 164, 180
Otranto 129
Ottoman (Turkish) empire 125, 129, 168
Oxford 15, 119
Oxfordshire 67
Pacific Ocean 20, 22, 25, 30, 34
Padua 127, 142
Páez, Pedro 26
*Pandosto: The Triumph of Time* (1588) 34, 36
*Parergon* 113
Paris 137, 142, 156-7
Peache of Vervins 137
*Pericles* 12, 114, 163
Persia 160
Persian Gulf 12
Peutinger Table 118
Philip Augustus (France) 60
Philip II (Spain) 30, 36, 83, 122, 130, 133, 134, 141, 151
Philip III (Spain) 134
Philippi 168
Philippines 30, 168, 172
Piedmont 122
Piri Reis 16, 168
Plancius, Petrus 164
Pliny the Elder 117
Plutarch 6
Poitiers 67
Poland 122, 141
Polo, Marco 12
*Poly-Olbion* 187
Pont, Timothy 65
Pope Alexander VI 21
Pope Clement VII 171
Pope Julius III 153
Pope Paul III 153
Pope Sixtus IV 129

Pope Sixtus V 153
portolan charts 12
Portugal 16, 122, 134, 151, 160, 163, 171
Prester John 12, 19, 26, 163, 163
*Principal Navagations* (1599) 34
*Prospect of the Most Famous Parts of the World* (1627) 110
*Prospect of the Most Famous Parts of the World* 65
Ptolemaic model 51
Ptolemy 16, 25, 33
Punta Delgada, battle of 34
*Purchas his Pilgrimage, or Relations of the World and the Religious observed in all Ages and Places discovered from the Creation unto this present* (1614) 26
Purchas, Samuel 26

*Questiti et inventioni* (1546)

Raleigh, Sir Walter 26, 28
Ravenna 142
Ravenspur 58, 94
Red Sea 26, 160, 164
Reformation 10
*Relaciones Geograficas* 36
Renaissance 6, 10
Ribeira, Diego 18
Ricci, Matteo 164
Riccioli, Giovanni 45
Richard II (England) 58, 129, 138, 168
*Richard II* 67, 68, 94, 182
*Richard III* 58, 60, 68, 75, 98
Richard of Haldingham [or Lafford] 8
*Robert Thorne's world map* 22
Rochester Bridge 58
Roman Empire 118
*Romani Imperii Imago* (1571) 113
Rome 113, 118, 152-3
*Romeo and Juliet* 142, 182
Rosselli, Francesco 148
Rousillon 122
Roussillon 141
Rudolf II (Emperor) 41, 42, 47
*Rudolphine Tables* 42, 47
Russia 33, 122, 154

Rutland 71
Rye 58
Ryther, Augustine 83
*Sacred Geography* (1584) 110
Safavid Empire 168, 171
Sahara desert 163
Sala dello Scudo 142
Salamanca 16
*Salla dello Scudo* 28
Santo Domingo 174-175
Saône river 122
Sardinia 122
Saris, Captain John 176
Saxton, Christopher 58, 60, 65, 68, 71, 72, 75, 76, 97
Scientific Revolution 10
Scotland 10, 63, 65, 83, 119, 129
Sea of Marmora 117
*Seaman's Secrets, The* (1595) 37
Seckford, Thomas 58
Selden Map 168, 169
Selden, John 168
*Selenographia* 45
Selim I 171
Selim II 6
Serse-Dingil 160
Seville 18, 22, 130-131
Shah Abbas 160
Shangdu 12
Sheppey 60
Shetland Islands 33
Sicily 19, 122
*Sidereus Nuncius* (The Sidereal Messenger 1610) 42, 52
Sigismund Vasa 141
Silesia 125
Skarburgh (Scarborough) 58
Slovenia 125
Smallburgh 91
Smith, Captain John 177
Somerset 186-87
*Somnium* (Dream) 1609 42, 47
Songhai Empire 163
South America 20, 25, 34
South Asia 30
South Pole 30
South-East Asia 21
Southampton 6
Southern Continent 19

Southwark 98, 104
Spanish Armada 67, 83, 114, 122, 138, 163
Spain 16, 28, 30, 34, 37, 58, 83, 122, 129, 130, 134, 137, 138, 171, 175, 177
*Speculum Britanniae* (Mirror of Britain) 62, 68
Speed, John 62, 65, 79, 85, 110, 113
Spitsbergen 33
St Albans 68, 98
St Bartholomew's Day Massacre 134, 157
Stanhope, Sir Michael 68
Stent, Peter 58
Strand 98
Stratford 180
Suffolk 68
Sufian 171
Süleyman the Magnificent 125, 126, 141, 168
Sumatra 25
Surrey 60
Susenyos 160
Sussex 60
Swan Theatre 187
Sweden 122
Swiss Confederacy 126
Switzerland 125
Symonson, Philip 58, 65
*Synonymia geographic sive populorum* etc (1578)
Syria 12, 114, 117, 125
Szigetvár, siege of 141

*Tamburlaine the Great* 19, 168
Tangier 134
Tarsis 26
Tarso (see Tarsus) 34
Tartaglia, Niccoló 60
Teixeira, Luis 34
Thames, river 83
Thanet 60
Tharsus 114
*The Chronicle of England* 98
*The Conspiracy and Tragedy of Charles, Duke of Byron* 138
The Hague 42

*The Invasions of England and Ireland …* (1601) 110, 114
*The Jew of Malta* 137
*The Madnesse of Astrologers* (1634)
*The Man in the Moone: or A Discourse of a Voyage Thither* (1638) 42, 47
*The Tales of Luqman* 57
*The Tempest* 6, 28, 38, 45, 47, 89, 109, 129, 134, 177, 180, 183
*The Winter's Tale* 28, 34, 36, 38, 141, 182
*Theatre of the Empire of Great Britain* 62, 65
*Theatrum Orbis Terrarum* (Theatre of the World) (1570) 34, 121, 151, 154, 176
*Theatrum Terrae Sanctae* 111
Thirteen Years' War 159
Thirty Years' War 138
Thorne, Robert 22
Thucydides 110, 116
Tibury 83
Tigre 163
Timbuktoo 163
*Titus Andronicus* 38, 47, 113, 164, 171, 185
Toul 122
Touraine 67
*Tratado da Sphera* (Treatise of Spheres) 33
*Treatise Against Judicial Astrology* 45
Trent, river 89
Tripoli 134, 164
*Troilus and Cressida* 20, 37, 38, 51
Tunis 6, 12, 134, 160
Turkey 117
Tuscany 45
*Twelfth Night* 19, 22, 34, 55, 75, 180
Twelve Years' Truce 137
*Two Gentlemen of Verona* 15, 133, 163, 183
Tyne, river 85
Tynemouth 58

Ulbadini, Petruccio 83
Union of Calmar 122
*Union of the Two Noble and Illustrious Families of Lancaster and York* (1548) 6

*Universale* (World Map, 1546) 34
*Urbis Hierosolyma Depicta* 111

van Adrichem, Christian 110
van den Keere, Peter 98, 109
van den Wyngaerde, Anton 101
van Doetichum the Younger,
 Johannes Baptista 179
van Linschoten, Jan Huygen 164
Vatican Gallery of Maps 145
Venezuela 26
Venice 6, 12, 23, 26, 28, 34, 36, 121,
 125, 126, 127, 142, 145

Ventidius 117
Verdun 122
Vere, Francis 125
Verneuil 184
Verona 142
Vicenza 127
Vienna 6, 125, 159, 182
Visscher, Claes 101, 107
*Vocabularium Saxonicum* 119
von Breitenbach, Bernard 110
von Wellenberg, Cardinal Lang
 48

Waghenaer, Lucas Janszoon 37
Wales 60, 62, 64, 65
Walker, John 93
Walmer Castle 60
Wars of the Roses 160, 171
Warwickshire 75
Webb, William 62
Webster, John 122
Wentworth, Thomas 138
West Africa 20, 21, 163
West Indies 26
Whitehall 98
Whitwell, Charles 58

William of Orange 83
William of Rubruck 12
Willoughby, Sir Hugh 33
Wiltshire 186-187
Windsor Castle 10
Wright, Edward 34

York 6
Yorkshire 58, 72

Zodiac 8, 38, 41, 55, 57
Zutphen 134

## Picture credits

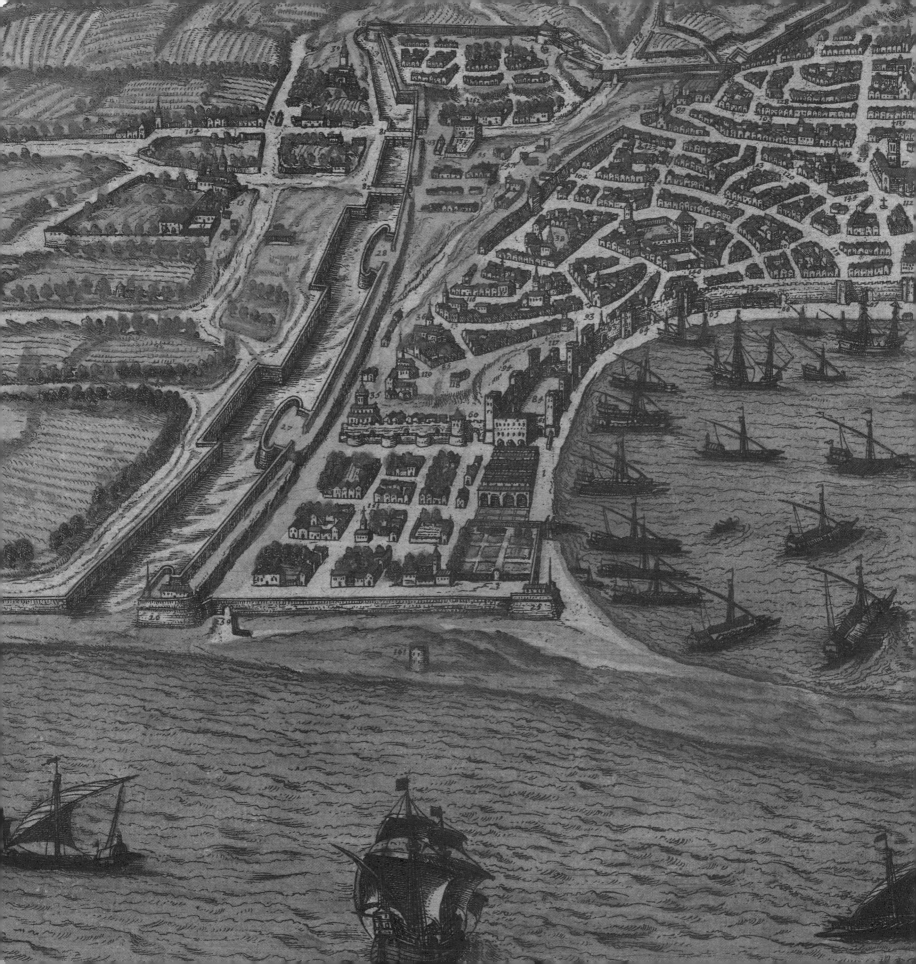